DISCOVER PCs

Computer Shopping List

Item	What to Consider	Web Page for More Info
Processor	80486 or Pentium	http://www.intel.com
Monitor	Large, no flickering	http://www.hercules.com/monitors
Keyboard	Full-size, comfortable	http://www.dgp.toronto.edu/people/BillBuxton/InputSources.html
Mouse	Comfortable, trackball easy to clean	http://www.altra.com
RAM	16MB, easily upgradable	http://sysdoc.pair.com/ram.html
Clock speed	At least 80MHz	http://www.sandybay.com/pc-web/clock_speed.htm
Hard drive	1GB drives common	http://members.gnn.com/MRosenthal/handtoc.htm#toc
PCMCIA slot	For notebook computers	http://www.rjbventures.com/pcinfo.html
Sound card	SoundBlaster-compatible	http://www.pcwebopaedia.com/sound_card.htm
Operating system	Preinstalled	http://www.microsoft.com
Loaded software	Brand names best	http://compusa.com
CD-ROM drive	Removable 4x (or faster)	http://www.infomagic.com
Printer	Inkjet or laser, color?	http://www.hp.com/peripherals/printers/main.html
Fax/modem	At least 28.8k baud	http://www.modemshop.com
General software, hardware, and Industry information		http://www.cnet.com http://oracle.uvision.com/idx/ http://www.pcwebopaedia.com

Helpful Technical Support Hints

What's Wrong?	How You Can Fix It
Low on RAM	Close unnecessary applications, upgrade to more RAM
Out of disk space	Erase, uninstall, or offload unnecessary applications and files; compress files with WinZip; upgrade to larger hard drive; or add a Zip drive
CPU speed crawls	Memory may be low, close unnecessary applications
Computer locks up	Reboot, run ScanDisk and Disk Defragmenter (Windows 95), close unnecessary applications
File opens as garbage	Make sure file isn't compressed, ensure file is in right format (and right version) for application
Error messages	Write down exact wording, reboot and try again, see if problem is reproducible, call manufacturer's technical support line if it persists
Printer doesn't print	Check all cable connections, printer power switch, and paper supply; turn printer off and on and retry; reboot computer and retry
Computer won't recognize floppy	Check if disk is formatted for the Macintosh, try it on another machine before reformatting and losing all data stored on it
Floppy gets stuck in drive or won't insert easily	Check metal shutter for damage, copy contents off disk and throw away
Can't find technical support number	Go to http://www.ozemail.com.au/~elwynw/tsp/ on the Web for links to many manufacturer's tech support pages

Important Information About Your Computer

Make and model: _____

Serial number: _____

Microprocessor type: _____

Speed: _____ **MHz**

RAM: _____ **MB**

Hard drive capacity: _____ **MB or** _____ **GB**

Monitor/display type: _____

Port for the mouse:	☐ COM1	☐ COM2	☐ COM3	☐ COM4
Port for the modem:	☐ COM1	☐ COM2	☐ COM3	☐ COM4
Port for the printer:	☐ LPT1	☐ LPT2	☐ LPT3	

Port for the  **:** _____

Port for the _____ **:** _____

Operating system: _____

Dealer name: _____

Dealer phone: _____

Technical support line(s):
_____
_____
_____
_____

Technical support e-mail contacts:
_____
_____
_____

Copyright © 1997 IDG Books Worldwide. All rights reserved.
For more information about IDG Books call **1-800-762-2974**.
ISBN 0-7645-3053-4

DISCOVER PCs

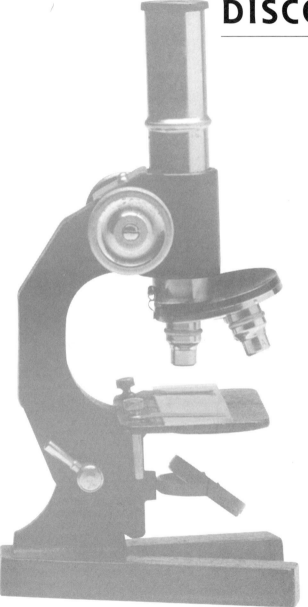

DISCOVER PCs

BY KATHERINE MURRAY

IDG BOOKS WORLDWIDE, INC.

AN INTERNATIONAL
DATA GROUP COMPANY

FOSTER CITY, CA • CHICAGO, IL •
INDIANAPOLIS, IN • SOUTHLAKE, TX

Discover PCs

Published by
IDG Books Worldwide, Inc.
An International Data Group Company
919 E. Hillsdale Blvd., Suite 400
Foster City, CA 94404

http://www.idgbooks.com (IDG Books Worldwide Web site)

Copyright © 1997 IDG Books Worldwide, Inc. All rights reserved. No part of this book, including interior design, cover design, and icons, may be reproduced or transmitted in any form, by any means (electronic, photocopying, recording, or otherwise) without the prior written permission of the publisher.

Library of Congress Catalog Card No.: 96-79752

ISBN: 0-7645-3053-4

Printed in the United States of America

10 9 8 7 6 5 4 3 2 1

1IPC/RU/QT/ZX/FC

Distributed in the United States by IDG Books Worldwide, Inc.

Distributed by Macmillan Canada for Canada; by Contemporanea de Ediciones for Venezuela; by Distribuidora Cuspide for Argentina; by CITEC for Brazil; by Ediciones ZETA S.C.R. Ltda. for Peru; by Editorial Limusa SA for Mexico; by Transworld Publishers Limited in the United Kingdom and Europe; by Academic Bookshop for Egypt; by Levant Distributors S.A.R.L. for Lebanon; by Al Jassim for Saudi Arabia; by Simron Pty. Ltd. for South Africa; by Pustak Mahal for India; by The Computer Bookshop for India; by Toppan Company Ltd. for Japan; by Addison Wesley Publishing Company for Korea; by Longman Singapore Publishers Ltd. for Singapore, Malaysia, Thailand, and Indonesia; by Unalis Corporation for Taiwan; by WS Computer Publishing Company, Inc. for the Philippines; by WoodsLane Pty. Ltd. for Australia; by WoodsLane Enterprises Ltd. for New Zealand. Authorized Sales Agent: Anthony Rudkin Associates for the Middle East and North Africa.

For general information on IDG Books Worldwide's books in the U.S., please call our Consumer Customer Service department at 800-762-2974. For reseller information, including discounts and premium sales, please call our Reseller Customer Service department at 800-434-3422.

For information on where to purchase IDG Books Worldwide's books outside the U.S., please contact our International Sales department at 415-655-3172 or fax 415-655-3295.

For information on foreign language translations, please contact our Foreign & Subsidiary Rights department at 415-655-3021 or fax 415-655-3281.

For sales inquiries and special prices for bulk quantities, please contact our Sales department at 415-655-3200 or write to the address above.

For information on using IDG Books Worldwide's books in the classroom or for ordering examination copies, please contact our Educational Sales department at 800-434-2086 or fax 817-251-8174.

For press review copies, author interviews, or other publicity information, please contact our Public Relations department at 415-655-3000 or fax 415-655-3299.

For authorization to photocopy items for corporate, personal, or educational use, please contact Copyright Clearance Center, 222 Rosewood Drive, Danvers, MA 01923, or fax 508-750-4470.

LIMIT OF LIABILITY/DISCLAIMER OF WARRANTY: AUTHOR AND PUBLISHER HAVE USED THEIR BEST EFFORTS IN PREPARING THIS BOOK. IDG BOOKS WORLDWIDE, INC., AND AUTHOR MAKE NO REPRESENTATIONS OR WARRANTIES WITH RESPECT TO THE ACCURACY OR COMPLETENESS OF THE CONTENTS OF THIS BOOK AND SPECIFICALLY DISCLAIM ANY IMPLIED WARRANTIES OF MERCHANTABILITY OR FITNESS FOR A PARTICULAR PURPOSE. THERE ARE NO WARRANTIES WHICH EXTEND BEYOND THE DESCRIPTIONS CONTAINED IN THIS PARAGRAPH. NO WARRANTY MAY BE CREATED OR EXTENDED BY SALES REPRESENTATIVES OR WRITTEN SALES MATERIALS. THE ACCURACY AND COMPLETENESS OF THE INFORMATION PROVIDED HEREIN AND THE OPINIONS STATED HEREIN ARE NOT GUARANTEED OR WARRANTED TO PRODUCE ANY PARTICULAR RESULTS, AND THE ADVICE AND STRATEGIES CONTAINED HEREIN MAY NOT BE SUITABLE FOR EVERY INDIVIDUAL. NEITHER IDG BOOKS WORLDWIDE, INC., NOR AUTHOR SHALL BE LIABLE FOR ANY LOSS OF PROFIT OR ANY OTHER COMMERCIAL DAMAGES, INCLUDING BUT NOT LIMITED TO SPECIAL, INCIDENTAL, CONSEQUENTIAL, OR OTHER DAMAGES.

TRADEMARKS: ALL BRAND NAMES AND PRODUCT NAMES USED IN THIS BOOK ARE TRADE NAMES, SERVICE MARKS, TRADEMARKS, OR REGISTERED TRADEMARKS OF THEIR RESPECTIVE OWNERS. IDG BOOKS WORLDWIDE IS NOT ASSOCIATED WITH ANY PRODUCT OR VENDOR MENTIONED IN THIS BOOK.

 is a trademark under exclusive license to IDG Books Worldwide, Inc., from International Data Group, Inc.

ABOUT IDG BOOKS WORLDWIDE

Welcome to the world of IDG Books Worldwide.

IDG Books Worldwide, Inc., is a subsidiary of International Data Group, the world's largest publisher of computer-related information and the leading global provider of information services on information technology. IDG was founded more than 25 years ago and now employs more than 8,500 people worldwide. IDG publishes more than 275 computer publications in over 75 countries (see listing below). More than 60 million people read one or more IDG publications each month.

Launched in 1990, IDG Books Worldwide is today the #1 publisher of best-selling computer books in the United States. We are proud to have received eight awards from the Computer Press Association in recognition of editorial excellence and three from *Computer Currents*' First Annual Readers' Choice Awards. Our best-selling *...For Dummies®* series has more than 30 million copies in print with translations in 30 languages. IDG Books Worldwide, through a joint venture with IDG's Hi-Tech Beijing, became the first U.S. publisher to publish a computer book in the People's Republic of China. In record time, IDG Books Worldwide has become the first choice for millions of readers around the world who want to learn how to better manage their businesses.

Our mission is simple: Every one of our books is designed to bring extra value and skill-building instructions to the reader. Our books are written by experts who understand and care about our readers. The knowledge base of our editorial staff comes from years of experience in publishing, education, and journalism — experience we use to produce books for the '90s. In short, we care about books, so we attract the best people. We devote special attention to details such as audience, interior design, use of icons, and illustrations. And because we use an efficient process of authoring, editing, and desktop publishing our books electronically, we can spend more time ensuring superior content and spend less time on the technicalities of making books.

You can count on our commitment to deliver high-quality books at competitive prices on topics you want to read about. At IDG Books Worldwide, we continue in the IDG tradition of delivering quality for more than 25 years. You'll find no better book on a subject than one from IDG Books Worldwide.

John Kilcullen
CEO
IDG Books Worldwide, Inc.

Eighth Annual
Computer Press
Awards ≥1992

Ninth Annual
Computer Press
Awards ≥1993

Tenth Annual
Computer Press
Awards ≥1994

Eleventh Annual
Computer Press
Awards ≥1995

IDG Books Worldwide, Inc., is a subsidiary of International Data Group, the world's largest publisher of computer-related information and the leading global provider of information services on information technology. International Data Group publishes over 275 computer publications in over 75 countries. Sixty million people read one or more International Data Group publications each month. International Data Group's publications include: **ARGENTINA:** Buyer's Guide, Computerworld Argentina, PC World Argentina; **AUSTRALIA:** Australian Macworld, Australian PC World, Australian Reseller News, Computerworld, IT Casebook, Network World, Publish, Webmaster; **AUSTRIA:** Computerwelt Osterreich, Networks Austria, PC Tip Austria; **BANGLADESH:** PC World Bangladesh; **BELARUS:** PC World Belarus; **BELGIUM:** Data News; **BRAZIL:** Annuário de Informática, Computerworld, Connections, Macworld, PC Player, PC World, Publish, Reseller News, Supergamepower; **BULGARIA:** Computerworld Bulgaria, Network World Bulgaria, PC & MacWorld Bulgaria; **CANADA:** CIO Canada, Client/Server World, ComputerWorld Canada, InfoWorld Canada, NetworkWorld Canada, WebWorld; **CHILE:** Computerworld Chile, PC World Chile; **COLOMBIA:** Computerworld Colombia, PC World Colombia; **COSTA RICA:** PC World Centro America; **THE CZECH AND SLOVAK REPUBLICS:** Computerworld Czechoslovakia, Macworld Czech Republic, PC World Czechoslovakia; **DENMARK:** Communications World Danmark, Computerworld Danmark, Macworld Danmark, PC World Danmark, Techworld Denmark; **DOMINICAN REPUBLIC:** PC World Republica Dominicana; **ECUADOR:** PC World Ecuador; **EGYPT:** Computerworld Middle East, PC World Middle East; **EL SALVADOR:** PC World Centro America; **FINLAND:** MikroPC, Tietoverkko, Tietoviikko; **FRANCE:** Distributique, Hebdo, Info PC, Le Monde Informatique, Macworld, Reseaux & Telecoms, WebMaster France; **GERMANY:** Computer Partner, Computerwoche, Computerwoche Extra, Computerwoche FOCUS, Global Online, Macwelt, PC Welt; **GREECE:** Amiga Computing, GamePro Greece, Multimedia World; **GUATEMALA:** PC World Centro America; **HONDURAS:** PC World Centro America; **HONG KONG:** Computerworld Hong Kong, PC World Hong Kong, Publish in Asia; **HUNGARY:** ABCD CD-ROM, Computerworld Szamitastechnika, Internetto online Magazine, PC World Hungary, PC-X Magazin Hungary; **ICELAND:** Tolvuheimur PC World Island; **INDIA:** Information Communications World, Information Systems Computerworld, PC World India, Publish in Asia; **INDONESIA:** InfoKomputer PC World, Komputek Computerworld, Publish in Asia; **IRELAND:** ComputerScope, PC Live!; **ISRAEL:** Macworld Israel, People & Computers/Computerworld; **ITALY:** Computerworld Italia, Macworld Italia, Networking Italia, PC World Italia; **JAPAN:** DTP World, Macworld Japan, Nikkei Personal Computing, OS/2 World Japan, SunWorld Japan, Windows NT World, Windows World Japan; **KENYA:** PC World East African; **KOREA:** Hi-Tech Information, Macworld Korea, PC World Korea; **MACEDONIA:** PC World Macedonia; **MALAYSIA:** Computerworld Malaysia, PC World Malaysia, Publish in Asia; **MALTA:** PC World Malta; **MEXICO:** Computerworld Mexico, PC World Mexico; **MYANMAR:** PC World Myanmar; **NETHERLANDS:** Computer! Totaal, LAN Internetworking Magazine, LAN World Buyers Guide, Macworld Netherlands, Net, WebWereld; **NEW ZEALAND:** Absolute Beginners Guide and Plain & Simple Series, Computer Buyer, Computer Industry Directory, Computerworld New Zealand, MTB, Network World, PC World New Zealand; **NICARAGUA:** PC World Centro America; **NORWAY:** Computerworld Norge, CW Rapport, Datamagasinet, Financial Rapport, Kursguide Norge, Macworld Norge, Multimediaworld Norge, PC World Ekspress Norge, PC World Nettverk, PC World Norge, PC World ProduktGuide Norge; **PAKISTAN:** Computerworld Pakistan; **PANAMA:** PC World Panama; **PEOPLE'S REPUBLIC OF CHINA:** China Computer Users, China Computerworld, China InfoWorld, China Telecom World Weekly, Computer & Communication, Electronic Design China, Electronics Today, Electronics Weekly, Game Software, PC World China, Popular Computer Week, Software Weekly, Software World, Telecom World; **PERU:** Computerworld Peru, PC World Profesional Peru, PC World SoHo Peru; **PHILIPPINES:** Click!, Computerworld Philippines, PC World Philippines, Publish in Asia; **POLAND:** Computerworld Poland, Computerworld Special Report Poland, Cyber, Macworld Poland, Network World Poland, PC World Komputer; **PORTUGAL:** Cerebro/PC World, Computerworld/Correio Informático, Dealer World Portugal, Mac*In/PC*In Portugal, Multimedia World; **PUERTO RICO:** PC World Puerto Rico; **ROMANIA:** Computerworld Romania, PC World Romania, Telecom Romania; **RUSSIA:** Computerworld Russia, Mir PK, Publish, Seti; **SINGAPORE:** Computerworld Singapore, PC World Singapore, Publish in Asia; **SLOVENIA:** Monitor; **SOUTH AFRICA:** Computing SA, Network World SA, Software World SA; **SPAIN:** Comunicaciones World España, Computerworld España, Dealer World España, Macworld España, PC World España; **SRI LANKA:** Infolink PC World; **SWEDEN:** CAP&Design, Computer Sweden, Corporate Computing Sweden, Internetworld Sweden, it.branschen, Macworld Sweden, MaxiData Sweden, MikroDatorn, Natverk & Kommunikation, PC World Sweden, PCaktiv, Windows World Sweden; **SWITZERLAND:** Computerworld Schweiz, Macworld Schweiz, PCtip; **TAIWAN:** Computerworld Taiwan, Macworld Taiwan, NEW ViSiON/Publish, PC World Taiwan, Windows World Taiwan; **THAILAND:** Publish in Asia, Thai Computerworld; **TURKEY:** Computerworld Turkiye, Macworld Turkiye, Network World Turkiye, PC World Turkiye; **UKRAINE:** Computerworld Kiev, Multimedia World Ukraine, PC World Ukraine; **UNITED KINGDOM:** Acorn User UK, Amiga Action UK, Amiga Computing UK, Apple Talk UK, Computing, Macworld, Parents and Computers UK, PC Advisor, PC Home, PSX Pro, The WEB; **UNITED STATES:** Cable in the Classroom, CIO Magazine, Computerworld, DOS World, Federal Computer Week, GamePro Magazine, InfoWorld, I-Way, Macworld, Network World, PC Games, PC World, Publish, Video Event, THE WEB Magazine, and WebMaster; online webzines: JavaWorld, NetscapeWorld, and SunWorld Online; **URUGUAY:** InfoWorld Uruguay; **VENEZUELA:** Computerworld Venezuela, PC World Venezuela; and **VIETNAM:** PC World Vietnam. 2/14/97

Welcome to the Discover Series

Do you want to discover the best and most efficient ways to use your computer and learn about technology? Books in the Discover series teach you the essentials of technology with a friendly, confident approach. You'll find a Discover book on almost any subject — from the Internet to intranets, from Web design and programming to the business programs that make your life easier.

We've provided valuable, real-world examples that help you relate to topics faster. Discover books begin by introducing you to the main features of programs, so you start by doing something *immediately*. The focus is to teach you how to perform tasks that are useful and meaningful in your day-to-day work. You might create a document or graphic, explore your computer, surf the Web, or write a program. Whatever the task, you learn the most commonly used features, and focus on the best tips and techniques for doing your work. You'll get results quickly, and discover the best ways to use software and technology in your everyday life.

You may find the following elements and features in this book:

Discovery Central: This tearout card is a handy quick reference to important tasks or ideas covered in the book.

Quick Tour: The Quick Tour gets you started working with the book right away.

Real-Life Vignettes: Throughout the book you'll see one-page scenarios illustrating a real-life application of a topic covered.

Goals: Each chapter opens with a list of goals you can achieve by reading the chapter.

Side Trips: These asides include additional information about alternative or advanced ways to approach the topic covered.

Bonuses: Timesaving tips and more advanced techniques are covered in each chapter.

Discovery Center: This guide illustrates key procedures covered throughout the book.

Visual Index: You'll find real-world documents in the Visual Index, with page numbers pointing you to where you should turn to achieve the effects shown.

Throughout the book, you'll also notice some special icons and formatting:

 A Feature Focus icon highlights new features in the software's latest release, and points out significant differences between it and the previous version.

 Web Paths refer you to Web sites that provide additional information about the topic.

 Tips offer timesaving shortcuts, expert advice, quick techniques, or brief reminders.

 The X-Ref icon refers you to other chapters or sections for more information.

Pull Quotes emphasize important ideas that are covered in the chapter.

 Notes provide additional information or highlight special points of interest about a topic.

 The Caution icon alerts you to potential problems you should watch out for.

The Discover series delivers interesting, insightful, and inspiring information about technology to help you learn faster and retain more. So the next time you want to find answers to your technology questions, reach for a Discover book. We hope the entertaining, easy-to-read style puts you at ease and makes learning fun.

Credits

ACQUISITIONS EDITOR
Greg Croy

DEVELOPMENT EDITOR
Stefan Grünwedel

TECHNICAL EDITOR
Matt Hayden

COPY EDITOR
Carolyn Welch

PROJECT COORDINATOR
Katy German

GRAPHICS AND PRODUCTION SPECIALISTS
Mario F. Amador
Laura Carpenter
Ed Penslien
Dina F Quan
Mark Schumann
Jimmy Young

QUALITY CONTROL SPECIALIST
Mick Arellano

PROOFREADERS
Desne Border
Andrew Davis
Stacey Lynn
Candace Ward
Anne Weinberger

INDEXER
Alexandra Nickerson

BOOK DESIGN
Seventeenth Street Studios
Phyllis Beaty
Kurt Krames

About the Author

Katherine Murray is a writer living in a farmhouse in the middle of a popcorn farm in southern Indiana. The author of more than 40 books, Katherine specializes in writing books for beginning-level computer users. Although the bulk of her writing is computer-related, Katherine has written two parenting books, a number of children's books, two books of poetry, eight plays, and numerous songs. A mom with three kids, Katherine runs her business from her home, where she can keep an eye on the kids and make sure the dogs, cat, birds, guinea pig, and cows stay out of trouble.

PREFACE

Discover PCs helps you explore the world of computers if you are learning about them for the first time. You'll find setup and startup information, beginning with the basics: What do systems offer now? What do you need? What do you want? In addition, this book offers a broad range of information on computers: what software programs work with them, how you can care for them, and what to do when they give you fits.

If you have had experience with computers before but haven't been using one for a while, *Discover PCs* will help you get a handle on what's changed while you've been away and bring you up to speed with the programs, peripherals, and PCs on the cutting edge of home and business computing. Once you've made your choices and settled in to work, you'll find out how the computer makes everything work and discover what you need to do to keep things running smoothly.

How This Book Is Organized

This book is broken up into four major parts:

Part One, "First, the Basics," is about the things you need to consider as you are preparing to drop the cash for your first personal computer. What kind of system do you want? What kinds of computers are out there? How are they used today? What features will you be sorry you skimped on? What is a must-have computer peripheral?

Part Two, "The Computer: Inside and Out," focuses on each major part of the computer, one at a time. You'll find a chapter on the system unit, mice, printers, keyboards — you get the idea.

Part Three, "On the Road to PC Productivity," assumes that you've purchased the system and now understand how most of the important things work. Now you get to put the computer together and begin using it. What does the operating system do? What if you want to take the PC traveling? This part of the book gets you moving in a new way: from desktop to phone line to Internet.

Part Four, "Preventing PC Pitfalls." I'm not saying it's inevitable, but things break. Disks crash. Monitors get screwy. Mice die. Hopefully it won't happen to you, but this part of the book focuses on what you can do — just in case. First you'll learn some basic care-and-feeding techniques for your PC. Then you'll discover important ways to communicate with those super-intelligent technical support people on the other end of the phone. As someone smart once said, "A pound of prevention is worth an ounce of cure" . . . or, um, something like that.

What's Next?

Now you are ready to get started. Be prepared to discover what a PC can do for you — at home or at work — and rest assured that your PC horizons will be expanded. Remember that you can have fun if you let yourself think about all the ways a PC can fit into your life. Be creative. Dream a little. And know that, especially when it comes to computers, what Walt Disney said is true: "If you can dream it, you can do it."

Acknowledgments

It takes a lot of people to make a book. From the publisher to the developer to the editor, and all the visionaries in between, a considerable number of people thought, planned, evaluated, and were connected with this book in some way. As the writer (that's the fun part!), I get to say thank-you to the group for the effort that produced *Discover PCs.*

Thanks to Walter Bruce, Greg Croy, Ellen Camm, Stefan Grünwedel, Kay Keppler, and Matt Hayden. And a special thank-you to Dr. Michael Mangas, Joy Deckard, John Sherman, and Julianne Williams, who contributed their stories for the real-life vignettes used in this book. Finally, thanks to the people who contributed their insight, tips, anecdotes, and PC Peeves — your experiences will help encourage and enlighten readers as they discover more about their PCs.

CONTENTS AT A GLANCE

Preface, ix
Acknowledgments, xi
Introduction, xxv

| QUICK TOUR | 1 |

PART ONE—FIRST, THE BASICS

1	COMPUTER POSSIBILITIES	9
2	MAKING A COMPUTER MATCH: A BEFORE-YOU-BUY GUIDE	21
3	CHECKING OUT COMPUTER TYPES	35

PART TWO—THE COMPUTER: INSIDE AND OUT

4	WHAT'S THIS SYSTEM UNIT THING?	49
5	THE LOWDOWN ON DISK DRIVES	63
6	MONITOR BASICS: THAT THING YOU LOOK AT	77
7	KEYBOARD CARE AND FEEDING	85
8	OF MICE AND OTHER POINTING DEVICES	97
9	POINTS ABOUT PRINTING	109
10	MODEMS, MODEMS	123
11	ADD-ONS YOU CAN OWN AND LOVE	133

PART THREE—ON THE ROAD TO PC PRODUCTIVITY

12	SETTING UP YOUR SPACE	143
13	STARTING OUT WITH THE OPERATING SYSTEM	151
14	PROGRAMS! PROGRAMS! READ ALL ABOUT 'EM!	167
15	TRAVELING WITH YOUR COMPUTER	195
16	GETTING ON THE INTERNET	205

PART FOUR—PREVENTING PC PITFALLS

| 17 | COMPUTER CARE 101 | 223 |
| 18 | PC PROBLEM SOLVING | 231 |

Discovery Center, 241
Index, 265

CONTENTS

Preface, ix

Acknowledgments, xi

Introduction, xxv

QUICK TOUR, 1

PART ONE—FIRST, THE BASICS, 7

1 COMPUTER POSSIBILITIES, 9

What Is a Computer?, 10
  A (Very) Little PC History, 10

What Can You Do with Computers Today?, 11
  PCs at the Office, 11
  PCs at Home, 12

Who Uses These Things?, 13

Fast-Changing PC Features, 13
  More Powerful Microprocessors, 13
  Amount of Disk Storage, 14
  Size of the PC, 14
  Amount of Memory, 14

Deciphering Computer Ads, 15
  Computer Terms to Know and Love, 16
  What Matters?, 17
  Beginning Your Computer Education, 18

A Good Read, 19

Summary, 19

2 MAKING A COMPUTER MATCH: A BEFORE-YOU-BUY GUIDE, 21

Things to Think About, 22

The Big Three, 23
  Software Considerations, 23

Compatibility 101, 23
Pardon Our Dust . . ., 24

Preferences, Preferences, 25
Keyboard Komplaints, 25
Mouse Mumblings, 26
Screen Scrutiny, 27
RAM Reminders, 28

The Significance of Speed, 29

Where Do You Get PCs?, 29

Before-You-Buy Questions, 31

PC Brainstorming, 31
Software Considerations, 31
Compatibility Issues, 32
Room to Grow, 32

Summary, 33

3 CHECKING OUT COMPUTER TYPES, 35

Today's Desktop Computers, 35
Desktop Basics, 36
Desktop Options, 36
Desktop Prices, 37

Carrying Around Portable Computers, 38
Notebook Basics, 38
Notebook Options, 39

A Computer in the Palm Is Worth Two in the Trunk, 41

A Peek at Peripherals, 42
Printers: An Optional Necessity, 42
The Modem: Connectivity and Cyberspace, 43
A CD-ROM of Your Dreams, 43

Scoping Out the Competitors, 45

Little Things Mean a Lot, 45

Summary, 46

PART TWO—THE COMPUTER: INSIDE AND OUT, 47

4 WHAT'S THIS SYSTEM UNIT THING?, 49

What's the System Unit For?, 50

System Unit Parts: Exposed!, 50

Power Up!, 51
Power Through: A Look Inside, 52

What in the World Is the BIOS?, 52

Chips Only a Mother(board) Could Love, 53
Put It All Together, It Spells m-o-t-h-e-r, 53
What Makes the Motherboard Proud? The Microprocessor, 53
RAM Chips and Dip: The Memory in Your Machine, 54

A Card in Every Port: Port Basics, 57

Power Supply? Big Deal!, 59

The Seven Deadly System Unit Sins, 60

More Power! The Uninterruptible Power Supply, 61

Summary, 62

5 THE LOWDOWN ON DISK DRIVES, 63

The Basics of Disk Drives, 64
Disk Drive Differences, 64
The Whole Point of Disk Drives, 64

Checking Out Storage Types, 65

The Facts About Floppy Disks, 67
Made of Tougher Stuff: 3.5-inch Disks, 67
How Dense Is Your Data?, 69

What's So Hard About Hard Disks?, 69
How Does the Hard Disk Work?, 69
A Hard Disk By Any Other Name, 70
More Storage! More Storage!, 70

CD or Not CD?, 71
CD Speeds and Options, 72
How Does the CD-ROM Drive Work?, 72

Doing Stuff with Disks, 73
Formatting Them, 73
Labeling Them, 74
Copying Them, 74
Erasing Them, 74

Major Storage Idea, 75

Summary, 76

6 MONITOR BASICS: THAT THING YOU LOOK AT, 77

Monitoring the Monitor, 77
The Display Adapter: Where It All Begins, 77
From the Adapter to the Monitor, 78

Important Monitor Qualities, 78
    Mono(tonous) or Color?, 79
    Is Size Everything?, 79
    Resolutions You Can Live With, 80
    A Quick Refresher Course, 81
    To Interlace or Not to Interlace?, 82
    Dual-Scan and Active Matrix, 82

Let's Get Comfortable, 82

Screen Add-ons, 83

Summary, 84

7   KEYBOARD CARE AND FEEDING, 85

Keyboard Basics, 85
    Your Average Desktop Keyboard, 86
    Not-a-Lotta-Room Notebooks, 87

Does Brand Matter?, 87

Keys to the Board, 88
    QWERTY Keys, 88
    Enter and Then Return, 89
    Which Way Did He Go?, 90
    It's Not My Function!, 91
    Num All Over and Scroll Locked, 91
    Specialty Keys, 92
    Escape! Escape!, 93

Healthy Keyboard Practices, 93
    Keyboard Care, 93
    A Keyboard in the Hands Is Hard on the Wrists, 94

Keyboard Add-ons, 95

Summary, 95

8   OF MICE AND OTHER POINTING DEVICES, 97

Pointing Devices: Why We Need 'Em, 97

Meet Your Mouse, 98
    Mouse Families: Serial and Bus, 98
    How Does the Mouse Work?, 99
    How Many Buttons Do You Need?, 99

Working with the Mouse, 99
    Moving the Mouse, 100
    Clicking and Double-Clicking, 100
    Dragging Items, 102
    Other Mouse Options, 102
    Cleaning Your Mouse, 102

Trackballs and Touchpads, 104
    Why a Trackball Isn't a Mouse, 104
    Touchy, Aren't You?, 106

Mouse Add-ons, 107

Summary, 107

9   POINTS ABOUT PRINTING, 109

When a Cheapo Printer Will Do, 110

When You Need a Good-Quality Printer, 111

How Does It Print?, 112
    Dot-Matrix Printers, 112
    Inkjets, 114
    Laser Printers, 116
    Thermal Printers, 118

Multifunction Centers, 118

Things to Worry about When You Use a Printer, 119
    Paper, 119
    Ribbons, Cartridges, and Toner, 120
    Switching from One Printer to Another, 120

Do-It-Yourself Business Cards, 120

Summary, 121

10   MODEMS, MODEMS, 123

What's a Modem?, 123

What Can You Do with a Modem?, 125
    A Modem and Then What?, 125
    Essential E-mail, 125
    New Worlds to Explore — Through the Phone Line?, 126
    Internet Mania, 127

Checking out Modem Types, 128
    External and Internal, 129
    How Important Is Speed?, 130
    The Software Difference, 130

Connecting a Modem, 131

Modem Extras, 131

Summary, 132

11   ADD-ONS YOU CAN OWN AND LOVE, 133

Scanners: Not Just Sci-fi Stuff, 134

Here's Looking at You, Kid: Digital Cameras, 136

Smile, You're on QuickCam, 137

P.C. Escher: Graphics Tablets, 137

Do Re MIDI, 138

Joysticks and Game Gear, 139

Summary, 140

PART THREE—ON THE ROAD TO PC PRODUCTIVITY, 141

12 SETTING UP YOUR SPACE, 143

Choose Your Space, 144

Plan Your Work Area, 144

Setup 101, 146
- Make a List, 146
- Get the System Unit Right, 146
- Eyeing the Monitor, 147
- Proper Printer Positioning, 148
- Cables, Cables Everywhere, 148

How Usable Is Your System?, 149

Let's Talk About Desks, 149

Summary, 150

13 STARTING OUT WITH THE OPERATING SYSTEM, 151

Flip the Switch!, 152
- What Happens During Startup?, 152
- System Checks and Other Automated Events, 152

What Is the Operating System Good For?, 154
- A Millisecond in the Life of Your Operating System, 154
- The System Versus Environment Issue, 155

Know Your Operating Systems, 156
- Microsoft Windows, 156
- Windows 3.1, 157
- Windows 95, 157
- DOS, 158
- OS/2, 160
- UNIX, 160

Installing or Upgrading Your Operating System, 161

Friendly Operating Tips, 162
  Windows's Likes and Dislikes, 162
  A Note About DOS, 164

Options, Options, 165

Summary, 165

14 PROGRAMS! PROGRAMS! READ ALL ABOUT 'EM!, 167

Why Do They Call It Software?, 167

Building Your Own Software Library, 168
  Word Processing, 169
  Spreadsheets, 172
  Databases, 173
  Games!, 174
  Communications Software, 176
  Web Page Design Programs, 177
  Graphics Programs, 178
  Desktop Publishing Programs, 180
  PIMs and Schedulers, 181
  Money Managers, 182
  Utilities, 183
  Educational Software, 183
  Fun Stuff and Edutainment Titles, 184

Finding Software, 185

Installation Issues, 187

Starting Programs, 188

Getting Help When You Need It, 190

To Upgrade or Not to Upgrade, 190

Keeping Your Programs Straight (and Safe), 192

Summary, 192

15 TRAVELING WITH YOUR COMPUTER, 195

What Is a Virtual Office?, 196

A Traveler's Guide to Computing, 196
  The Occasional PC Traveler, 197
  The Mobile Computerist, 197

What Do You Need for PC Travel?, 198
  The Hardware, 198
  The Software, 199
  The Other Stuff, 199

Preparing Your Computer, 200

The International PC, 201
    Is Your PC AC/DC?, 201
    Can You Plug a Square Peg into a Round Hole?, 202
    Où Est le Téléphone?, 202
    (Almost) Online and Ready, 203

Leaving a Paper Trail, 203

Summary, 204

16 GETTING ON THE INTERNET, 205

What Is the Internet (Am I the Last Person on Earth to Know)?, 205
    What Exactly Is a Network?, 206
    A Little Internet Evolution, 207

How Do I Get There?, 207
    First Things First: The Speed Issue, 208
    Using a Commercial Service to Get on the Internet, 208
    Accessing with an Internet Service Provider, 209

How Will I Use the Internet?, 211
    The World's Biggest Card Catalog, 211
    Kids on the Net, 212
    E-mail for Everyone, 213
    The News About Newsgroups, 214

Discover the World Wide Web, 215
    What Do I Need to Get on the World Wide Web?, 215
    There's No Place Like Home (Page), 216
    How Do You Create a Home Page?, 217
    Navigating the Web, 218

Web Page Organizers, 219

Summary, 219

PART FOUR—PREVENTING PC PITFALLS, 221

17 COMPUTER CARE 101, 223

A Basic System Self-Care Guide, 223

What Your System Needs, 224

Diverting Display Disasters, 225

Keyboard Care, 225

Mouse Mothering, 226

Protect Your Printer, 227

What Your Software Needs, 228
What You Need, 228
Back Up the Easy Way, 229
Summary, 229

18 PC PROBLEM SOLVING, 231
Ten Common PC Potholes, 231
Hardware Headaches, 236
Software Struggles, 236
What You Need to Tell Tech Support, 237
The Best Troubleshooting Advice Ever, 238
First Aid 95, 239
Summary, 239

Discovery Center, 241
Index, 265

INTRODUCTION

I'm lucky to find time to write these days. "Mom, can I use your computer?" is a common question at our house. So common, in fact, that even though I have another computer for my kids to use, they prefer mine because it has a faster modem.

And I'm not alone. Today all over the globe we've got parents arm-wrestling teenagers away from computer keyboards. The computer has been discovered as the next best thing to the telephone as a communication device. In fact, my teenager goes online to chat in cyberspace and talks to local friends on the phone at the same time. (Something I should have considered before I put in that second phone line.)

And the attraction isn't limited to adults and teens. In my house, there's an eight-year-old who wants to use Microsoft Bookshelf and a three-year-old who demands equal time playing Math Rabbit. If the dog could figure out how to use the mouse, I'm sure he'd be up here sniffing out his own ideas.

Just a few years ago, PCs were special equipment we used to accomplish a particular task. If you needed to automate your small business's accounting system, you invested in a computer. If you published manuals or brochures, you could cut printing costs and headaches by doing the desktop publishing yourself on a PC.

If you worked in a large company, you may have used computers to enter billing information, update a database, perform analyses, or do any number of other tasks. But the idea of owning one seemed ludicrous. What would you use a computer for at *home*? Why would a small, struggling business spring a few thousand much-needed dollars for something as luxurious as a computer?

Today, you can flip that question around and ask, "What *can't* you use a computer for at home?" Interested in recipes? There are programs to help you record, file, organize, and even create your favorite recipes. Basic home maintenance things like creating a billing system, maintaining a home inventory, and keeping important information like Social Security numbers, medical insurance data, and student IDs are now the part of the domain of the family computer. And there are also programs for the letters you write, the checkbooks you balance, the taxes you prepare, the family trees you grow, and games — don't forget the games!

That doesn't even peek into the world of cyberspace. If your computer has a modem, there are worlds you can explore that were unavailable to most of us normal folk just a few years ago. The information superhighway used to be a Ph.D.'s Autobahn to research; now it is capturing our imaginations, quenching our thirsts for knowledge, and luring us away from our television sets. Whether you're into surfing for fun or profit (or both), you can use the various Internet search tools and the visually pleasing World Wide Web to extend your data reach around the world and back.

These are just a few of the things home users are doing these days. In the balance sheet of the business world, computers have moved from the Luxury column into the Necessity column. As computers have gotten more powerful, they've also grown more affordable. Most businesses today don't have trouble justifying the cash outlay for their first PCs.

The traditional small business uses — organizing mailing lists, keeping databases current, writing reports and training materials, performing financial analyses, forecasting, and more — have been expanded and enhanced. Now, in addition to those things, we publish on the desktop. We write and record music. We capture and edit video.

And in an even more esoteric world, computers are performing virtual surgery, a training ground for future surgeons. They are building buildings, composing symphonies, creating multimedia training events, and running television stations. They keep track of your local library's holdings and can search through other library stacks all over the globe. They instantly update the stock of your local 7-Eleven and log your phone number in when you call your insurance agent.

Still not convinced? You may be happy with the way things are running right now — without a computer, thank you very much. You can balance the checkbook just fine using your calculator. You can figure your taxes on paper. You use the card file your grandmother gave you back in 1972 to store your favorite recipes. You never needed a presentation program to get up in front of prospective clients before — what's wrong with an overhead projector?

The computer won't take any of your favorite tools away or completely replace your comfortable way of doing things. Think of the computer as an add-on; something that can (and will) make boring tasks faster, complicated tasks easier, and difficult tasks more accurate. Educate yourself gradually and try out the things that interest you first. You may be surprised to find out how quickly you want to learn more.

If you're in a work environment, you may not have much choice about whether or not you're going to use a computer. Someone may thrust a computer program in your hands, lead you to a PC, and say, "Try this." There's not a lot you can do about that. Just go at it with an open mind and keep these things in mind:

* You're not going to break the computer
* We've all been beeped at
* If you take the proper precautions, you won't lose any of your work

What will computers do tomorrow? One thing, for certain: much more than we expect of them today.

PCs QUICK TOUR

IN THIS CHAPTER YOU LEARN THESE KEY SKILLS

GET THE PC YOU REALLY WANT   PAGE   2

SET UP THE PC JUST RIGHT   PAGE   4

USE THE PC   PAGE   4

SOLVE BASIC PC PROBLEMS   PAGE   6

If you're just starting out with your PC — or just now thinking about making that first PC purchase — take heart. It's not as hard as it looks. Yes, there are volumes written about which computer to buy, what programs you need, and how to handle all the hardware headaches. Sure, everything seems overwhelming and hard to figure out.

But getting a PC and moving past that first uncomfortable "I-don't-know-what-to-do" stage really takes only four steps:

1. Get the PC you want.

2. Set up your PC.

3. Start using the PC.

4. Solve PC problems.

In this Quick Tour, we'll hit all the basics of those four major steps, and you'll be well on your way to PC proficiency.

Step 1: Find the PC you want

Most of the people I interviewed for this book told me that the absolute worst part of their PC experience was the prepurchase turmoil. "Which one should I buy? What if I make a mistake and I'm sorry later?" Here are some tips to help you get the PC you want and need

* If there is a particular program you need to run on the PC, make sure you get a PC powerful enough to run it. (This will also help you determine which type of PC to get. If you will be using a program that runs only in Windows, you know you need an IBM-compatible computer that can run the version of Windows the program needs.)

* If you need to be compatible with a computer at the office, look for something similar (same brand, same software, same amount of RAM, and so on.)

* Consider what you need the computer to do now and what you might need a year from now. Get enough computer so that you can easily grow into any new tasks (Internet access? Multimedia?) next year.

* Educate yourself. Perhaps the most important part of making that computer purchase is in finding out what's available. Go to a computer store and play with the machines. Decide what you like and what you don't like. Read computer magazines and review the reviews. Talk to other computer users, but don't make your decision based solely on the advice of a salesperson. Get some good, old-fashioned hands-on experience with a PC that suits you before you make your decision.

What kind of computer do you need? There are desktop computers, notebook computers, IBM, Apple, Compaq, and much, much more. Most desktop computers include a system unit, monitor, keyboard, and mouse (some are sold without the monitor — check the ads carefully). You'll probably want to add a printer, too.

Most notebook computers can do anything the desktop systems can do, but they are packaged in a notebook-sized chassis and are made to be portable. The system unit, monitor, and keyboard are all part of the notebook computer, and instead of the mouse, you may have either a trackball or a touchpad.

A question that's often difficult for people to answer is, "Where should I get the computer?" Best advice: Check out local computer stores and retailers that carry computers. Those people are nearby, and if you have a problem you know you can contact a real human being about it. But before you write the check, compare prices and technical support availability with mail-order houses. You may pay a little more for a computer from a dealer close to home, but, depending on your budget and your comfort zone, it may be a good investment.

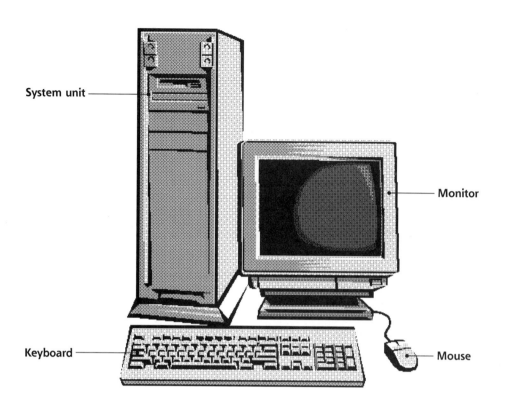

QUICK TOUR

Step 2: Set up the PC

Now you've got the PC and you're ready to set it up. Choosing the right location, and arranging the components so you're comfortable, means that you'll be more likely to use your new PC, which means you're more likely to get your investment's worth. Whether you're setting up your PC in the office or at home, stick with these guidelines to make sure you and your PC are comfortable with each other:

- Set up an area reserved especially for the PC
- Make sure you've got a fairly large work surface (with room for books, the mouse and mouse pad, a light, and room for real pen-and-paper writing)
- Choose an area that's out of the family (or company) traffic flow
- Make sure your monitor is positioned in such a way that you don't catch any glare from outside light
- Choose a good, supportive chair that enables you to sit up straight — but not stretch — to reach the keyboard
- Allow plenty of room for your PC — don't cram it up against the wall, stack things on top of it, or use it as a plant stand

Try the setup for a week or so and then reevaluate. If you aren't happy with the way things feel, if the kids keep knocking the books off the desk when they play MechWarrior or you've spilled coffee on the keyboard twice the first week, you need to rethink things. Make a few changes and watch what happens. Soon you'll settle into a place and position that's comfortable for you, and your investment in time, money, and effort will begin paying off.

Step 3: Use the PC

Sounds easy, doesn't it? Using your PC means simply loading the programs you've got — you do have programs, don't you? — and starting to produce that output you've been yearning for. Ready to do a family budget? How about a letter to Aunt Edna? Maybe you'd like to try sending e-mail to your brother in Barcelona. All these tasks are part of the "use your PC" stage.

Many PCs sold today come with programs already installed. You'll probably get Microsoft Windows 95 and several programs that help you get things done. You might have Microsoft Office, a popular suite of programs that gives you the ability to write documents, create spreadsheets, organize data, and more. You might have a few games, as well, such as 3D Pinball or the ever-popular (and addictive) Minesweeper.

Whatever programs are included on your system, you've got to fire up the PC in order to start them. The first steps to using your PC are these:

1. Make sure everything is plugged in.
2. Push the power button (or flip the switch to On, if you've got a switch to flip!).

Your PC goes through a series of self-checks, making sure everything is working properly, and loads any programs it uses automatically at startup. Then you are presented either with a DOS prompt or a desktop with folders or windows. What you see at this point depends on the operating system your PC uses to interact with programs and with you. The Windows 95 desktop looks something like this:

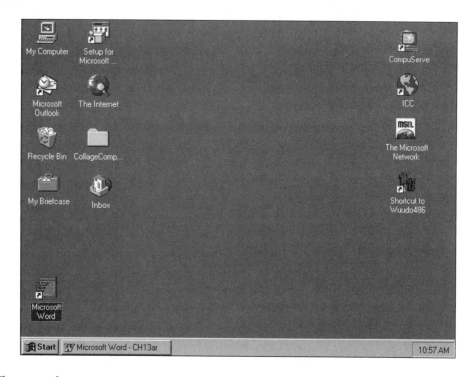

The steps for starting a program vary, too, depending on your operating system. If you're using DOS, which means you don't have a desktop like the one shown here, you must type a command at the DOS prompt, which looks somewhat like this, if you're starting the game Mario's Early Years:

```
C:\> MEYCD
```

NOTE Check your program documentation to see what command you enter to start the program of your choice.

Once the program starts, you're ready to roll. Use the program, experiment, play, whatever. When you exit the program, you are returned to the operating system which, again, is probably either the DOS prompt or the Windows desktop.

Step 4: Solve PC problems

Whoever first said, "An ounce of prevention is worth a pound of cure," must have had a PC. Many of the problems PC users experience could be avoided with a little preventive maintenance. The first cardinal rule of healthy PC use is the following:

Back up important files

Back up means simply to make copies of the files you really, really need. Then if something fails, you're not panicking until someone, somehow, recovers them. If you don't have many files to back up, you may just want to save the files to a disk and put the disk away somewhere safe. If you have a number of files to safeguard, consider getting a backup program that will copy all modified files for you from week to week so you have a complete backup of your PC whenever you need it.

The following are a few common PC problems and potential solutions:

* **A dead mouse**. Make sure the mouse cord is plugged in.
* **An error message during printing**. Check the printer for a paper jam; make sure the cable is plugged in both to the printer and the system unit.
* **An error message when you're trying to open a file on a disk**. Use ScanDisk to determine whether there's something wrong with the disk.
* **A locked up computer**. Press Ctrl+Alt+Del to reboot; if you're given an option to close the program that is not responding, exit that program and see whether the PC stabilizes.

Avoiding Lockup

To avoid a system lockup, follow these guidelines:

* Save your file every 10 to 15 minutes.
* Don't leave a number of programs running at once.
* Don't autoload programs you don't really need.
* Keep an eye on how much RAM you're using.
* Delete unneeded files on your hard drive to keep as much space free as possible.

This QuickTour gives you just a simple overview of what PCs are about. Turn now to the rest of the book to learn many more details about the world of personal computers.

PART ONE

FIRST, THE BASICS

THIS PART CONTAINS THE FOLLOWING CHAPTERS

CHAPTER **1** COMPUTER POSSIBILITIES

CHAPTER **2** MAKING A COMPUTER MATCH: A BEFORE-YOU-BUY GUIDE

CHAPTER **3** CHECKING OUT COMPUTER TYPES

When you're investigating your first PC purchase, the choice may seem overwhelming. It may reassure you to know that many new computer users find making the initial decision — Which one should I get? What software do I need? — is the most difficult part of purchasing and using a PC. Once you make it through this startup stage, the rest will be clear sailing (well, hopefully). This part shows you what computers are being used for today and helps you make educated choices about what to look for in your own personal PC. When that's over, you can move on to the easy stuff.

THE DIGITAL DOMICILE: COMPUTERS IN THE HOME

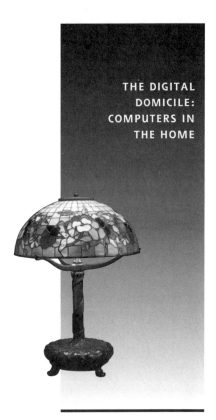

Joy Deckard is an unusual find on the World Wide Web. If you visit her home page, you'll find her photo, several pieces of her artwork, and information on how she does what she does. She's used color, style, formatting, and links to make her Web page a pleasant and informational place to visit. In addition to being an artist and Web page designer, Joy Deckard is a grandmother, a gardener, an innovative cook, and a publisher.

"I never saw a computer before December, 1992," said Joy in an online interview. "That's when my daughter asked me to buy her 386 with 8 megs of RAM and an old dot-matrix printer that was so loud it scared the cat." Joy began putting together booklets, publishing a cookbook of recipes for diabetics, and researching old family recipes that she worried her family might lose track of if they weren't preserved for the children. The computer bug had bitten, and Joy continued upgrading her system to make use of new technologies. Today she has a state-of-the-art system with full desktop publishing and Web publishing capabilities. She talks often with her daughters over the Internet. Yes, "talks" is the word — they can connect and speak *and* type to one another. The video cameras probably aren't too far off in the future.

On the day we talked by phone, Joy had just received the newest addition to her PC family: a digital camera. Now she can take pictures of her artwork, or artwork she compiles for online catalogs for other artists, and capture them in digitized form, ready to be uploaded to the artists' Web sites or to the catalog locations.

What's out there in Joy Deckard's future? Probably all kinds of things. If there's a creative idea to be explored and a PC way to do it, we can be sure Joy is already excitedly planning the best way to accomplish it.

CHAPTER ONE
COMPUTER POSSIBILITIES

IN THIS CHAPTER YOU LEARN THESE KEY SKILLS

LEARN WHAT A COMPUTER IS   PAGE 10

DISCOVER WHAT COMPUTERS ARE DOING TODAY   PAGE 11

FIND OUT WHO IS USING COMPUTERS   PAGE 13

KNOW WHICH COMPUTER FEATURES ARE EVOLVING THE FASTEST   PAGE 13

DECIPHER THE COMPUTER ADS   PAGE 15

If you've been hesitant to join the ranks of PC owners, you may be waiting to see what a personal computer can do before you purchase one for yourself. If you're a business owner, you want to make sure the payback will be worth the investment. If you're thinking about getting a computer for your home, you want to make sure it is something your family will use and that it will be compatible with both office and school.

NOTE The computer you use in business may be different from the ones your kids use at school. Be sure to find out which computers your family members are familiar with so that your first home PC is compatible with their needs.

This chapter takes you through some basic computer background. After a brief introduction explaining how the computer got to be the computer, you will have a chance to see how computers are being used today and how they may perhaps be used tomorrow. This chapter ends up with an introduction to computer ads, so you can decipher for yourself what the acronyms and promises mean in terms of real hardware and software.

What Is a Computer?

You may be surprised when you spend a little time thinking about the answer to this question. Yes, that off-white box and monitor sitting on your desktop is a computer. But, chances are, so is your phone and perhaps your answering machine. And the clock on your desk may be running silently off a little microchip inside. Your car may rely on computer parts to do some of its self-checking functions; the microwave you just used to warm up your coffee relies on computer technology to give you the temperature you want at the time you want it.

But computer parts do not a computer make. A computer, according to *Webster's Ninth*, is "a programmable electronic device that can store, retrieve, and process data." Not only are you putting information in (like setting the amount of time and power level for the microwave), but you are getting information out (no, not the cup of coffee!). Consider that letter you've been meaning to write Aunt Nell. You sit down at your computer, fire up the word–processing program, type the letter at the keyboard (there's the putting–in part), and save the file (that's storage). Now you can get the data out either by printing the file or by copying it to a data disk. And you can retrieve the data over and over again without any loss of data quality, which is another perk. If you want to write a letter to Aunt Nell and then make copies to all 11 other aunts, you can do that easily using a personal computer. (Just don't forget to change the names!)

So we've established that a personal computer is different from all the other pieces of equipment you may use on a daily basis that rely on computer technology to streamline or enhance qualities they already have. You will use your personal computer—that system with a system unit, monitor, and keyboard—to perform a variety of tasks more easily and accurately.

The *system unit* of your computer is the part that does all the computer's processing; the *monitor* shows you what you're working with; and the *keyboard* is like a typewriter keyboard, enabling you to enter and edit data. Chapter 3 explains the various parts of your computer system in more detail.

A (Very) Little PC History

That PC sitting on your desk or on the store shelf is the latest in a chain of evolutionary developments that has spanned many decades. Computers were once room-sized pieces of equipment. Known as *mainframes,* these megacomputers ran corporations, stored enormous amounts of data, and kept up with operations that were lost on the general public. You wouldn't use a mainframe to write a letter to Aunt Nell; you'd use a mainframe to track, report on, and control the power generation in the south district.

Minicomputers, a smaller version of the mainframe, also organized, stored, and controlled massive amounts of data. Both mainframe and minicomputers are still in use today, although they are the general property of large corporations that have the need and the finances to support them.

The microcomputer, which is the small desktop model you use at the office or at home, is the computer for the masses. More than two decades ago, hobbyists began experimenting with computer technology in order to create a more "personal" computer.

Today the machines we purchase are much easier to use than the computers assembled years ago. You can buy a complete system at your neighborhood Wal-Mart, with the software already loaded, the operating system set up nicely for you, and all the bells and whistles you'll ever want. You can load it up, take it home, open the boxes, and plug it in. If you have just purchased your system or are considering purchasing one, take some time to look through Chapter 12, so you can get your workspace organized right from the start.

What Can You Do with Computers Today?

The changes in hardware and software and the fact that computers have gotten more powerful and easier to use have enabled many businesses to computerize in a way they'd never thought possible. Computers at home have changed the definition of homework forever and have expanded the research and socialization possibilities (watch that one, if you have teenagers!) beyond anything we'd imagined before.

Let's take a look at how computers are routinely being used, both in the business world and at home.

PCs at the Office

When I was working as a book editor many years ago, I worked for one of the first publishing companies to perform online editing. What this meant, back then, was that we used computers to edit our books. Today, *online* means something different—now the term is used to describe being connected to the Internet, an online information service, or network.

Our jobs back then involved word processing. That was it. Typing, backspacing, removing text, adding other text. We thought, we typed, we thought some more.

Today, that same job still involves thinking and typing. It also sometimes involves doing financial forecasting and tracking, researching on the Internet, using an e-mail utility to trade messages with and check on authors, and perhaps video conferencing, graphics work, and database management.

In other industries, the reach into other capabilities has continued. The advertising agency that used an early PC to record and print data for mailing labels now uses a faster, more powerful machine to send and receive e-mail from clients, design logos, compose jingles, edit video clips, create multimedia presentations, design portfolios, storyboard ideas for client proposals, keep track of financial data, log project time, design and post Web pages, and calculate, record, and print paychecks.

Or consider the doctor's office. Remember all those colored folders? The one the doctor brought in that lists every symptom you've had for the last seven years? Today, you're a computer file, along with all your various illnesses and treatments. Automated voice-mail answers your call: "Press 1 to make a new appointment, press 2 to cancel an appointment, press 3 to have your prescription refilled." Your responses are logged in so they know when you called and why. And maybe they will even send your charges directly to the insurance company by modem, so you don't have to mess with the paperwork.

PCs at Home

Only those seriously interested in computer technology had a computer in their living room in the early '80s. As the decade drew to a close, PCs and PC-compatibles, largely fueled by an expanding game industry, and Apple computers, thanks to spreading popularity in the schools, started to dot desktops across the country.

Few of us anticipated that the PC phenomenon would grow to the point that the line between office work and homework would become blurred. Today a growing percentage of office workers spend at least a portion of their work week at their own home computers—up to 19 percent of the entire working population. We can now take our reports home to finish them, check on e-mail from clients, work on spreadsheets and charts, and accomplish just about anything on the home front we can do with our office computers. And some of us have given up the commute altogether (Hallelujah!) to run our own SOHOs (that's small-office-home-office) from the place of our choosing, whether it's an easy chair in the den or office space we carve out in the basement or attic.

Computers are also being used at home for a variety of household management tasks. Need a way to organize your bills? Use your home computer. Having trouble balancing your checkbook? There's a program that can do it for you. You can track the inventory of your home, keep track of recipes, write letters (or e-mail) to friends and relatives, help your children with their homework, connect to the Internet, and even shop online.

And the educational benefits add yet another facet to home use. Hundreds of programs are available for your children—from toddler to college-age—that can help them work on everything imaginable. From their first glimpse of the alphabet to chemistry tables to French, your kids can explore and practice using almost unlimited educational resources.

In all this talk about functionality, we shouldn't forget the fun factor. Computer games today rival those available in arcades; the animation, music, and action available with today's PCs will hold anyone's interest. And if gaming isn't your cup of tea, you can use the computer as a tool for any number of other hobbies, including music composition (now you can write, record, and edit music on your PC), video production (you can capture, edit, and incorporate video clips in other applications), and floor plan and garden designs. All you need is the relevant software installed.

Who Uses These Things?

It's not surprising, these days, to walk into a day-care center and see three-year-olds pointing and clicking through a colorful computer program. Schools all the way up, from K through 12, now include computers as part of their regular curriculum. No matter where you travel, you won't have to look far to find PC technology assisting in education. And PCs are popping up in other places, as well. You can find them in offices, stores, libraries, banks, even restaurants.

No matter what your age, no matter what your occupation, chances are that you will be using a computer soon, if you aren't already.

Fast-Changing PC Features

Earlier in this chapter, you learned that as the PC evolved, certain features changed faster than others. Some of these features are mentioned here.

More Powerful Microprocessors

As computers have changed, they have gotten progressively faster. The earliest PCs had the 8088 microprocessor; then a jump was made to a chip known as an 80286. Since that time, we've had 80386 and 80486 (you hear them referred to as 386 and 486 chips), and recently the Pentium. New standards are in the works. (In Chapter 3, you learn more about what the microprocessor does and how it processes information.)

The speed of the microprocessor is measured in megahertz (MHz), and a microprocessor may be available in different speeds. One system, for example, could advertise a 133MHz Pentium while another advertises a 90MHz Pentium. Both computers use the same type of microprocessor, but the 133MHz operates at a much faster speed than the 90MHz.

Amount of Disk Storage

The first PCs didn't have any storage capacity at all. Then floppy disks arrived, capable of storing only minimal amounts of information. When the first hard disks were made available, they stored only 20MB of information—just a fraction of the amount of data that can be stored on today's computer. Don't be surprised to find hard disks of up to 2Bs (gigabytes) or more on your new computer. (A *gigabyte* is approximately one billion bytes of information.) That's no small difference when you compare the storage capacity with the 20MB hard drives of yesterday.

Size of the PC

Today's computers have changed shape several times since the earlier systems were available. In general, technology gets smaller as it improves. (Remember how big your TV remote control used to be?) We've gone from large desktop models to "small footprint" models that take up less room on your desktop. You can choose from a horizontal look or a tower configuration, depending on how you arrange your office and the amount of room you've got. And other choices abound as well: Now you can select not only from desktop models but from laptop, notebook, and even palmtop computers to get the size and portability you need.

A new marketing idea has sprouted "kid-sized" mice, monitors, and keyboards. You'll find these computer components in primary colors with oversized controls for easy button pushing and built to stand up to some intense tapping.

Amount of Memory

When you're new to computers, the term *memory* is one of those catch-all words that seem to mean four or five different things. Let's define it here to bypass any ambiguity: Your computer's memory is the bank of chips in which information is stored while you're working with it. The amount of memory your system has depends, in part, on how many memory chips you have and how many chips your system is built to support.

Memory is often referred to as *RAM,* an acronym for random–access memory. When you first turn on your computer and start a program, the program is loaded from the hard disk storage into your computer's RAM. When you work on a file, it is stored in RAM. When you turn off the computer, all information in RAM is wiped away. In order to keep that file you were working on, you must save the file to disk, which copies the file from your computer's RAM and stores it on the disk under the file name you specify.

Your computer has another kind of memory known as *ROM*. This memory is read-only memory. The computer stores certain programs in ROM, such as the power-on self-test it runs through when you first turn on your system.

Deciphering Computer Ads

If you're shopping for a computer on your own, you may find the ads somewhat confusing. What do all the different acronyms mean? How do you know when you're getting a good system? What things should you ask when you call?

Most computer ads give you the basics of the system:

- Memory
- Speed
- Microprocessor
- Storage capacity of the hard disk
- Capacity of the CD-ROM, if there is one
- Size and type of floppy drive
- Type of video graphics card
- Number of expansion slots

NOTE If you plan to find out what the Internet fuss is all about, you'll also need a modem. Most manufacturers can easily add a modem to the setup you purchase, and the cost is minimal compared to the overall purchase price of the system. Even if you're not sure you will use it, invest in a modem. You'll be glad you have it later.

The sections that follow introduce you to some of the cryptic phrases and acronyms you'll find in ads. You'll also find out what issues are most important as you begin your computer education. But first, a general caveat for the computer purchaser: Remember that computer manufacturers are not by and large a dishonest lot. They are, after all, trying to sell you something. They want to hook your attention and show you what a great deal they are offering. Some *are* really great deals. Others are less so. Figure 1-1 shows you a representative example of the ads you have to watch out for.

The moral? Read the ads carefully. What might look like a great deal may have the words "Monitor sold separately" tucked away in small print at the bottom of the ad. You will be real happy with your purchase until the computer arrives and the monitor is missing. Read everything in the ad, and then read it again. And then ask someone else to read it and tell you what they think. And before you call to place the order, write down a list of questions to ask so you are sure of what you're getting before you order it.

Figure 1-1 When you see an ad that sounds too good to be true, examine it. You'll find out what's really for sale—and what's *not* included.

Computer Terms to Know and Love

Through the course of this chapter, we've been through some of the terms you'll see in the computer ads. RAM is a common acronym, for example, telling you how much random-access memory the computer has. You've also learned that the microprocessor is the brain of your computer, the main chip that controls all the processing going on.

Here are some additional terms that you'll see in the computer ads:

* **Infrared transceiver**—a feature that enables you to use a light pen or other infrared pointing device in place of a mouse.
* **Serial and parallel ports**—the ports on the back of your computer to which you can connect other devices such as printers, scanners, graphics tablets, and more.
* **Speakers**—built-in or external speakers that give you good quality sound for multimedia programs, games, and other applications with sound effects, voiceovers, and music.
* **Sound board**—the plug-in card that enables you to have quality sound on your computer. The sound board is often an add-on device that you can use to record and play music and take full advantage of sound effects on multimedia games and programs.
* **Touchpad**—the pointing device available on some notebook computers that you use by simply touching the sensitive pad to move the cursor and carry out operations on the screen.

What Matters?

The most important features for you will be the ones that make sure you get your work done most efficiently. Memory makes a big difference—the more the better! The earliest systems had only 64K of memory—that's only 64,000 bytes of information (a byte is roughly equivalent to one character). By comparison, most systems sold today have at least 8MB and are often expandable up to 80MB. For most general purposes, 32MB is a good investment. For applications that involve sound and video, you'll be happier with the maximum memory you can get for your particular computer.

The speed of the processor also is important to many people, especially if they have a fast system at the office and a slow system at home. The slow system will begin to fray your nerves as you sit and wait for the cursor to reappear while you're typing a letter. You will notice the speed of your system (or the relative slowness of it) when you are doing tasks that require a lot of processing, such as sorting large databases; opening and closing programs; switching among open applications; searching for phrases, files, and folders; and working with graphics-intensive files and applications.

Depending on what you will use the computer for, the type of monitor and the availability of video RAM (memory that's reserved strictly for video use on your system) can have a lot to do with how happy you are using the machine. In ads for laptop and notebook computers, you'll see the terms *active matrix* and *dual-scan*. Both terms refer to the way the image is updated on the screen, and active matrix is higher quality than dual-scan. You can also see active matrix screens in the dark; whereas dual-scans rely heavily on ambient light for reflection. (For more information about display issues, see Chapter 6.)

Having a floppy drive is important for moving files back and forth from one system to another. Most systems come equipped with a 3.5-inch disk drive, usually 1.44MB capacity, meaning the disks you insert in the drive can store up to one and a half megabytes of information. Older systems may have a 5.25-inch floppy drive, which uses a larger diskette made of mylar. Generally, these larger disk drives are not included as part of a system package; you may need to request that the manufacturer install a 5.25-inch drive or add one by cable to the back of your computer. Unless you are already using a computer with a 5.25-inch drive and have a need to be compatible with that machine, however, you will be fine with a single 3.5-inch drive on your computer.

If you plan to play games or rely on reference works as part of your computer time, you will benefit from investing in a CD-ROM drive. Such a drive enables you to run a program from a CD-ROM disc—sometimes a very large program that would otherwise occupy a good portion of your hard disk. CD-ROM drives are different from disk drives in that you cannot write information to them—your computer can only read information off the CD to run the program. The faster the CD-ROM drive (expressed as 2×, 4×, etc.), the better, particularly if you play CD-ROM games.

The number of expansion slots controls how much you can expand your system. If you're buying a computer for your home office right now and don't want to invest a lot of money, at least get a system that you can expand in the future. If your computer has room to grow, you'll be able to add items to it later—perhaps a modem, a CD-ROM drive, a trackball or joystick, a graphics tablet, or other add-ons.

Beginning Your Computer Education

This chapter has made the point that the computer industry is an ever-changing world of fast hardware and powerful programs. From the mundane to the magnificent, computers are being used for a world full of purposes and potentialities.

As you begin to look for the computer that's right for you, ask yourself a few questions:

- What tasks am I most concerned about?
- What will I use it for right away?
- What might I be interested in later?
- What types of applications interest me the most?
- What kind of tasks do I need the computer for?
- Will I use this computer at the office or at home?
- What features would my ideal computer include?
- How many people will be using my computer? What are their preferences?

As you begin to consider the answers to these questions, you'll get a clearer picture of what you're looking for in a system. That way, you'll know it when you find it.

The next chapter helps you explore the different types of computers available. You will check out the major competitors and see what kinds of systems they are offering, as well.

BONUS

A Good Read

Since you are starting out to explore the possibilities of a PC, stop by your local newsstand and check out the computer magazines. You'll find publications on PCs, Macs, the Internet, and more. One good magazine for home computer users—especially those of us with kids—is *Family PC*, published by Ziff Davis. Each month, you'll find articles about how to use the PC you've got, what to look for in a new PC, and what's coming in the future. Best of all, you'll find hardware and software reviews that may prove valuable.

Summary

Whether you are considering a computer for your home, office, car, or bathtub (*bathtub?*), be sure to do some homework before you shop. The amount of information out there is staggering, and you don't have to become an expert PC enthusiast overnight. But knowing what a PC is capable of doing-and knowing what you want your own computer to accomplish-will help you recognize the perfect system when you find it.

Some Web Sites to Hit

WEB PATH

ComputerScene on the Web:
http://www.cscene.com

MegaBytes & Internet Weekly:
http://www.megabytes.com

CoProductions for Cinema, Television, and Multimedia:
http://www.coproductions.homee.html

CHAPTER TWO

MAKING A COMPUTER MATCH: A BEFORE-YOU-BUY GUIDE

IN THIS CHAPTER YOU LEARN THESE KEY SKILLS

KNOW WHAT TO CONSIDER BEFORE YOU BUY   PAGE 22

DECIDE WHAT YOU NEED   PAGE 23

HIT ALL THE OPTIONS   PAGE 25

LEARN WHERE TO GET YOUR COMPUTER   PAGE 29

ASK THE RIGHT QUESTIONS   PAGE 31

No, you're not the only person in the world to be still thinking over that initial personal computer purchase. The television advertisements would have you think that most people have the latest computer system and are already fully connected to the Internet and chatting around the globe.

Perhaps you've been waiting to see how it would really benefit you to have a computer at home. Maybe you didn't want to spring for a PC in your small business until you were absolutely sure it would pay for its investment.

PC prudence is a wise thing. If you take the time to examine your needs and the computer market in the same careful fashion that you shop for an automobile, you will find yourself amply rewarded. By educating yourself, you can ensure that you won't buy technology that is faddish or short-lived. In any event, you will now benefit from the way prices have been dropping and continue to drop for computer systems. A few years ago, you would have paid double what you'll pay now for a system twice as powerful.

With the tremendous growth in the computer market comes people who are reasonably knowledgeable about computers and willing to assist you when you want to buy one. But be careful—don't blindly take advice from just anyone. Do as much research as possible by yourself, since it will enable you to evaluate any advice you receive.

Today computers are often sold fully equipped, loaded up with software galore. Games, programs, spelling checkers, calendars, you name it—you can probably find it on your preconfigured PC (and you may still be discovering new programs months after that initial purchase).

Another boon—free or (more likely) low-cost software. With the easy access of the Internet, you can find programs of all kinds waiting at the other end of your phone line.

But enough proof that waiting has had its advantages. The time is drawing near for you to jump in with both feet. You've seen that it's time to make the leap, but in which direction should you go?

Things to Think About

Now you know you want to get your first computer, but a question looms: Which one? Finding the computer that best matches your particular needs will take a little analysis and a little more education. You may find that you have a number of questions rattling around in your head. The most common new-user questions are these:

- What's more important, the computer (*hardware*) or the programs (*software*)?
- How much will I have to spend to get a good system?
- Should I get one at home that is compatible with the one at the office or in school?
- What type of computer package should I get?
- Do I need the extras, like a printer, a modem, speakers, and so on?
- Is purchasing a used system a good financial decision or a poor risk?

The sections that follow answer several of these questions. You'll find answers to the remaining questions sprinkled throughout the rest of the chapter.

The Big Three

The bulk of the decision you make about the type of system you purchase will involve three factors:

* The type of software you need to use
* The other systems you need to be compatible with
* The possibility of future expansion

Software Considerations

Without software, your computer would be a big expensive paperweight. Software enables you to do what you do—write letters, create spreadsheets, print mailing labels, send e-mail.

When you are preparing to purchase a computer, you need to think about why. Do you want to be able to finish writing reports at home so you won't have to stay so late at the office? If so, what kind of software program do you use at the office? You'll need something compatible at home.

Do you want to get a system that will give your kids an educational advantage in school? If so, find out what the schools are using. And you'll need to check into the various educational programs available—what offers them the most information in the subject areas they need? Programs abound that will help children grow into writers, artists, scientists, or simply help them expand their knowledge base and give them a wealth of resources from which to choose. In any case, you need to find out what software you'll be considering—either to go along with the school's computers or not—and then make sure you get a computer that will run the programs you're interested in.

Compatibility 101

An important issue when you're considering the purchase of your first computer is *compatibility*. Do you use a computer at work that you need to be compatible with at home? Make sure you purchase a system that will be compatible with other computers you may be using on a regular basis.

For some applications, you can go back and forth between different machines. For example, files created with Microsoft Word for Windows can be read on a Macintosh loaded with Microsoft Word for Macintosh. But not all programs are so flexible. If you use a particular spreadsheet program on your Mac at work, you may not be able to use it on your PC at home.

And if you use the latest version of software at work (or on a friend's machine), you won't be able to read any files created with that software on a machine that is loaded with an older version of the software. For example, Word for Windows 2 cannot read files created with Word for Windows 6.

You should also strive to be compatible in terms of the power of the machine. Suppose, for example, that you use a PC at work. It's equipped with 16MB of RAM and has a Pentium processor, which enables it to run programs that require speed and a significant amount of memory. Suppose, also, that you use Windows 95 on that system, along with Word for Windows 95 and other Microsoft Office applications. Since you use a PC at work and are familiar with the software it uses, it makes sense to purchase a home computer that runs the same software. If you can, try to get a machine that's equally powerful as well—it's difficult and annoying when you're hobbled by computer limitations.

Pardon Our Dust . . .

Especially if you're having trouble swallowing the $2,000 to $4,000 initial investment, you may doubt that you'd ever want to expand the capabilities of the system you buy. But as you get more comfortable with the purchase and the technology, there will undoubtedly be add-on items that call your name. A faster modem? Better speakers? A joystick? A CD-ROM? A graphics tablet? The industry is ripe with peripherals for your picking.

When you make that purchase, be certain that the computer gives you room to grow. Ask the computer salesperson how you can add to this machine before you buy it, and find out what the procedure is. (Do you need to take the system back to the store or ship it back to the manufacturer? Do they have an on-site technical department?)

SIDE TRIP

POSSIBLE EXPANSION IDEAS

* A great sound card if you like to play games
* A video camera that mounts on your monitor so others can see you
* A faster modem
* A tape backup for data storage
* A graphics tablet if you like to draw
* A joystick for the virtual pilot in you

Preferences, Preferences

Once you've determined the type of system you need in order to be compatible with computers at work and school, software- and hardware-wise, you can start asking yourself what you like and don't like in a system.

The best way to find out what your peculiarities are is to go to a store and try out several different systems. And don't simply push a few keys, either—spend some time giving that keyboard a workout. Compose a letter to Aunt Mabel. See whether you can find your way around in the operating system (described later in the book).

Click the mouse, play with the monitor brightness. Speak into the microphone and see how well (or how poorly) it picks you up. And if you find that some or all of these features are disabled on the system, ask a salesperson to help. And if they can't help, forget the system. A computer isn't meant to sell itself. If the salesperson can't figure it out on the floor, how will you master it at home?

Here are some features people have been sorry they didn't spend more time thinking about before they wrote the check:

* The responsiveness of the keyboard (or lack of it)
* The type of mouse or trackball
* The size, type, and quality of the screen
* The amount of RAM
* The speed of the microprocessor

Keyboard Komplaints

When you type on the computer keyboard, do the keys feel sluggish or are you aware of the quick action? Is there a mushy, rubbery feel or a clean click? Do you hear a key action (usually a key click) or do you hear only the sound of your fingers releasing the keys?

Fast typists are often much fussier about keyboards than slower typists. This is my prime complaint with most computer systems I try; if the keyboard feels "slow," I feel like it's holding me back, which, in the face of looming deadlines, can drive me crazy.

Keyboard feel is very much a personal preference, however. Some people prefer a slower keyboard, while others want that high-response rate. Just be sure to try out several so you get a feel for which you like best.

Another issue is the size of the keyboard itself. Some systems have small keyboards that are designed to take up less space on your desktop. Others are full size, including a separate numeric keypad with numbers and cursor movement keys out to the right. (For more information about how keyboards work, how you can take the best care of them, and what kind of options are available, see Chapter 7.)

If you wind up with a great system that has a rotten keyboard, what can you do? Take heart—keyboards are easy to replace, and there are now carpal tunnel-friendly keyboards (manufactured by Microsoft and other companies) that take some of the stress and strain out of your hands and wrist joints. You can pick up a replacement keyboard for between $79 and $150. (And having a replacement nearby—just in case you spill that coffee—isn't such a bad idea.)

> **SIDE TRIP**
>
> ### THINGS TO NOTICE ABOUT THE KEYBOARD
>
> * Is it full size?
> * Does it have a separate numeric keypad?
> * How do the keys feel?
> * Do you hear a key click?
> * Is the size of the keyboard comfortable for your hands?
> * Does it have a long enough cord so you can position it as needed on your desk?

Mouse Mumblings

The mouse is another small, seemingly insignificant device that can make a world of difference in how well—and how often—you use your computer. Most desktop systems come equipped with a traditional mouse, a small, almost oval-shaped device connected to the computer with a cord that resembles a mouse tail. On the mouse are two (or sometimes three) small buttons that you click when you select items on the screen or choose a particular software program installed on the computer.

Like the keyboard, your mouse has its own personal responsiveness rate. The buttons click a certain way. The mouse will feel either comfortable in your hand or not. Experiment with the mouse and practice using it—don't just give it a few arbitrary clicks.

Not all computers come equipped with a mouse. Some—usually laptop computers—have a device known as a *trackball*. Trackballs are like upside down mice: You spin the little ball directly. Some people think trackballs are great; others find the rolling approach to pointer movement distracting and difficult to master. Trackballs are also sensitive to environmental influences; things like everyday dust, M&Ms candy residue, and even smoke build-up can interfere with the contact points and cause the pointer to skip and jump across the screen in a terribly annoying way. (If you find this happening at your house, take heart—Chapter 17 discusses computer care and feeding issues and includes remedies for a wayward trackball.)

An improvement on the trackball is the *touchpad*. In this case you slide your finger across the pad to move the pointer on the screen. It's better than the trackball because there are no moving parts to get dirty or broken.

If you are considering a portable system that includes items like a touchpad or trackball, be sure to ask the salesperson about service issues. How hard are they to use? Can you also attach a mouse? How do you clean them? How difficult are they to replace?

Be sure to spend plenty of time experimenting with the pointer device on the system you are considering. It's one of your primarily tools for interacting with your computer. If you're not happy with the way the device works, it's going to impede your progress with your system and perhaps color your entire computing experience.

Of course, you can purchase a better mouse if you get a great system with a lousy mouse. The Microsoft mouse is the standard, and it is available in a number of styles and colors, but other companies sell well-designed mice as well, such as Logitech and Genie. For more information on mouse types and options, see Chapter 8.

Screen Scrutiny

An important personal preference is the size of the monitor, or screen, you choose. Computer monitors come in a variety of sizes. Laptop and notebook computers, for example, have small screens. A full-sized system, on the other hand, may have a 14-inch monitor, a 17-inch monitor, or even a 20-inch monitor. Some monitors can be turned to show full pages of information, and others can show two full pages on the screen at once.

The most telling feature a monitor has to offer is screen quality, which is usually referred to as the *screen resolution*. Resolution has to do with the number of dots projected on the screen to create the display. The greater the number of dots, the higher the resolution and the better the monitor.

Another important factor in most monitors is the *refresh rate*. This term refers to the way in which the images are drawn (and redrawn) on the screen. As you'll learn in Chapter 6, when you explore in more detail how monitors work, the faster the refresh rate, the better the image holds steady on your screen.

Another important issue for laptop and notebook owners is the type of display technology used: active matrix or dual-scan. Of the two, active matrix is the better quality, and you'll pay slightly more for it. If having high-quality screen images is important on your laptop or notebook, however, you'll be glad you made the investment.

SIDE TRIP

IMPORTANT DISPLAY ITEMS

* The size of the screen
* Screen resolution—the higher, the better
* Refresh rate—the faster, the better
* Active, passive matrix screen (on laptops)

RAM Reminders

The amount of memory included in the standard computer today has increased in astronomical proportions since the first personal computers. Today's computers are sold with a minimum of 8MB, and most manufacturers offer systems starting with 16MB and going through 128MB or more.

As computers have become more affordable and more powerful, their thirst for available RAM space has also grown. This is due not to the changing hardware itself but to the ever-changing software developed for the hardware. Microsoft Windows 3.1 limped along on a system with 4MB of RAM a few years ago; today you need at least 8MB (and preferably 16MB to avoid computer lock-ups) to use Windows 95.

Most other software programs have followed suit. If you can run Lotus 1-2-3 using 4MB, think how much better, faster, and smoother it will operate with 8MB. And imagine how much faster that Asteroids game will be!

Not only can more memory give you a smoother operation and access to more powerful programs, but it enables you to run several programs at once. When the amount of RAM in your system is limited, so is your ability to use multiple programs. One program might lock up, costing you important data. Another might simply refuse to work.

The best pre-purchase advice? Settle on the amount of memory you think you need to run the applications you want; then go one increment higher, adding either 4MB or 8MB, depending on what your computer can accommodate. In other words, if you think, "I can get by with 8MB," get a system with 16MB. If you know you need 16MB, get 32MB. You get the idea.

You can always upgrade your system at a later time and add memory as needed, providing that your system still has room for more RAM. (Most systems sold today can take at least up to 128MB.) But upgrading can be a hassle, especially if you have to give up your system for a few days while a registered technician does the dirty work. Better to get the system with the RAM you want, right off the bat.

So, know how much you need, and then buy more.

The Significance of Speed

We just discovered the importance of having enough memory in your system, but there's another item you don't want to cut corners on: your microprocessor. The microprocessor in your computer is the single chip that controls all the processing. This chip operates at a certain speed, which is measured in megahertz. The earliest microprocessors (8088 and 80286) were excruciatingly slow by today's standards and wouldn't even be able to run the programs we run today. The 80286 evolved into the 80386, and the 80486 arrived quickly on the scene. As microprocessors have evolved, they have become faster and more powerful. Today's standard is the Pentium chip, available in speeds from 80MHz to 166MHz—the faster, the better.

When you are investigating your first computer purchase, you may think that speed doesn't have a whole lot to do with you. After all, going from no computer at all to simply having a computer is a pretty amazing increase in speed! After considering the type of work you plan to do with your computer (word processing, checkbook balancing, whatever), you may consider settling for a slow 486 or a low-MHz Pentium. But this might be a bad decision.

A word of advice: Get the fastest system you can afford. Remember that speed doesn't simply mean how quickly the characters appear on the screen after you press the keys (although that is part of it). It also means how long you wait when you open and close programs. Speed controls the amount of time it takes for a file to be saved to disk, how quickly you can switch from one running application to another, and a variety of other things. The speed of your computer may affect—and perhaps frustrate—you in ways you don't even recognize. Even if you don't feel the need for speed, don't sell yourself short if you can afford it.

Where Do You Get PCs?

You won't have to look very far to find PCs for sale. Your local neighborhood discount store no doubt has a sampling. The impulse to buy a computer that looks good on a store shelf may be powerful, especially if you have been thinking about the purchase for a while.

Most people buy computers in one of two ways: from a retail store or through mail order. Each has its benefits. When you purchase a computer from a retail store—specifically a computer retail store—it gives you the comfort of talking with knowledgeable people about the system you're considering. What do they think you need and why? What sells the best? Which systems have a high breakdown rate? Is there one type of computer they would recommend over another?

NOTE The opinions of the salesperson are based on his or her experience, so take them as such. Remember, a salesperson is primarily interested in whether you actually buy a machine, not so much in which kind you buy. So you still need to make your own informed decision about what works best for you.

With a retail computer store you also may have a technical support department at your disposal, ready to solve problems like, "Hey, this printer doesn't work!" when you get the system home and unbox it. Most retail computer stores offer a period of free question-and-answer support as well as on-site or in-store service for a limited time. They may also offer service contracts (which is a great idea if you run a small business with several computers and your computer provider has a good technical support department and fair rates) for varying periods of time.

Other retail stores may have PCs right beside the washing machines or down the aisle from the sporting goods. In these computer aisles, you may not find a very knowledgeable salesperson. If the computers are set up so that you can use them, chances are the mouse, keyboard, and any other items are cabled down and restricted so no damage can be done. The downside is that you can't really get enough experience with the system—or input from someone who's familiar with it—to make an educated choice in the computer aisle. If the prices appeal to you in the discount store, get some experience with a system somewhere else —perhaps in a computer retail store, at the office, at a friend's house, or whatever—so you'll be able to spot the features you like best and know the ones you want to avoid.

Some computer retail stores are not offering new PCs but are instead selling reconditioned, used PCs. How reliable are they? That depends on the talent and training of the store's technical support staff, the quality of the hardware they are reconditioning, and how heavily the computer has been used in its previous incarnation. If you are considering purchasing a used computer, spend plenty of time with the system you plan to buy. Ask the technical support staff about the reliability of the computer and find out how helpful they will be if you run into problems with it later.

Many users are happy purchasing computers from mail-order houses. They simply call an order line after reviewing the models and order the computer they want. The whole process isn't any more difficult than ordering a pizza. Because mail order doesn't provide you any hands-on experience with a computer, you need to educate yourself about the computer you want before you purchase it. Check out popular PC magazines for reviews on the system you are considering. *Computer Shopper* and *PC Magazine* are good sources. Ask friends and coworkers. Also find out what guarantees the company offers in case you are not happy with your investment.

Before-You-Buy Questions

Whether you decide to purchase your computer from a retail computer store, a department store, or a mail-order company, be sure to ask these questions:

* How well does this computer sell? (But beware of jumping on the hype bandwagon.)
* Have there been any problems with it?
* What kind of warranty do you offer?
* Do you offer technical support? For how long? Is it free?
* What is the process if I want to upgrade the system later?
* If I'm unhappy with this purchase, what recourse do I have?

Remember that because computers are available in so many different places these days, you have more options. If you don't like the answers to the questions you ask, shop around. Good companies will stand behind the products they sell and be willing to cultivate a relationship with you, the buyer. It might take a little looking, but you'll find the company with the computer you want.

BONUS

PC Brainstorming

The best way to guarantee your happiness with the PC you select is to educate yourself about your choice before you make it. You have a number of things to think about, such as what programs you'll need to use, what types of computers you may need to trade files with, and what PC items you might want to add later. As you investigate different computers, use the checklists and sample table in this section to identify important and not-so-important computer qualities.

Software Considerations

What programs do you use at work? _____
_____

What programs are used at school? _____

What programs are you interested in? _____

What programs have been recommended to you? _____

Write down the programs you'd like to look at: _____

_____

_____

_____

_____

Compatibility Issues

You can use a table like the one here to list the computers your new system needs to be compatible with at school, work, and home.

Computer	Floppy Disk Size	RAM	Storage	PC or Mac?

Room to Grow

What items might you want to add later?

_____ modem

_____ printer

_____ trackball

_____ joystick

How many expansion slots does the computer have? _____

How does the seller handle upgrades? Do you do it yourself or do you send or bring the system back to the company? _____

FIRST, THE BASICS

Summary

Many computer users rate the purchase of the computer system the hardest part of their PC experience. So take heart—you're almost over the hard part! In the next chapter, you learn about the different types of computers out there: desktop PCs, notebook PCs, and more.

Some Web Sites to Hit

Tips for buying and selling computers online:
http://www.trade-direct.com/html/tips.htm

PC World Personal Shopper:
http://www.pcworld.com/hardware

ZDNet:
http://www5.zdnet.com/

CHAPTER THREE

CHECKING OUT COMPUTER TYPES

IN THIS CHAPTER YOU LEARN THESE KEY SKILLS

LEARN WHAT YOUR DESKTOP CHOICES ARE   PAGE 36

LEARN ABOUT PORTABLE COMPUTERS   PAGE 38

DISCOVER WHAT'S HANDY ABOUT PALMTOPS   PAGE 41

GET "MUST-HAVE" ADD-ONS FOR YOUR COMPUTER   PAGE 42

When you begin looking into the purchase or adoption of your first computer system, you quickly realize that there are many different types to choose from. Depending on what type of system you want and what you plan to do with it, there are any number of different options available.

Today's Desktop Computers

Chapter 1 explained the PC metamorphosis from the room-sized mainframe to the cumbersome but moveable desktop system. It was a major jump. Today's desktop computer sits atop your desk (see Figure 3-1) and includes the following components:

* The system unit
* The monitor
* The keyboard
* The mouse

35

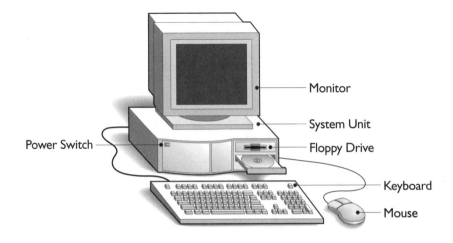

Figure 3-1 A typical desktop PC

Desktop Basics

The desktop computer is a combination of several different pieces of equipment that are connected to the system unit through cables. The system unit houses the microprocessor, the disk drives, perhaps the CD-ROM drive, and the necessary items that receive data from and send data to the other computer devices.

Desktop Options

You'll find desktop systems available in a variety of colors and configurations. Some have two disk drives; others won't. Some come equipped with a CD-ROM drive. Some send along speakers. No matter what the bells and whistles of your particular system are, every desktop system will have at least the system unit, the monitor, the keyboard, and the mouse connected together by cables.

The system unit is the most variable item of the bunch. In a traditional desktop system, the system unit is a rectangular box, with the disk drives and/or CD-ROM drive positioned on the front of the unit. The system unit may instead be set vertically, in what's known as a tower configuration. You can easily position a tower unit under your desk and connect it by cable to the monitor on top, giving yourself more clear desk space and making it easy to insert and remove disks as needed. Figure 3-2 shows a tower system unit.

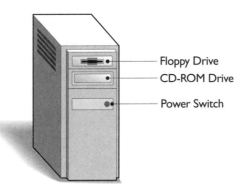

Figure 3-2 A tower system unit

SIDE TRIP

REASONS FOR BUYING A DESKTOP COMPUTER OVER OTHER MODELS

* You want full computing power and a computer that doesn't need to be portable.
* You want a full-sized screen and full-sized keyboard.
* You plan to keep the computer connected to various external items, such as a tape backup unit, a printer, the phone jack, and so on.
* You want to get the greatest amount of power and expandability for your money.

Desktop Prices

Small businesses often rely on desktop computers for the bulk of their computing tasks. As technology has evolved, computer components have become, for the most part, cheaper to make. This lowering of the cost has carried through to the desktop computer system. Depending on what you need, you can purchase a good, fast system for around $2,000. When you begin adding to the basic features of the system, however, such as more RAM, a bigger hard disk, a CD-ROM drive, multimedia features, and more, the price grows incrementally. State-of-the-art standalone PCs begin in the neighborhood of $4,000 and rapidly move to higher ground.

Another difference in cost depends on the manufacturer of the machine. IBM offers high-quality machines with a number of options, but they also come with a high price tag. A different brand of IBM-compatible computers may offer the same features at a lower cost. You'll have to weigh the considerations such as brand loyalty or importance, service agreements, dependability, and so on before you buy.

Carrying Around Portable Computers

Portable computers are taking PCs into the world in a big way. You'll find them at baseball games, on airplanes, in restaurants, on the shoulders of people walking downtown at lunchtime. Portable computers can go with you to the beach, to the doctor's office, to school, and back to the office. You can be within a dial tone's reach of your e-mail, the latest stock quotes, and contractor bids if you've got a notebook (with modem) at your disposal. And that's just the beginning.

Not all portables were all that portable. Larger than briefcases — and just as heavy — the original "portable" computers had small screens, a flip-down, detachable keyboard, and a handle affixed to the back of the unit so you could lug the thing around. Carrying one through an airport was enough to make you swear off portable computing forever. They were aptly nicknamed "luggables."

Today's portable computers are something like 8-by-11 inches in size and may weigh from five to eight pounds. Some, like the IBM ThinkPad Slimline, boast widths of under two inches, which makes the system smaller than most three-ring binders you carry back and forth to meetings or school. Most people these days call them laptops or notebooks, rather than portables. Notebook is the newer term.

Notebook Basics

The notebook computer is a single item — as opposed to the desktop computer that is one system comprised of many pieces. It is built with monitor, system unit, and keyboard attached in one piece. The system opens to reveal the monitor, which is a screen of ten to twelve inches, depending on the model you've selected. Figure 3-3 shows an example of a notebook computer.

Figure 3-3 A notebook computer

The notebook computer can fit neatly inside a briefcase, a bookbag, or in a satchel-style carrying case. A built-in pointer device, which could be either a trackball or a touchpad depending on the notebook model you get, keeps you from having to mess around with external items and cables.

The notebook computer functions as any desktop computer might; in fact, if you prefer to use a larger screen and full-sized keyboard, you can plug these items into the notebook when you're at your home station or office.

Notebook Options

Smaller technology sometimes comes with a higher price. For the same computing power you can get in an average PC, you will pay the same or perhaps more for a notebook. This is especially evident in the more powerful notebooks. For those who need to take their work with them, notebooks offer a wonderful solution, and the flexibility is worth any increased cost.

Similar to desktop PCs, costs range greatly for notebooks. If you get a relatively low-end system, you'll pay $1,500 to $1,800. Here's an example of a passable notebook:

✳ 100MHz Pentium microprocessor
✳ 8MB RAM (upgradeable to 40MB)
✳ 10.4-inch dual-scan monitor

- 810MB hard drive
- 1.44MB disk drive
- PCMCIA slot
- SoundBlaster-compatible sound card
- Windows 95 preinstalled
- Touchpad
- Loaded software

All this for an advertised price of $1,699. Sounds pretty good. But what's missing? There's no modem, so if you plan to use the notebook to check e-mail and send files back and forth to clients or to school, you'll need to add one. And there's no CD-ROM drive, which may or may not be a necessity depending on how you plan to use the machine.

NOTE Depending on the model of notebook computer you purchase, expanding the system may be a challenge. Some notebooks are easy to expand — you simply replace one hard drive cartridge for another, plug in some more memory, or add a docking station, which gives you access to all your desktop PC components. Other notebooks may be harder to expand. Talk to your computer dealer about expandability issues before you buy.

A more powerful notebook will set you back quite a bit more. Here's a higher-end system with some additional features:

- 133MHz Pentium processor
- 12.1-inch active matrix display
- 16MB RAM, upgradable to 80MB
- 1.2GB removable hard drive
- Removable 4× CD-ROM drive
- 28.8 fax/modem

This particular system has a price tag of $5,299, and it is one of IBM's top ThinkPad notebook models. You'll notice something interesting about this notebook — both the hard drive and the CD-ROM drive are removable, which means that you can use these two important items with your desktop computer at home or at work if they are similarly equipped.

That's really the ultimate in portability — being able to take your data, reports, letters, and spreadsheets with you, along with your reference materials, and then putting them back into the larger, more comfortable system when you

SIDE TRIP

get home.

DO YOU NEED A NOTEBOOK?

You could benefit from a notebook computer if:

- You spend a lot of time stalled in traffic jams on the highway (in your carpool or at a rest stop).
- You go to visit clients as part of your business and need to get work done while you're there.
- You need access to e-mail while you travel.
- You would like to be able to enter notes or orders into a computer wherever you are, rather than first write them by hand and then enter them later at the desktop computer.
- You frequently go off-site to research projects and gather information.
- You don't have a lot of desk space at home to devote full time to a computer.
- You don't use a computer every day, so you don't want it on display every day.
- You like the idea of using it in a café.

A Computer in the Palm Is Worth Two in the Trunk

Computers get even smaller yet. Have you seen the language translators in your local Wal-Mart? Many different palmtop computers — just slightly larger than a calculator or TV remote control — are now available to perform a specific task. Some track names and addresses for you; others are electronic DayTimers; still others do more elaborate financial analyses and have the capability to print reports and fax information.

Hewlett-Packard produced a palmtop a few years ago, as did Apple. Both machines were based on the idea of instant use — pull the thing out of your pocket, make a few notes (the Apple Newton MessagePad palmtop can actually be taught to understand your handwriting) and then dump the data later, via cable, back into your larger system at home or at the office.

These palmtops average a hefty $700 in price and have not enjoyed widespread success; for just a few hundred dollars more, you can up your computer's power into the notebook range.

A Peek at Peripherals

This section explains some of the *peripherals* — that is, the add-on devices — that may or may not be included as part of your system purchase.

We should say right off the bat that some computer manufacturers consider monitors a peripheral. If you are purchasing your computer from a computer ad, be sure to read the fine print closely. If the desktop system looks like a great one and it weighs in at a friendly $799, chances are there's a "Monitor sold separately" note somewhere on that page. (Don't be surprised if the keyboard is extra, too!)

Apple computers — the Macintosh line — are ordinarily sold without monitors. Some IBM-compatibles also resist the temptation to make the computer a complete package, preferring to allow users to make the monitor decision on their own.

But, in broad terms, peripherals are those items that you connect to your computer, whether you are using a desktop or a notebook computer. We'll take a quick look at different peripherals in this chapter, and you can check out Chapters 8 through 10 for more in-depth information on how the peripherals work and how you will use them. Here are the peripherals you may be interested in as part of your initial computer purchase:

* Printer
* Modem
* CD-ROM drive

Printers: An optional necessity

At some point you will need a printer. Depending on how difficult the initial purchase is for you, you may be tempted to wait to purchase a printer at a later date. Best advice: Don't. Printers are available today for $150 that produce readable, you'll-be-glad-you-did-it quality. You can choose from dot matrix (a standard, which used to be the scourge of printing quality but has improved with age) and ink jet, two low-end but passable printing techniques that enable you to print output for a low-dollar investment. You may even be able to get into ink jet color printing for under $400.

NOTE See Chapter 9 for a complete discussion of different printers and what they do.

If your printing needs are more of a priority, you'll need to consider a laser printer, which takes you into a different cost bracket. While laser printers begin around $800 and go up into thousands of dollars, the Okidata LED laser costs about $250 and produces perfectly passable output. PostScript laser printers are the highest of the lot, sometimes hitting as high as the $4,000 mark.

The modem: Connectivity and cyberspace

Especially if you are considering a notebook computer, a modem is another one of those get-it-even-if-you-don't-need-it items. Even if you aren't particularly interested in either e-mail or Internet access right now, a modem is a relatively low-cost item that can be a great benefit.

A modem is a device that enables your computer to send and receive data through the phone lines. The data might be electronic mail messages, files, reports, spreadsheets, even songs or video clips. Many modems sold today are actually faxmodems, which mix both fax and modem features so the device can function as either one.

Modems that are sold with systems are usually included in the computer, plugged into one of the computer's expansion slots. You then plug the phone line into the back of the computer and into the phone jack on the wall.

Other modems are available, as well. You can purchase an external modem, which is a small box-like device with little red lights on the front. It connects to the back of your computer and you connect the phone line to the external modem. On notebook computers, the modem often plugs into a PCMCIA slot though the use of a card and a small cable, which attaches to the phone jack.

Modems range in cost from $170 to $300. The speed of the modem is it's most important feature, and the fact that it mixes fax and modem capabilities. Today's highest speed standard is 33.6Kps (that's kilobytes per second).

NOTE Modems are covered in Chapter 9, where you'll learn more about how modems work.

A CD-ROM of your dreams

You may have heard the splash created when CDs first dropped into the computer market. What has turned out to be a very popular peripheral among those people who use their computers for a substantial percentage of time per day is still dragging a little in popularity among new users. What is a CD-ROM drive and do you need one?

If you've purchased software—or, as you will learn when you begin to investigate software purchases—you've noticed that many programs are available on both CD and disk. Some are available only on CD. Programs that use multimedia to convey their information—such as *Just Grandma and Me*, a CD-ROM book by Living Books—need massive amounts of storage space to hold all the sound, video, animation, text, and program files involved with that program.

And that's the beauty of the CD: massive storage space.

The CD has become very popular for reference works. You'll find encyclopedias, histories, anthologies of literature, medical books, legal information, entire publications, and collections of just about everything else—your favorite games, favorite songs, favorite applications, favorite fonts—all on CD.

So if you're into massive amount of information and use reference works heavily, and if you have students or future students at your house who would benefit from various CD libraries, a CD-ROM drive is a wise addition to your computer.

We should make the point clear, however, that the CD-ROM is not a storage device similar to a disk drive, in which you create a file and store it to the disk in the drive. You can't store anything on a CD-ROM. The information is on there, burned forever on the surface of the disk. When you use the CD to play a game, load an encyclopedia, or whatever, the program simply loads the information from the CD into your computer's RAM. But we'll talk more about RAM in Chapter 4.

CD-ROM drives, when they are packaged with the computer system, appear to play a pivotal role in the overall cost of the system. Desktop systems without CD-ROM drives are generally around $2,000; desktop systems with CD-ROM drives general weigh in at $3,200 or more.

This price increase isn't totally the responsibility of the CD-ROM drive, however; prices for CD-ROM drives range between $100 and $400. CD-ROM programs are multimedia applications, which mean they need a sound board, good video, and plenty of RAM in order to operate correctly. These items, combined with the cost of the CD-ROM drive, inflate the cost of your average, everyday PC.

One more option on the CD-ROM drive side: Speed. When CD-ROM drives were first introduced, there was only one speed, and that wasn't very fast. Today, you'll find CD-ROM drives rated as 2×, 4×, 6×, and 8× speeds. You'll pay more for the faster drives, but as a general rule, get the fastest CD-ROM drive you can afford.

> **NOTE** Although the CD-ROM drives you purchase as part of your computer system are read-only devices, meaning you cannot save files to the CDs in the drives, there are peripherals now available that do, in fact, enable you to write to a CD. These are called CD-R recorders, and they allow you to create your own CD, which is beyond the reach of most users' needs (and checkbooks).

Scoping Out the Competitors

As you investigate the offerings of different computer manufacturers, you'll notice that the same names keep popping up. Don't be surprised to see these:

* IBM
* Apple
* Compaq
* NEC
* Toshiba
* Texas Instruments

These tried-and-true computer companies continue to introduce new and improved systems and to offer not only name-brand recognition but the dependability of their reputations. In other words, you know they will be around tomorrow, after you've put your system together and find out that your mouse is dead. Some companies, like the ones you may find in a small ad in the back of a computer magazine, may not be around tomorrow to help you cure your PC headaches.

Many other companies exist in addition to the top names. When you find a system you like, check it out thoroughly, ask questions about the company, and be sure to educate yourself about their technical support policies. (For more information on before-you-buy items, see Chapter 2.)

BONUS

Little Things Mean a Lot

As you think about the computer you are destined to have, remember that the purchase of the system itself isn't all you have to deal with. Little extras can make your computing life a lot easier. When you're checking out various computers and getting an idea what you like (and can afford), look at things like mouse pads, wrist pads, disk boxes (protective plastic boxes that store disks), and power surge protector strips (long strips with multiple plugs that help cut down on cord clutter and can protect your system in the event of a power spike on your electric line).

Most of these items cost $10 or less and they will make you a much happier camper. And, as in the case of the wrist pad, which protects your wrists from carpal tunnel syndrome, they may make you a *healthier* camper, too.

Summary

Here's the bottom line to finding the system you like. Make sure that it:

* Runs the software you need.
* Is compatible with other computers you use and rely on.
* Offers some upgrade possibilities.
* Fits within your budget.

Keep asking questions until you are satisfied with the answers and feel confident in your purchase. Then take it home, unbox it, set it up (we'll help you with that in Chapter 12), and prepare to be occasionally aggravated, but, more often than not, amazed.

Some Web Sites to Hit

Dell Computer:
http://www.dell.com

Compaq Computer:
http://www.compaq.com

IBM Computer:
http://www.pc.ibm.com

NEC Computer:
http://www.nec.com

PART TWO

THE COMPUTER: INSIDE AND OUT

THIS PART CONTAINS THE FOLLOWING CHAPTERS

CHAPTER 4 WHAT'S THIS SYSTEM UNIT THING?

CHAPTER 5 THE LOWDOWN ON DISK DRIVES

CHAPTER 6 MONITOR BASICS: THAT THING YOU LOOK AT

CHAPTER 7 KEYBOARD CARE AND FEEDING

CHAPTER 8 OF MICE AND OTHER POINTING DEVICES

CHAPTER 9 POINTS ABOUT PRINTING

CHAPTER 10 MODEMS, MODEMS

CHAPTER 11 ADD-ONS YOU CAN OWN AND LOVE

Did you always wonder what actually goes on inside the system unit? Did you feel that your discovery of PCs wouldn't be complete unless you knew how the information got from the keyboard to the screen? This part of the book walks you through the different components in your system, telling you how each of them works and which items you need to watch out for. Nuts and bolts — with some electricity thrown in.

PCs AND PROFITS: COMPUTERS IN BUSINESS

John Sherman is the owner of Sherman & Company Public Relations, a small public relations and marketing firm. His PC — one of the four now used in his business — was with him on the day he opened his doors back in 1991.

In John's business, he spends quite a bit of time and focus producing printed materials; creating, writing, and editing brochures, newsletters, business cards, flyers, and more. To accomplish these tasks, he needs a good word processor (he uses WordPerfect), a page design program (PageMaker), and a good quality printer (a laser printer for quality output; a DeskJet 550C to print in color). He also uses Quicken to manage the financial aspect of his business and stay on track budget-wise and tax-wise.

He's looking at the possibility of adding a scanner to be able to import high-quality graphics and photos, and he may soon network the computers in his office so file transfers will be easier and applications can be shared. One "definite" on his to-do list is subscribing to CompuServe so his clients can reach him and his employees via e-mail whenever necessary.

What does John say to startup business owners? "Whatever your business is — you need a computer. You need word processing if nothing else, and you need a good printer. Something with enough power and memory to print letters and get reports done. Have good-looking letterhead and business cards and a fax line, or don't even get in business. People won't take you seriously. You can get by with a single computer and a single printer, if you have to, but you definitely need one."

CHAPTER FOUR

WHAT'S THIS SYSTEM UNIT THING?

IN THIS CHAPTER YOU LEARN THESE KEY SKILLS

FIND OUT WHAT THE SYSTEM UNIT IS FOR PAGE 50

DISCOVER THE DIFFERENT PARTS OF THE SYSTEM UNIT PAGE 50

LEARN WHAT THE BIOS IS PAGE 52

GET YOUR CHIPS IN ORDER PAGE 53

FIND OUT MORE THAN YOU EVER WANTED TO KNOW ABOUT PORTS PAGE 57

KNOW WHY THE POWER SUPPLY IS IMPORTANT PAGE 59

IDENTIFY THE SEVEN DEADLY SYSTEM UNIT SINS PAGE 60

Who says hardware has to be boring? Still systems run deep—as it were—and there is a lot going on inside that cool metal box when you flip the power switch on. What does your computer do and how does it do it? The system unit is the key to everything.

This chapter takes you on a tour around the outside of the system unit and then the inside. You'll learn what happens when you first power up your system, what parts of the system unit make everything work smoothly, which gadgets can really mess things up if they go bad, and more.

What's the System Unit For?

The system unit is the central piece of your computer, the component inside which the data is actually processed. When you type that letter to Aunt Frieda, the characters are sent as electronic signals from the keyboard to the system unit. When you click the mouse, the click is registered in the system unit. When you choose a command and your computer begins searching for all text files containing the words "Belgian waffles," the search takes place in your system unit.

The system unit is more than just a processing machine. (I'll talk about the actual chip that does the processing in a minute.) The system unit controls all the in-going and out-going of the data on your computer.

The data from the keyboard goes in through a cable. The data to the monitor goes out through a cable to the screen. Disk drives housed in the system unit allow you to transfer files to and from your computer. You can read the information on a CD and use it in documents, play games, look up resources, and so on —in effect, putting the data into your computer's RAM. (More about RAM, which is your computer's temporary storage space, later in this chapter.)

And when you want to print a file? That's right—out through a port in the back of your system unit, through a cable, and to the printer. And when you get bitten by the Internet bug and want to begin sending e-mail to relatives in far-away places (which is the best place to have relatives, don't you think?), the e-mail you send travels out of your modem port, through the phone line to the jack and—poof!—out into cyberspace.

System Unit Parts: Exposed!

The system unit of your computer includes a number of different components, all lumped together into this one supremely important piece of hardware. Some of these things you may not care a whit about—and hopefully you'll never need to know where they are and what they do. However, in the unfortunate event that something quits working and you need to be able to describe what's happening to a technical support person, knowing your way —generally—around the system unit isn't a bad tool to have in your belt of computer knowledge.

Basically, you need to know something about the motherboard, the microprocessor, the disk drives, the ports, the BIOS, the RAM and ROM twins, and the power supply (see Table 4-1).

And a bunch of other little things along the way.

Let's catch the little things first. (I cover disk drives in Chapter 5, so you have that to look forward to.)

TABLE 4-1 System Unit Verbiage You Should Know

Term	Description
MOTHERBOARD	The main board inside the system unit of your computer.
MICROPROCESSOR	The single chip that is responsible for all the data processed in and by your PC.
SYSTEM UNIT	The hardware component to which your keyboard, monitor, mouse, and other pieces are attached. It contains disk drives, the CD-ROM, and includes ports to which other PC parts can be connected.
DISK DRIVE	The slot on the front or side of your system unit that enables you to insert a disk and write or read data to or from the disk.
CD-ROM DRIVE	A drive that reads information from a CD.
BIOS	The set of PC startup instructions permanently burned on a chip (or chips) on your PC's motherboard.
ROM	*Read-only memory,* the set of chips that contains important instructions about the way your PC operates. Some PCs include applications programs in ROM, as well.
RAM	*Random-access memory,* the erasable memory chips that store programs and data during your current PC work session.
CARDS	Plug-in cards that enable your system unit to send data to and from the other components in your system. Your monitor relies on a graphics card; your mouse uses a mouse card; you hear multimedia sound because of the sound card in your PC.

Power Up!

The power switch on your computer may or may not be red. It may say On/Off. It might say 1 or 0. It might not say anything at all. The switch might be a round button like the one on my laptop. It might be a tan rounded rectangle, like the one on the front of my desktop computer that my two-year-old son Cameron loves to push . . . and push . . . and push.

Power Through: A Look Inside

If you've seen the Intel commercials and gone careening with the camera through the inside of the system unit, you know that there are all kinds of strange looking items in there. Green or black plastic boards with little silver tracks running in straight lines up, down, and across. Small items resembling the fake trees on a youngster's train set dot the landscape. You see black rectangles arranged in blocks of four, or eight, or more. You'll find cables—perhaps big, flat, gray cables, and other smaller wires and whatnots—strung about in a seemingly disorganized fashion. And somewhere in the middle of it all, you may find a small rectangular or square chip. That's the brain. The microprocessor (see Figure 4-1).

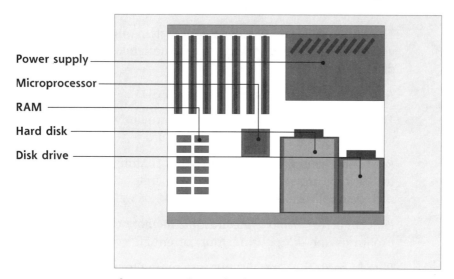

Figure 4-1 The inside of the system unit is a highly ordered miniature world.

Good thing the data knows where it's going! If we had to direct traffic inside the system unit, we'd soon give up and take the typewriters and adding machines out of the attic.

One of the first places that starts to hum after flipping the switch is the motherboard. It contains a singularly important chip: the microprocessor. It also contains the chips that tell your computer how to start itself, something called the BIOS.

What in the World Is the BIOS?

The BIOS of your computer is the Basic Input/Output System, a set of startup instructions on a chip on the motherboard of your computer. The BIOS also helps turn software instructions into hardware instructions your computer can understand.

How do you interact with the BIOS of your computer? You don't. The BIOS exists solely to tell the computer what it should do when you first turn the power on. For example, it checks to make certain that your RAM is OK, that your hard drive exists, that your floppy drive is alive, and so on. This process, which takes five to ten seconds, is called the Power On Self Test (POST for short). When the POST is done, the computer begins to load the operating system from your hard disk.

Although we're concerned here with the BIOS for your PC, you may also have a BIOS that controls your monitor (that's video BIOS) and a BIOS that starts the hard disk (that's hard disk BIOS). We all need a set of instructions to help us get started in the morning. Your PC is no exception.

Chips Only a Mother(board) Could Love

BIOS is one of the residents on your PC's motherboard. The motherboard is the mother of all boards, the main board of circuitry inside your system unit. On the motherboard, you'll find other chips as well, including the microprocessor, the BIOS, and your computer's RAM.

Put It All Together, It Spells m-o-t-h-e-r

One of the things you don't want to hear from a technical support person: "We'll need to replace the motherboard." Although the board itself isn't usually all that expensive, replacing it can be a delicate operation.

Every item you add to your computer—that printer, the modem, a graphics tablet, a keyboard, everything—connects to a port on your system unit that is connected to a board which plugs into the motherboard (that is housed in the system unit that Jack built!).

The motherboard is an important piece of system equipment. It is susceptible to things like water spills, dust particles, and smoky environments, so keep that cover on your system unit at all times.

What Makes the Motherboard Proud? The Microprocessor

You've already heard that the microprocessor is the brain of your computer. Hard to believe that a single chip—something smaller than a quarter—is responsible for the entire operation of a piece of equipment that cost you thousands. (Oops, sorry to remind you.)

Yet the microprocessor is that all-important piece that controls all the input and output your system has to give you. In fact, the microprocessor is so important that your computer is probably named for the microprocessor it has. A 386, 486, or Pentium system is so named because it uses a 386, 486, or Pentium microprocessor. Each of these processors offers a different standard in terms of the speed of data processing. Generally speaking, the 486 is faster than the 386. The Pentium is faster than the 486 (which is faster than the 386). You get the idea. The only catch is that some microprocessors are slower than others, so it is actually possible to put a very fast 386 microprocessor in a machine that surpasses the speed of a low-end 486, but it's not something you need to worry about. Most systems you purchase today will have either a high-speed 486 or a Pentium microprocessor inside. And if you see additional letters following your chip's name—such as 486DX or 486SX—that means the processor is a cousin to the basic 486. An SX chip is a little faster than the original processor, and a DX chip is faster yet.

You learned in Chapter 2 that the higher the microprocessor number, the better off you are. Pentium Pro is today's highest available standard, although new, faster, and better chips are no doubt just around the corner.

Not only is the type of microprocessor you've got important, but the speed of your particular microprocessor contributes to how quickly your computer can sort through the 1,000 client labels you want alphabetized. You'll see the speed of the particular microprocessor listed in megahertz. The faster the better.

RAM Chips and Dip: The Memory in Your Machine

Another important item that your computer can't do without is its RAM, or random-access memory. When it comes to RAM, your computer may have 4MB, 8MB, 16MB, or more. RAM is actually a series of chips plugged into the motherboard of your system.

In your particular system, your RAM may be single IC chips like those shown in Figure 4-2, or they may be what's known as a SIMM (Single Inline Memory Module), which are 1MB modules of memory that hold several chips and plug directly into the motherboard.

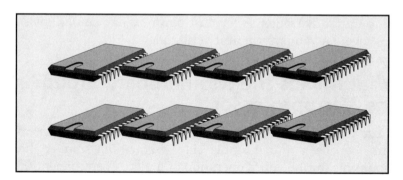

Figure 4-2   The RAM in some computers is a set of memory chips placed on the motherboard.

THE REASON WE NEED IT? I FORGET . . .

What does RAM do for your computer? It helps it remember things. Important things. Things like, "What program am I using here?" "What sentence did she just type?" "What command did she just undo?"

The RAM in your computer stores everything your computer needs to know about the current work session. For example, if you sit down to write an e-mail message to cousin Elmo, you may—depending on what software you've got on your computer—start Windows 95, open Microsoft Exchange, and create the e-mail message. The RAM of your computer stores the information it needs to run Windows 95 and Microsoft Exchange, plus it holds onto that e-mail message until you either send it or save it in a file.

WHAT RAM ISN'T

RAM isn't disk storage—that's what the hard disk and the floppy disks are for. When you install a program, it is stored on the hard disk of your machine. Some programs require 20MB or more of disk space in order to store all the necessary program and data files. When you run the program, the program files that the software needs to run are loaded into RAM. When you end your worksession and turn off your computer, the contents of RAM are erased.

Your computer stores what it needs for the current work session in RAM. When you turn the computer's power off, everything in RAM is erased.

THANKS FOR THE MEMORY

It is possible to add to your computer's memory banks, but you need to know what you're doing. For best and easiest results, let a professional do it. Most computer service departments can pop in more RAM for a nominal service fee above and beyond the price you pay for the RAM chips themselves.

One other note: Computers are different when it comes to how much memory they can handle. Consult your computer manual, your technical support person, or the manufacturer to find out how much RAM your particular make and model is equipped to use.

Few of us will get through PC life without seeing the dreaded "Out of memory" error message. You can reduce your chances of being caught unaware by following these guidelines:

* **Know how much memory your computer has.** If you are using a Windows 95 computer, you can check this out by choosing Start→Settings→Control Panel, and double-clicking System. On the bottom right side of the General tab you will see the Computer settings, beneath which is listed the amount of RAM installed in your machine.

* **Know how much memory your computer is using.** When the System Settings dialog box appears, click the Performance tab. In the System Resources line, you'll see the percentage of memory you have available (see Figure 4-5).

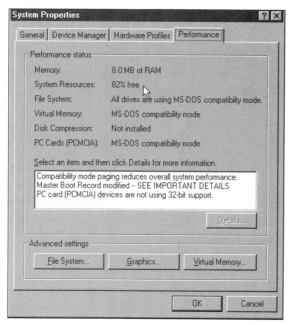

Figure 4-3 Check your System Resources if you suspect your available RAM is dwindling.

* **Keep an eye on memory when you're using several open applications.** The greater the number of open programs you've got going, the higher the demand on the RAM in your system. And, to free up RAM, close any open applications you're not currently using.
* **Save your files frequently.** The best way to recover from an "Out of memory" lockup (and it does happen) is to make sure you save your files every few minutes. Each time you make a major change to that document, spreadsheet, report, graphic, whatever—make sure you've saved the changes. That way, even if you do get caught in a lockup, your work will be protected.
* **Reduce the number of programs that run automatically.** Some programs load automatically at startup if you've got them included in your Startup folder. If you're maxing out on available RAM, try removing the programs you don't need.

SIDE TRIP

YOU KNOW YOU'RE RUNNING OUT OF MEMORY WHEN...

* Your pointer freezes.
* You click a menu in the menu bar and it doesn't open.
* You move from one open program to another and the computer responds v..e..r..y s..l..o..w..l..y.
* One program leaves pieces of itself in another program's window. RAM is getting so tight that the screen update can't happen; when the video starts to mess up, lockup is coming soon. Save that file!
* "Beep." You click the mouse button. "Beep." You press a key. "Beep."

X-REF For information on how to step around, if not bypass, lockups, see Chapter 18.

A Card in Every Port: Port Basics

You may be sensing that the motherboard seems to hold all the important items together, through a series of connections, connectors, and chips. The microprocessor is on the motherboard inside the system unit. So is your computer's RAM.

Other important elements, also plugged into the motherboard, are the cards that work with the various components in your system. A *card* is like a small computer board that plugs into a slot on the motherboard. Remember when we were talking about expansion slots in Chapter 2? The cards tell your computer how to operate with—and send data to and from—the other parts of the system.

For example, the video card in your system tells your computer's BIOS how to interact with the computer monitor. It may have its own RAM to help lighten the load of the microprocessor in your system. It may include its own video accelerator to speed up screen updates. It carries the chips responsible for the type and quality of the display you see.

On a typical desktop computer, the video card on the motherboard has an outlet on the back of the system unit. This outlet is called a *port*, and it is the place where you plug in the monitor cable (see Figure 4-4). Thus, as you work with your program, the video information is sent to the video card, processed, and sent through the cable to the monitor so you can see the results of your actions as you work.

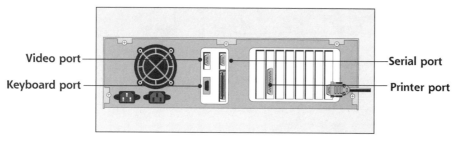

Figure 4-4 The port is the connection point between the cable and the card for the computer component you're adding.

Here we're just using the video card as an example because it's easy to explain. You have other cards and ports on your system, as well. There's a printer port, usually labeled LPT1. The LPT1 port is what's known as a *parallel port*. There's a COM port and perhaps a COM1 and COM2 port. The COM port is known as a *serial port*, which has nothing to do with what you feed it and everything to do with how the data is transmitted through the port.

> **SIDE TRIP**
>
> ### DO I HAVE TO KNOW ABOUT PARALLEL AND SERIAL PORTS?
>
> One look at the back of your system unit will tell you that the outlets are in different sizes and shapes. The chances that you'll try to plug the long-mouthed, 25-pin printer cable into the little round 9-pin connector are pretty remote, unless you flunked shape recognition in Kindergarten.
>
> You'll see terms like *parallel* and *serial* bantered about in books such as these from time to time, but don't spend too many minutes scratching your head over them. They both refer to the way data moves through the port. When you think "serial," think "series"—one after another. When you see the word "parallel," think of two parallel lines. That's the basic difference in the way data flows through the ports. The same data gets transferred at basically the same rates.
>
> The most important thing is that you get the cables that fit into the ports built for them.

If you are using a notebook computer, the ports will be slightly different. You will have a printer port, a mouse port, and other ports on the back of your system unit (which is connected to the monitor). You may also have PCMCIA slots, which enable you to plug in cards for different devices. The two most popular devices used with PCMCIA slots are fax/modems and CD-ROM drives.

Power Supply? Big Deal!

If the Great Gardening Shears in the Sky suddenly cut through the power lines that connect your house to the outside world, what would happen?

Exactly.

That's what the power supply does for your computer. Most computers are equipped with adequate power supplies. It's not something you need to worry about or consider changing, unless you, during the course of your computer experience, add a number of different items to your computer that draw off that same power supply.

Occasionally we hear horror stories of dead power supplies. The victimized users claim complete innocence: They just walked in and there it was, feet up, on the desk.

There are really only two rules for keeping your power supply happy:

* **Don't overload it.** If you add devices to your system that pull on the power, ask your friendly local computer tech whether you should have a stronger power supply put in. This is a straightforward process, although not one you should do yourself without some expert assistance, which just requires taking the cover off the machine, detaching a couple of cables, and unscrewing a few screws. Still, the power supply is such an important part of your system that its replacement is best left to the pros.

* **Don't block the fan.** Your power supply needs the help of a cooling fan to keep it operating within its own comfort zone. If you position your computer too near a wall, or otherwise block the little air holes the hamsters need in order to breathe, you might come in and find it feet-up one day.

> **TIP** What? You don't have a "friendly computer tech" and don't know where to find one? Don't be surprised if you haven't thought about it before—most computers don't come with a human technical support helper packaged right inside the box. But inside your computer manual you will find a phone number that can lead you to a helpful party. And the salesperson at the computer store should be able to connect you with their technical support department, which may be a guy named Bob who comes in every other afternoon and fixes broken PCs. If you don't have a tech support phone number and there's no Bob in your local computer store, get out the phone book and look under "Computers." You should be able to find several computer stores or fix-it shops in your area that can answer your questions and get you back on the road to happy computing.

> **NOTE** The power supply still relies on electric current to fuel your computer, so we're not talking batteries here. If you use a notebook, you may work with rechargeable batteries, which are a different issue altogether. For more information on preparing your batteries and your system for life on the road, see Chapter 15.

The Seven Deadly System Unit Sins

Putting anything except a disk in the drive. You may not be guilty of it, but your toddler will be. That little slot looks like a place for mail, don't you think? Watch your Post-it notes and loose disk labels—and for goodness' sake, don't dig anything out with a screwdriver!

Hitting it. Remember that the disk drive is delicate machinery, and rough stuff will cost you a trip to your nearest technical support bench. Besides, who would hit a poor unoffending system unit? After all, it's not a vending machine.

Shaking it. I did this once and I was sorry. I had this idea that something was loose inside. I had moved the system unit from one place to another and thought I heard something rattling. So I shook it, to be sure. Yup, something was loose all right. The difference was that, before, the system was working and after, well . . . suffice it to say that the computer tech got everything back together again after a certain investment in both time and moolah.

Turning it sideways. This is not an aggressive action, like hanging someone out the high-rise building by his heels. This is a practical, "Hmmm . . . what if I use this system unit like a tower unit and put it under my desk?" kind of problem. If your system unit isn't specifically built to be a tower, don't make it into one. The hard disk isn't meant to turn on a vertical axis; it is comfortable horizontally. You may not see any hazardous results right away, but you may down the road, in terms of wear and tear on your machine.

Using magnets to hold notes on the side of it. Let's just get this clear: Magnets and electronic data do not like each other. The magnetic field sucks the data right off the disk (more or less) and can do all kinds of weird electronic tricks with your favorite data files if the magnet is close enough to your hard disk or disk drive. For maximum data protection, use Post-its for those must-stick notes.

Messing in the system unit just for the heck of it. You don't want to take the cover off your system unit for any reason you can avoid. For one thing, it's a real chore to get all of those screws back in straight. For another, there are just way too many things that could accidentally go wrong when you explore beyond your depth. So be warned: Don't go swimming in the system unit without an experienced computer guru swimming buddy.

Overdoing the on-off thing. Don't nervous people make you nervous?

Once I was interviewing at a company and the discussion turned to computers. He wanted to show me something on his PC and, for some reason, when he flipped the power switch, the computer seemed to be coming up a little slowly. He looked at me, huffed something under his breath, and turned the computer off and back on again. Again, the computer yawned and started to wake up. The man huffed a little more loudly and turned the system off and on again.

I could just see it. Sometime in the future, he appears in my office doorway early in the morning. "Where's that report you were writing?" I blink. "Well, I—"

He huffs and steps closer. "Where's that report you were writing?" His voice is raised about a half-decibel.

"I planned to—"

He's jumping up and down now. "The report! I need that report! Confound it, how many times—"

Sheesh. No thanks. And, by the way, the time your computer takes to start up is really a service to you. You're supposed to take a few deep breaths, a few mental deep knee bends. Prepare yourself for the day. And keep your hands off that power switch.

NOTE No matter what kind of computer you are using, power down gently when you can. Close the programs you are using, get to the prompt or desktop level, and choose the necessary Exit commands. When your system says "OK to turn off your computer," go ahead. If you must turn the computer off because it is totally locked up and you can't do anything else, count to 10—slowly—before you flip that switch back to On. Your system will thank you for it.

BONUS

More Power! The Uninterruptible Power Supply

Remember the Great Gardening Shears in the Sky? That doesn't happen to many of us unless you consider the number of times your computer has been rebooted because of a sudden power surge, a nearby lightning strike, or some other act of nature like your three-year-old tripping over the power cord.

One answer to sudden losses of power—which can mean *huge* losses of data, effort, and time if you haven't saved your files—is to invest in an *uninterruptible power supply*. The UPS supplies your system with power until the power is restored, and protects your files against spikes and surges that could corrupt your files and damage your data. UPSs run from about $90 upwards into the hundreds. You'll find them in computer retail stores and in all the mail-order catalogs.

Summary

In this chapter, you've learned about the major players in the system unit. Inside that boring gray or tan box lurks the equipment that brings the miracle of computing right to your fingertips. The microprocessor makes all the data processing happen; the BIOS tells your computer what to do with information and how to respond; the RAM stores the programs and data you work with; the ports are the doorways through which the data passes on its way to other components in your system; and the power supply gives them all juice.

The next chapter helps you explore the whys and wherefores of the disk drives, which are also a part of the system unit but important enough to deserve some space of their own.

Some Web Sites to Hit

WEB PATH

Motherboard HomeWorld:
http://users.why.net/uruiamme/

Motherboard Information Page:
http://www.dfw.net/~sdw/mboard.html

Power-On Products (power supplies):
http://www.power-on.com/

CHAPTER FIVE

THE LOWDOWN ON DISK DRIVES

IN THIS CHAPTER YOU LEARN THESE KEY SKILLS

DISCOVER THE BASICS OF DISK DRIVES   PAGE 64

CHECK OUT STORAGE TYPES   PAGE 65

FIND OUT THE FACTS ABOUT FLOPPY DISKS   PAGE 67

KNOW WHAT'S HARD ABOUT HARD DISKS   PAGE 69

UNDERSTAND WHAT CD-ROM DRIVES ARE AND AREN'T   PAGE 71

DO STUFF WITH DISKS   PAGE 73

Denise was confused. She was thrilled to have a new computer and was having a blast writing letters to friends and creating and printing greeting cards right on the spot. But each time she turned the power off, her work disappeared. Every time she wanted to print a new card, she had to retype the text in her word processor before she clicked the Print button.

The problem? Denise wasn't saving her files. She was using her computer like a souped-up typewriter.

It's a true story and one that most of us, thankfully, haven't experienced. And yet it typifies what using a computer would be like if we couldn't save the information we enter, edit, and enhance. If we can't use the PC to make our lives easier, what's the point?

Disk storage—whether you're talking about saving files or small programs on a floppy disk or installing large, complicated programs on your hard disk—is all about keeping hold of the work you've already done. This chapter introduces you to the different disk storage choices you have available.

The Basics of Disk Drives

Your computer has at least one disk drive. Most computers, in fact, have two: one hard disk drive and one smaller disk drive into which you place a floppy disk that has your stored files on it.

Disk Drive Differences

Three different computer components are generally called *disk drives*:

* The 3.5-inch drive in the front of your system unit. (If you have an older computer, you may have a 5.25-inch drive on your system.)
* The hard disk inside your system unit. This is not a drive you can see, move, touch, or label (unless you've got a removable hard disk, but that's another story).
* The CD-ROM drive either installed in or attached to your system unit.

Let's start by weeding out what's *not* a disk drive. The CD-ROM drive, although *drive* it is called, does not enable you to store data. You can't save a file to a CD. The CD-ROM drive is designed so that users can only read data from the surface of the CD, not write data to it, which is the operation that would be required if you were to save a file to the CD. If you want to save information on a CD, you need a CD-R drive, which enables you to burn information on the surface of the CD. The CD-R drive is more expensive than either traditional CD-ROM drives or hard disks with enormous storage capacities.

For more dirt on CDs and their drives, see "CD or Not CD?" later in this chapter.

The Whole Point of Disk Drives

The disk drives in your computer enable you to store data. That spreadsheet you created to decide whether you should buy a new sailboat will vanish—poof!—if you exit the program and turn off your computer before you save the file. The file is stored only in your computer's RAM until you save it, and RAM is erased when you turn your computer's power off.

When you save the file, the program you are using works with your computer's operating system to store the data away in a place—on a disk in the disk drive or on your computer's hard disk—where you can find it again later.

So saving is the important part. The difference comes in the type of disk on which the data is saved.

You can save a file to the 3.5-inch disk, which you pop into the disk drive on the front of your system unit. But you can also save the same file to the hard disk that is enclosed within the body of the system unit—you don't have to insert anything into anything. In fact, with the hard disk, the only evidence you see that anything at all is happening when you save a file is that most programs, thankfully, tell you so ("Saving file HIMOM.DOC to C:\"), and you'll see a little light flashing on the front of the system unit. (You may even see the letters HDD, for hard disk drive, to one side of the light.)

Checking Out Storage Types

The early PCs offered only one type of disk storage: floppy disk drives. Soon a bigger, clunkier option was available—the mind-blowing 20MB hard disk. Today you won't find a 20MB hard disk, even if you search under the biggest PC scrap heap you can find. Hard disks of 300, 500, and 850MB are now the norm. And 1GB drives are so common they don't even raise eyebrows anymore.

But still we need different types of disk storage. Having a huge hard disk is a great thing, but you still need the floppy to move files back and forth (even if your computer is networked, via cable, to other computers). You will need that floppy drive (see Figure 5-1).

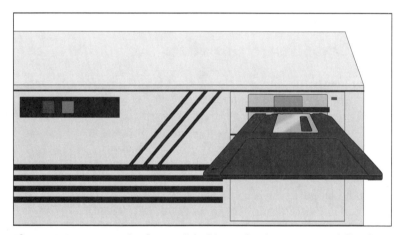

Figure 5-1 You use the floppy disk drive to load programs and files from a disk onto your computer. You can also copy programs and files from your computer onto the floppy disk.

On the hard disk, you can store large volumes of information without having to insert anything into anything (the hard disk is enclosed in the system unit). Different types of hard disk drives are available in addition to the one that's already in your computer. You can get external hard disks, which plug into your computer via cable, or removable hard disks, which enable you to pop out the hard disk cartridge and take it home with you, exchange it with other machines, or put it away for safekeeping. Either way, the hard disk gives you the same benefit: lots of room for data.

CD-ROM drives give you a way to access massive amounts of information from one compact source. If you do a lot of reference work, you'll enjoy the wealth of information at your fingertips; but if saving massive data files is your thing, get the largest capacity hard disk you can afford.

Tape backup units could be considered a storage device, but they are more for oops-the-power-went-off-and-we-lost-the-file kinds of problems. That is, you don't normally work with tape backup units on a daily basis; you use them only to keep a safe backup copy of your entire hard disk's contents. You can either buy a tape backup unit that fits inside your PC (you may have to request that it be added to a new system) or you can add an external one via a cable that plugs into your system unit. Backup software is included with the backup unit, although other programs—including one with Windows 95—will do the backup for you as well.

In a nutshell, the amount of information each storage medium can store is the most important difference between floppy disk drives and hard disks. The CD-ROM can't store information, and the tape backup unit is used for its safety-net potential.

SIDE TRIP

The We-Can't-Avoid-It Glossary

No matter how hard we try, we simply can't avoid using some technospeak to explain the hows and whys of computers. In any discussion of memory or storage space, you're going to see the abbreviations K, MB, and GB, so I've defined them here, where we're talking about the capability of one type of disk storage to hold more information than another. If you're clued in to what the abbreviations stand for, the differences between the following storage devices should be pretty obvious.

Bit. A bit is a single electronic pulse, the smallest amount of data that flows in and out of your computer. Each bit is a binary 1 or a 0, which is an "on" or "off" pulse. Because computers can count only in binary (1 = 1, 2 = 10, 3 = 11, 4 = 100, 5 = 101, 6 = 110, 7 = 111, and so on), they must process information one bit at a time.

Byte. Bits are divided into groups of eight, called a byte of information (pronounced "bite"). One byte of information is roughly equal to one character.

K. A kilobyte, written as K, is approximately one thousand bytes of data (actual size: 1,024 bytes). The earliest computers had only 64K of RAM, compared to today's 8MB (actually 8,388,608K) or more.

MB. A megabyte, written as MB, is one million bytes of information. The real number for 1MB is 1,048,576 bytes. Now we're talking! What's the difference between a thousand and a million bytes? A million bytes is a thousand kilobytes. Think in dollars rather than bytes—then it's easier to understand.

GB. A gigabyte, written as GB, is upwards of one billion bytes of information, or one thousand megabytes. In actuality, it's 1,073,741,824 bytes, or characters. Can you imagine? If that were a speech, how long would it take from beginning to end?

Another important difference among the storage types is speed. If you open a file that's stored on a floppy disk, you'll find yourself waiting and waiting for it to open, but if you load a copy of that same file that's stored on the hard disk, you'll find that it opens quickly.

The Facts About Floppy Disks

Back in the Stone Age days of PCs, the original IBM PC had one 5.25-inch disk drive. The 5.25-inch drive wrote your files out to a 5.25-inch disk, which was larger in size, smaller in capacity (meaning it couldn't store much information), and more vulnerable to damage or data corruption than today's computer disk. Thank goodness times have changed!

Whether you are talking about yesterday's standard disk or today's disk, the 3.5-inch variety, disk drives work by writing or reading information to and from the surface of the disk inserted in the drive slot. Recording heads read and write the information onto the exposed disk material. The drive also writes an index (called an *FAT,* or *file allocation table*) on the disk, so it knows where to find the information it has stored on that disk. Each disk has its own FAT that is updated every time a file is saved to the disk.

Made of Tougher Stuff: 3.5-inch Disks

The downsizing from 5.25-inch disks to 3.5-inch disks was not a sudden jump. Early Macintosh computers introduced the smaller standard many years ago, and it's only been in the last five years (which is like half a century, when you're talking computer shelf life) that 3.5-inch disk drives have become the standard in most new PCs. Figure 5-2 shows a typical 3.5-inch disk.

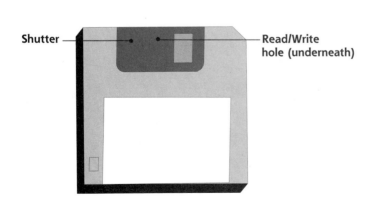

Figure 5-2 The 3.5-inch disk is handy for transferring files from one computer to another.

The 3.5-inch disk is enclosed in plastic, making it pretty safe from such elements as cigarette ashes, cat hair, dust, and melted M&Ms. The recording surface of the disk is covered with a piece of metal called a *shutter*.

When you pop a 3.5-inch disk into the drive, the spindle grabs the spindle hole (which is visible only on the back of the disk) and the drive slides the shutter open, revealing the read/write hole. When you want to remove the disk, you push the button on the drive; the disk is then pushed out so you can reach it easily.

TIP Many software programs sold automatically on a CD-ROM disk are also available on 3.5-inch disks for those customers who haven't yet purchased a CD-ROM drive. Only older programs are available on 5.25-inch disks. In addition, some computer systems sold today— usually recycled or refurbished PCs—come with both a 3.5-inch and 5.25-inch disk drive, which solves the problem for you if you are having a difficult time swapping 5.25-inch floppies with coworkers or friends.

SIDE TRIP

DISK DO'S AND DON'TS

Even though 3.5-inch disks are fairly sturdy beasts, these common-sense safety tips will protect your data:

- Keep disks away from magnets.
- Don't pry off the metal shutter (it's supposed to be there).
- Don't touch the surface of the disk with your finger (you have to slide the shutter over to do it).
- Don't submerge the disk in water.
- Label the disk clearly, with a felt-tipped pen.
- Don't throw a bunch of disks together in your desk drawer and expect them to work forever.
- Keep disks in a disk box to protect them from dust, spills, and so on.
- Don't leave disks in the sun.
- Don't layer disk labels upon old disk labels; take the old one off and then put the new one on.

How Dense Is Your Data?

Life is complicated enough, you may think, with floppy disks, hard disks, and CD-ROMs to worry about. But there's another issue to consider: *density*.

Floppy disks come in two densities. The density of the disk means, roughly, how much data you can cram on any one disk. High-density disks hold more information than low-density disks. You get the idea.

In fact, 3.5-inch high-density disks store 1.44MB of data, while low-density disks store only 720K (about two memos to Mom). So which one is better? If your disk drive supports high-density disks (check your computer manual to be sure, but every new computer sold today has high-density drives), go for the highest amount of storage you can get. The high-density disk will give you more room for your money and will provide a better-quality, longer-lasting disk to boot.

When *shouldn't* you get high-density disks? When your drives are low-density drives or when you need to be compatible with ancient computers that have only low-density drives.

Low-density drives cannot read high-density disks. But high-density drives can read low-density disks.

What's So Hard About Hard Disks?

Unless you purchased your computer from some guy named Guido who pulled the PC out from under his trench coat, handed it to you, and ran away, you probably have a hard disk in your system unit. No self-respecting computer manufacturer would sell a standalone PC today without one.

And if hard disk space makes you happy, you might think this is a great thing. All that open hard disk space—kind of like the wild frontier. You can put anything you want on that hard disk. Wonderful things. Fun things.

Except for one thing. Almost parallel to the growth in storage capacity, programs have gotten larger and larger. Years ago, having a program that took up 1MB of storage space was a seriously hefty program. Today, it's not unusual to lose 8MB, 20MB, even 33MB to a single application on your hard disk. And if you're turning over 33MB to one program, it's safe to say that an 80MB hard drive suddenly doesn't look so big.

How Does the Hard Disk Work?

Like its smaller cousin, the floppy disk drive, the hard disk works in much the same way as the floppy disk; recording heads read information from and write information to the surface of the disk. The disk just happens to be enclosed in a case. The disk itself is not plastic but a hard platter (hence the name *hard disk*). You may also see the term *fixed disk* used to describe hard disks because the disk is nonremovable and therefore "fixed" inside the unit.

A Hard Disk By Any Other Name

You've got the "massive storage" idea, so you understand the need for the largest capacity hard drive you can afford. What, then, are your other options?

In the last section you read about nonremovable disks—those run-of-the-mill hard disks enclosed inside your system unit. Another kind of available hard disk enables you to remove the hard disk (which is still enclosed in a plastic case for protection), move it to another computer, and use it there. This device is called a *removable hard disk* (no big surprise there).

Generally, PC users who have invested in removable hard disks love them and swear by them, taking disks to and from work and home with religious zeal. And it's good practice. Not only does it give you the added benefit of having access to important data at the drop of a hat, but it safeguards data against prying eyes and fingers, or natural — and not-so-natural — disasters.

More Storage! More Storage!

Are you one of those people whose closets are filled to the brim? Do you never have enough storage space? Do you still have shoes from the '80s? Couldn't make yourself part with that Sonny and Cher belt buckle?

If you find that you keep accumulating files you can't bear to part with, you've got one of two options. You can buy bigger and bigger hard drives. But that's just like building a larger and larger closet for those retro clothes and lava lamps. Sometimes the answer to dealing with huge amounts of data is to make the data smaller. If you're stuck with a certain size hard disk and don't plan to upgrade anytime soon, you can compress the files on your hard disk to give you more room in which to work.

Data compression does just what it sounds like. It compresses the data so that it takes up less room.

Several data-compression utilities are available today, including DriveSpace, which comes with Windows 95. Other compression utilities are available from Norton Utilities and other companies, but I won't recommend one over any other because, frankly, I don't use them. Data-compression programs have a reputation for eating data once in a while, and I'd rather not take the risk. If you plan to use a data-compression program, be sure to back up your files first.

Some people like data-compression utilities because compression gives them more space — sometimes lots more space. The downside, however, is that an error in the compression could cause you to lose some of your data.

A safer option is to use a file-compression program like PKZIP or WinZIP, which simply compresses a file or a group of files. You have control over how, when, and where the files are compressed, and you can decompress them when you need to use them. This option doesn't give you the massive amounts of available storage in one swoop like data-compression utilities do, but it is a lot safer.

> **TIP** A common problem you may run into sooner than you think occurs when you're running low on disk space. The first clue? Files take forever to save. Your programs start to do strange things—lock up, leave the dialog box on the screen, display odd errors. When you run low on disk space, clean everything off your PC that you definitely don't need and compress the files you do need on hand, but not for everyday use. Taking files off your computer doesn't mean deleting them; you can save them to disks or tapes and put them away for safekeeping. And don't be afraid to uninstall programs you no longer use; as long as you were working with a legal copy, you can install the programs again later if you need them.

CD or Not CD?

Your sparkling new PC may or may not have a CD-ROM drive. Depending on what you were willing to spend, whether your kids were with you ("Please, Mom, I want to play *Myst* . . . er, I mean, use *Microsoft Bookshelf*! We need a CD-ROM drive!"), and what type of deal the retailer was offering, your decision to purchase a CD-ROM drive may have been either a planned or surprise blessing.

Throughout this chapter, I've made the distinction between a "real" drive and a CD-ROM drive. On a disk drive and a hard disk, you can store the files you create. The letter to Aunt Penelope, the spreadsheet for your accountant, the newsletter for the gardening club—all these files you can store on a floppy disk or your hard disk.

On a CD-ROM, you can't store anything you create. The "ROM" in CD-ROM stands for read-only memory, which means you can read information *from* the disk but you can't write anything *to* it.

A CD-ROM drive enables you to read data from a CD-ROM. For example, you might pull a picture of posies for your gardening newsletter from a CD-ROM collection of art. (You can even slip in a music CD and play it through your speakers; the storage technology on both disks is identical.)

But you're not going to be storing any data on those CD-ROMs. Not unless you, at some point, need your own CD-R (for recording) drive and are willing to invest thousands in the possibility. It should be noted here that CD-R drives are great if you need to record large amounts of data that will not be deleted or modified. For example, a thriving doctors' office might invest in a CD-R drive to store all its patient records in an electronic archival system. The doctors need to have access to this information; the CD-R enables them to store huge amounts of information or data that must be preserved in its original state. CD-Rs are especially useful for users who create large files—perhaps graphics or multimedia projects that take up incredible amounts of disk space—that don't need to be stored on the hard disk. CD-Rs also save the day for people who publish large volumes of proprietary information and who need to be able to circulate it at will (things like legal briefs or elaborate financial analyses, for example).

It's unlikely, however, that the general population needs such equipment, so we'll focus here on the CD-ROM drive that you're likely to find in your friendly neighborhood PC.

CD Speeds and Options

If it drives you crazy to wait for your games to update the screen, for graphics to be loaded, and for sound effects to play, invest in the fastest CD-ROM drive your budget will allow. CD-ROM drives are advertised in many different speeds—2X, 4X, 6X, and 8X—but many CD titles today do not yet take advantage of higher-speed capabilities. Still, if you invest in the speed-capable device today, when the titles catch up, you'll be at the front of the pack. (Unless, of course, the pack jumps over you and goes right to 10X speeds—which *could* happen.)

Other CD-ROM options include multi-disk changers, which enable you to load several CDs at once and then move among them easily, like different drives on a computer. If you use reference works a great deal, perhaps in a legal or financial setting, having a multi-disk changer might save you some serious CD-swapping time. But it's a perk and a relatively new one at that, so expect to pay more than you would for a regular CD-ROM drive.

How Does the CD-ROM Drive Work?

Using a CD is similar to using a disk. You push the CD-ROM door (or button, if there is one) and a tray opens. You place the CD in the drive (usually printed side up—check the instructions for your particular drive) and gently push the door closed (or press the button again).

 TIP Some CD-ROMs fit into a container called a CD caddy. You then put the entire caddy back into the drive.

The reading device in the drive then scans the disk's file allocation table so it knows what's on the disk and tells your computer, through the CD-ROM software and your operating system, what programs and/or files are now available for use.

You access the data from a CD-ROM as you would from any other disk in a drive.

When you're ready to remove the CD, you simply push the door (or push that button) and the door opens. You can remove your CD and replace it in its box.

X-REF For more information on taking care of disks and discs, see Chapter 17.

Doing Stuff with Disks

No matter how you slice them—and you *shouldn't* really slice them— disks are not difficult to use. This section lists some of the most common procedures you should follow with your new PC.

Formatting Them

Before you can use a disk, it must be prepared to store data. You can purchase formatted disks (they say "formatted" right on the box) or unformatted disks. If you need to format the disks yourself, don't panic—it's a simple procedure. Your operating system actually does it for you. To format a disk, use the following procedures:

* With DOS, enter **FORMAT A:** (if A is the drive with the disk you want to format) at the command prompt and press the Enter key.
* With Windows 3.1, start the File Manager, open the Disk menu, and choose Format Disk. Then follow the screens.
* With Windows 95, right-click on the 3 1/2 Floppy (A:) icon in the My Computer folder and choose Format from the popup menu.

TIP Especially if you're formatting a disk using DOS, be careful. It's easier to make a mistake with DOS and format the wrong disk, which could result in a loss of data (perhaps a massive loss of data if you accidentally format your hard disk).

What does the format do? Earlier in this chapter you learned about the FAT, or file allocation table, which keeps track of where the different files are stored on the disk. It's like a table of contents your disk uses when the program you are using searches the disk for a particular file. Without the FAT, the program wouldn't be able to tell where the data you want is stored.

Once a file has been formatted the first time, reformatting the file simply removes all the data from the disk, in effect wiping it clean. You can reformat a disk when you've been having trouble with it or when you no longer need the data you've stored there.

Labeling Them

Once you format the disk, stick a label on it. There won't be any data on the disk, but the label will remind you that the disk has been formatted; when you save a file to the disk, you can write the filename on the label. Here are a few pointers for dealing with disk labels:

- Use labels that fit the disk.
- Don't let the label overlap the metal shutter.
- Make sure no edges of the label stick up (otherwise the label could cause the disk to jam in the drive).
- Write on the label using a felt-tipped pen.
- If the filename is cryptic, add a description so you'll remember a year from now what's on that disk.

Copying Them

The process for copying a disk is one of the functions of your operating system. (See Chapter 13 for almost everything you'd ever want to know about operating systems.) Copying a disk simply means making a copy of whatever is on the disk and placing it on an empty disk, either a floppy disk or on your hard drive. To copy a disk, use the following procedures:

- With DOS, you can use the DISKCOPY or XCOPY command to copy an entire disk (the command you use depends on the version of DOS you're working with). Type DISKCOPY /? or XCOPY /? at the command prompt for detailed instructions.
- With Windows 3.1, copy a disk by starting the File Manager, opening the Disk menu, and choosing Copy Disk.
- With Windows 95, right-click on the $3 \frac{1}{2}$ Floppy (A:) icon in the My Computer folder and choose Copy Disk from the popup menu.

Erasing Them

You may want to erase a disk from time to time. Erasing removes any data currently stored on the disk, freeing up room to store more files on the disk. The exact process of erasing the disk will depend on your operating system:

- With DOS, you can use the ERASE command. That's actually **ERASE A:*.*** if the disk you want to erase is in drive A. Be careful with this command! You don't want to accidentally type the letter of your hard disk (usually C) after the ERASE command! Type **Y** at the "Are you sure?" prompt and press Enter.

- With Windows 3.1, you start the File Manager, open the File menu, and choose Delete. When the Delete dialog box appears, type **a:*.*** and click OK. Then click Yes to All to proceed.
- With Windows 95, open Windows Explorer and click on the 3 1/2 Floppy (A:) icon. Open the Edit menu and choose Select All. Then open the File menu, select Delete, and click Yes in the dialog box to proceed.

NOTE Although there are add-on programs that enable you to recover accidentally-erased files, for the most part erased files are gone. Be very careful before you erase a disk and, when in doubt, keep it.

BONUS

Major Storage Idea

If you're interested in the most-storage-for-your-dollar game, you might want to check out yet another type of disk drive. The Zip drive is a kind of mutant —not really a disk drive and not really a hard disk. Removable cartridges enable you to store up to 100MB of data, and the whole kit and kaboodle is relatively inexpensive. Most users I've talked with who use Zip drives store extra large files—such as sound and video files—on them and move them from computer to computer. Zip drives keep you from having to hassle with compressing files enough to get them on traditional disks. Iomega is the manufacturer of the "original" Zip drive, although there are others on the market now. The cost is just over $100 for the drive and around $15 per disk for the storage. Check PC catalogs and talk to your local computer retailer to find out more.

Summary

This chapter has shone the light on the mysteries of disk storage, illuminating the differences between floppy disks, hard disks, and CD-ROM drives. Our friend the 3.5-inch disk is the most common "portable" storage device available today, useful for moving files among computers and carrying them home to work on them over the weekend (ugh!). Hard disks offer terrific amounts of data storage, expanding our horizons to billions of data bytes. CD-ROM drives enable us to gather information in huge quantities but are still read-only in nature.

The next chapter introduces you to your PC's monitor. Together we'll explore how you see what you see and how your computer helps you see it.

Some Web Sites to Hit

Article on how to add a second disk drive:
http://www.pcworld.com/hardware/storage
 _backup/articles/mar97/1503p248a.html

Iomega (Zip drives):
http://www.iomega.com

Seagate Technologies (disk and tape storage):
http://www.seagate

CHAPTER SIX

MONITOR BASICS: THAT THING YOU LOOK AT

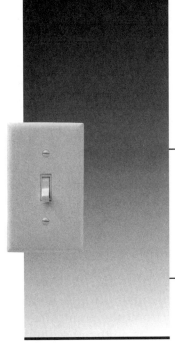

IN THIS CHAPTER YOU LEARN THESE KEY SKILLS

DISCOVER HOW A MONITOR WORKS   PAGE 77

FIND OUT ABOUT IMPORTANT MONITOR QUALITIES   PAGE 78

GET COMFORTABLE WITH YOUR MONITOR   PAGE 82

You may not recognize the value of a good monitor until you use one that's not so great. A wavering screen will give you headaches. One with a high-pitched electronic whine will make your dog howl. A screen that's too small will have you squinting as you write long passages of text.

This chapter introduces you to the monitor component of your PC hardware. You'll learn how it does what it does, what makes a good monitor good, and what different types of monitors are currently available.

Monitoring the Monitor

The monitor itself is only one part of the display system of your computer. Sure, it's the part you see. But the unseen part—the display adapter that plugs into the motherboard of your system—controls what you see on the screen.

The Display Adapter: Where It All Begins

The display adapter, which is also called the *graphics card*, controls everything you see on the screen. Expansion slots are slots on the motherboard that hold plug-in cards for other items you add to your computer system (like a printer, a mouse, or a monitor). The graphics card plugs in to one of those slots on the motherboard.

The display adapter is a kind of translator; it receives information from the microprocessor and turns it into information that can be displayed on the screen. When you press a key, the information goes from the keyboard to the microprocessor; then from the microprocessor to the graphics card. The card turns the signal into information that can be displayed on the screen, and the letter or key you just pressed appears a fraction of a second after you pressed it. All this happens so quickly that the individual character appears before you type the next one.

 TIP Some display adapters have their own memory, known as *video RAM*, which takes some of the video processing off your system's microprocessor and enables the graphics card to display data faster without slowing down other processing.

From the Adapter to the Monitor

The display adapter transmits the data to the monitor through a cable. The information is sent to an *electron gun*, which electronically paints the inside of the monitor, back and forth each line at a time, causing the phosphors on the inside of the screen to glow and the image you see to appear—and remain—before your eyes.

After a fraction of a second, however, those glowing phosphors begin to fade, and the inside of the screen must be repainted. The screen must be repainted again and again and again. The only time this stops is when you turn the monitor off.

 X-REF You'll see different acronyms used to refer to the different display adapters: EGA, VGA, and SuperVGA. You'll learn more about how these different adapters affect the quality of the display in the "Resolutions You Can Live With" section later in this chapter.

Important Monitor Qualities

A number of things contribute to your overall monitor happiness. Do you want color? If so, how many colors? How quickly does that electron gun repaint the screen? What's the resolution like? Is your monitor interlaced?

THE COMPUTER: INSIDE AND OUT

Mono(tonous) or Color?

Although color monitors—and the number of options they present—far outweigh the variety of monochrome monitors available, single-color monitors are still out there.

You may be wondering why in the world anyone would be interested in a single color monitor these days. Simple. Text work. In those applications that are text-intensive, you may be happier with a simple black-and-white screen than you would with one in full color. (However, many applications let you choose the colors you want to use, including black and white.)

When color monitors first appeared, they were capable of displaying only red, green, and blue (and their combinations). Today, over 16 million colors are available in a wide range of monitor styles and sizes. Some monitor ads even claim "unlimited" colors. When the after-dinner talk turns to monitor color options, use the terms in Table 6-1 to help you banter with the best of them.

TABLE 6-1 Computer Monitor Color Options

Standard	Called	Number of Colors
4-bit color	16-color mode	16
8-bit color	Pseudo color	256
16-bit color	High color	32,000
24-bit color	True color	16+ million

Is Size Everything?

How important is the size of the monitor? That's purely a personal preference issue. Some people love the little 9-inch diagonal screens on the original Macintosh computers; other people go cross-eyed trying to read the text on the minuscule monitor.

When you're talking about monitor size, you should know that, as with television sets, the ads give you the diagonal measurement. A 15-inch monitor means "this monitor has a 15-inch display area measured diagonally from one corner to another." You'll find monitors in a variety of sizes, from 15 inches up to 21 inches. (That's a big monitor!)

TIP When you are monitor shopping, read the ads carefully. Typically, you'll see an ad that claims "15-inch monitor!" In small print, it'll say something like "13.7 viewable area." The larger measurement is the size of the monitor itself; the smaller measurement is how much of the screen you can actually see through the plastic case. Make sure you're happy with the viewable area measurement before you buy it.

Resolutions You Can Live With

One of the most important issues you'll wrestle with is screen resolution. The *resolution* of the monitor refers to the quality, or sharpness, of the display. A monitor with low-resolution has badly formed characters and worse graphics. A high-resolution monitor shows clear, crisp images and easy-to-read text.

One of the keys to resolution is the size of the dots used to paint the screen. When the electron gun hits the screen, it runs across a grid (imagine the screen in your kitchen window). The open area in the grid (the space between the mesh in the screen) picks up the electronic charge. From the outside, these grid areas look like dots. And these dots are called *pixels*.

The smaller the space between the holes in the grid, the smaller the pixels. And the smaller the pixels, the greater the number of pixels that can be displayed on the monitor, which translates into a better screen display for you to spend all day gazing into.

In the monitor ads, you'll see this referred to as the *aperture grille pitch* or the *dot pitch*; the smaller this number, the better. In other words, a 0.28 dot pitch is better than a 0.30 dot pitch. See Figure 6-1.

The issue of resolution—the more dots there are, the better the quality—is true for print quality as well as display quality.

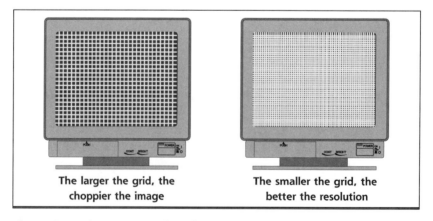

Figure 6-1 The greater number of pixels that can be displayed on the monitor, the clearer the picture.

Early graphics cards and monitors displayed text and graphics at a low resolution. The first monitor/card combos were CGA (color graphics adapter) and EGA (enhanced graphics adapters). They displayed fewer pixels than the screen resolutions offered today. The resolutions were written as a kind of horizontal-by-vertical measurement; for example, one adapter might be able to display an image 800 pixels wide and 600 pixels tall. Over the years, the standards have changed. Table 6-2 shows what you'll find today.

TABLE 6-2   Graphics Cards and Screen Resolutions Available Today

Graphics card	Resolution
VGA	640 × 480
SuperVGA	800 × 600
Extended VGA	1024 × 768
Ultra VGA	1280 × 1024

When you're buying a monitor, don't purchase anything less than VGA (in fact, you may have trouble finding anything less than VGA) and purchase the highest quality you can afford.

A Quick Refresher Course

As it paints the display on the screen, the electron gun inside the monitor moves back and forth and from top to bottom. How quickly the gun moves is known as your monitor's *refresh rate*. The refresh rate can be a very important characteristic in the quality of your display; if the gun moves quickly enough, you never notice the phosphors fading in the top-left corner of the screen. However, if the refresh rate is slow, the screen begins to fade before it is repainted, which causes the screen to flicker or waver annoyingly. Don't settle for a refresh rate of less than 72Hz. That will keep your display fresh and clear, and your eyes will thank you for it.

TIP   As you are considering what kind of monitor to buy, keep the following guidelines in mind:

* 0.30 dot pitch or smaller
* VGA or higher
* Refresh rate of 72Hz or greater

To Interlace or Not to Interlace?

Even a 72Hz refresh rate won't do your eyes any good if it's an interlaced monitor. *Interlaced monitors,* which are rapidly disappearing from the marketplace, redraw every other line of the screen each time they refresh the screen, which gives it a noticeable flicker. *Noninterlaced monitors* repaint every line of the screen every time they repaint the screen. This means that it takes an interlaced 72Hz monitor twice as long to fully paint the screen as a noninterlaced monitor. If you can possibly avoid an interlaced monitor, do so, even if it's cheaper. Don't buy one except as a last resort, and then plan to replace it soon.

Dual-Scan and Active Matrix

When you're looking into the purchase of a notebook computer, you'll see the terms *dual-scan* and *active matrix.* Dual-scan, the lower of the two standards, updates the screen display in interlace fashion (which may or may not be noticeable on the smaller screen size of the notebook).

Let's Get Comfortable

One of the most important features of your monitor has nothing to do with dot pitch, refresh rate, or interlacing. It's an important consideration: How do you feel when you're using it?

If you're not comfortable using your monitor because of your (and its) physical position, you'll be dissatisfied, whether you're using a top-of-the-line $1,500 monitor or a $198 blue light special.

You shouldn't be scrunched over or stretching up in order to get the best vantage point; your monitor should be roughly at eye level so you can sit comfortably while you are working with it. If you are continually looking up, your neck will let you know; if you're always looking down, your back will begin to ache.

TIP Some manufacturers also sell monitor stands that have tilting or swiveling bases; you can then tilt the screen so that it looks down or up at you, even if you can't move the entire monitor.

Are you sitting close enough to the monitor that you can read text easily? Don't make your eyes work overtime—staring into a gleaming monitor for hours on end is hard enough.

SIDE TRIP

FIVE STEPS TO REDUCING EYESTRAIN

1. Make sure your monitor is placed at eye level.
2. Use indirect lighting in your workspace to minimize screen glare.
3. Set the contrast and brightness controls on your monitor to comfortable levels.
4. Choose soothing colors for your applications and desktop environment.
5. Break up long periods of screen-intensive work; take at least a five-minute break from the screen every 30 minutes.

BONUS

Screen Add-ons

Here are a few products you can add to your monitor to make both you and it happier.

Tempered glass filters can help you reduce glare and cut down on eyestrain. They also block up to 99 percent of the radiation transmitted by the monitor. Filters such as these cost anywhere from $19 to $39.

A copy clip is a simple addition that can make your life easier. It simply attaches to the top of your monitor and extends to the right or left (whichever you prefer) and then holds the document you're working with so you no longer have to move your eyes back and forth from the desk (or wherever the page is set down) to the screen.

A swivel base enables you to turn the monitor easily any which way you need to. Up a little, down a little—it makes no difference to the monitor.

Summary

The monitor isn't as mysterious as you might think. It's not like the television, which pulls signals from the air or through a cable from a broadcaster who-knows-where. You know where the signal comes from: right there inside the system unit. The monitor receives its direction from that all-important-device, the display adapter. The electron gun inside the monitor receives the electronic pulses from the adapter and paints the inside of the screen, creating the picture you see.

You can choose from a number of different monitor sizes and styles, but the most important issues are screen resolution and refresh rate.

The next chapter helps you watch your Ps and Qs by taking a close look at the keyboard.

Some Web Sites to Hit

WEB PATH

Dell Computer:
http://www.dell.com

Viewsonic (computer monitors):
http://www.viewsonic.com

PC World **article on "Top 10 17-inch Monitors" (March, 1997):**
http://www.pcworld.com/hardware/monitors/articles
 /mar97/1503p235.html

CHAPTER SEVEN
KEYBOARD CARE AND FEEDING

IN THIS CHAPTER YOU LEARN THESE KEY SKILLS

DISCOVER FULL-SIZED AND NOTEBOOK KEYBOARDS   PAGE 86

LEARN WHETHER BRANDS MATTER   PAGE 87

KNOW THE BASIC PARTS OF THE STANDARD KEYBOARD   PAGE 88

FIND OUT HOW TO TAKE CARE OF YOUR KEYBOARD — AND YOURSELF   PAGE 93

Where did your old typewriter go? It didn't really disappear; it only changed form. The typewriter you used to feed carbons and corrector tape is now part of a PC system of reusable data that makes life easier and reduces the amount of time you spend typing — especially *retyping*.

It's what you use to type that letter to Aunt Edna.

It's the thing you use instead of the adding machine when you're attempting to balance your checkbook.

It's even your partner in playing *Space Invaders* and *War of the Cubic Zirconia*. Your old Smith-Corona would be proud.

Keyboard Basics

Even though all keyboards do basically the same thing, several things make keyboards different from each other. Figure 7-1 shows a typical PC keyboard.

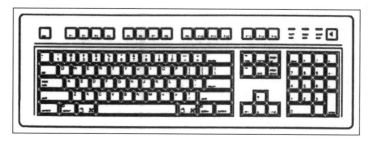

Figure 7-1 A full-sized keyboard includes separate cursor keys, function keys, and a numeric keypad.

SIDE TRIP

TEN WAYS YOUR PC KEYBOARD IS NOT A TYPEWRITER

* It doesn't have corrector tape.
* It doesn't have a sliding carriage.
* You don't have to change type balls (remember those?).
* You don't have to constantly (re)adjust the page before you type.
* Jammed keys? Never!
* No more messing with typewriter ribbons.
* You don't have to reposition the envelope 15 times before you get the return address placed right.
* It won't walk across your desk on its little rubber feet.
* You don't have to listen to your keyboard hum (or go tat-a-tat-tat).
* It can fix your typos for you automatically!

Your Average Desktop Keyboard

The keyboard with your PC desktop system more than likely includes the following areas of keys:

* The basic letter and number keys (known as the "QWERTY keys")
* A set of cursor keys
* A separate numeric keypad
* Function keys along the top
* Special keys, including Num Lock, Scroll Lock, and more

Not-a-Lotta-Room Notebooks

If you are using a notebook computer, you'll notice a keyboard different from the one shown in Figure 7-1. The notebook keyboard is smaller on all scales (see Figure 7-2). The keytops themselves are smaller; the cursor keypad is usually incorporated along the edge of the letter keys. The spacebar, which is traditionally located across the bottom of the keyboard, is half that size on a laptop.

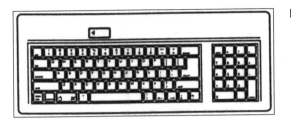

Figure 7-2 A notebook keyboard is smaller but includes all the essential keys.

Does Brand Matter?

Once upon a time, the keyboard came with the system you purchased and you never thought a whole lot more about it. IBM had its keyboard and the Macintosh had its keyboard (which was smaller than the IBM's but no one seemed to notice).

IBM and Apple computers both introduced extended, full-sized keyboards, the luxury versions that gave you every key you could ever want with more-than-adequate room for pressing. Today it's not only the major brands in the mix but also a variety of smaller companies — some created just to provide add-on components — that are bringing a number of options to the keyboard market.

Oh, you'll still get the standard keyboard with the PC you purchase. In fact, the standard layout for new desktop systems is still the IBM Enhanced Keyboard. But now, should you decide to upgrade to a fancier keyboard, you have a number of options.

You'll find *wave keyboards*, which literally bend the shape of the keyboard from its rectangular shape into an extended *S*, reducing the stress and strain your hands and wrists suffer when you are typing for prolonged periods. One such keyboard is the GlidePoint WaveKeyboard, produced by Cirque.

Another type of wave keyboard raises the midsection so the place where your index fingers would reach is higher than the points your little fingers reach. Again, the idea is to lessen stress on joints and muscles. The Truform Ergonomic Keyboard, produced by Addesso, is available for both PC and Macintosh computers. You can also get a pointer on the keyboard, which you can push as you would a mouse button.

Another enhanced keyboard is the slimline model, which is shorter in stature so your wrists don't have as much of a reach to the top of the keyboard. The Alps Enhanced Windows 95 Keyboard includes special keys designed for Windows 95 applications and boasts both an Erase-Eaze key (a built-in Undo key) and a special dust-resistant coating.

You'll also find keyboards that offer wrist rests, built-in trackballs or touchpads, or specially programmed keys. The most important thing is to remember that if you're not happy with the keyboard you've got, chances are you'll be able to find one you like better. Be prepared to do a little shopping and some experimenting before you decide.

TIP Having a backup keyboard is not a bad idea. You can get keyboards inexpensively — from $50 to $100. That way, in the event that the cat knocks over your Dr. Pepper, you have a spare to use while your regular keyboard is drying on the line.

The most important thing is to get a keyboard that's comfortable to use. Cheap keyboards usually feel cheap. Their keys have a hollow feel to them, and the keyboards are so light they can inch away from you as you pound on them. Higher-quality keyboards generally have a more solid feel, stay anchored on the desk, and have the kind of key responsiveness you'll feel good about using day after day.

Keys to the Board

All keyboards have certain keys in common. Of course, we all need the basic letter keys and the number keys. You also need cursor keys, which enable you to move the cursor on the screen instead of using the mouse. Depending on what programs you use, you may or may not use the function keys. And the numeric keypad — a luxury reserved for full-sized keyboards — is a necessity if you want to be comfortable entering long columns of numbers accurately.

QWERTY Keys

On any keyboard, you'll find the standard set of alphanumeric keys. These keys are often called the *QWERTY* keys. Why? Because Q, W, E, R, T, and Y are the first six keys along the top row of the keyboard.

TIP   *Alphanumeric* is a math major's word, which refers to all the keys on the keyboard that are alphabetic, numeric, or symbolic: 2, 6, 8, A, Y, W, M, /, *, (, etc.

The QWERTY keyboard is arranged as follows: a rectangular arrangement of three rows of letters with symbols toward the right (always in the same order), a row of numbers and symbols above, and the spacebar below, within easy reach of either thumb.

> **SIDE TRIP**
>
> ### Typing 101
>
> There she is now, class, with her pince-nez pushed to the end of her nose. She's got her finger on the timer. Ready, set, go! The buzzer rings and you've got to type as many words as you can — correctly — in 60 seconds.
>
> You don't emerge from a typing class without being marked one way or another. If you did well, you came out of class feeling that you were a good typist. If you did poorly, you were branded "all thumbs when it comes to typing." Even if you've had therapy to counteract the experience, the label sticks. When you look at the computer keyboard, that familiar sense of failure looms.
>
> The good news is that your computer will make you a better typist, whether you've had a typing class before or not. The idea that you can make mistakes — and easily correct them — removes about 98 percent of the intimidation, which is ordinarily what causes the errors anyway. If you've ever watched anyone type with intensity, you've seen that they rarely goof up. When we're sweating about typing each letter, errors abound.

Enter and Then Return

If you were a Smith-Corona typist before your journey into PCdom, as I was, you were accustomed to pressing the carriage return key to move the type head down to the next line so you could continue typing. That carriage return key has become the PC's Enter key.

NOTE   With word-processing programs, you don't need to press Enter at the end of each line of text because the program automatically moves the cursor to the next line as you approach the end of the line (a feature known as *word-wrapping*).

Enter is the "Do it!" key. When you press Enter, the computer carries out some action. You've chosen the necessary commands to rename a file, and you entered the new name you want in the provided space. Now you simply need to tell the computer to complete the operation. Press Enter.

TIP Because pressing Enter has an air of finality about it, know what you're doing before you press it. Especially if the action is something as important as deleting a file or a folder, the operation is worth a second look before you continue.

Which Way Did He Go?

All keyboards, no matter how small, have cursor keys in common. Table 7-1 shows how these keys appear on your keyboard.

TABLE 7-1 Cursor Keys and Names

Key Symbol	Key Name
→	Right-arrow key
←	Left-arrow key
↑	Up-arrow key
↓	Down-arrow key

Most keyboards have two sets of cursor keys: one stand-alone set to the right of the QWERTY keys and another set that does double duty as a numeric keypad, on the far right side of the keyboard (see Figure 7-3).

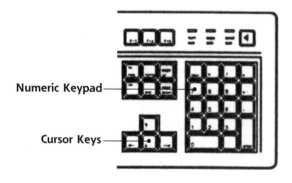

Figure 7-3 Both the cursor keys and the numeric keypad enable you to move the cursor.

It's Not My Function!

It escapes me why we really need the function keys, but someone, somewhere, must have a good reason. Typically, the function keys — labeled F1 through F12 (or F15 on some keyboards — are located above the horizontal row of numbers on your keyboard and are used to carry out some operation quickly. For example, to start the spelling checker in Microsoft Word for Windows, you can press the function key F7. This saves you from having to open a menu and choose a command.

But outside of Microsoft Word, the F7 key may or may not do anything. It's entirely up to your software. Windows 95 makes use of some function keys; Windows 3.1 uses others. DOS (that age-old operating system) uses still others for things like copying files and such.

Some people never use their function keys, preferring to let them gather dust at the top of their keyboards. Other people use them all the time. If you choose to use them, they can make your life a little easier; if you don't, no one will ever know.

Num All Over and Scroll Locked

Above the cursor keys on the full-sized keyboard, you've got some nifty little keys that cause lights to come on. Before you use them, it may not be apparent what they do. *After* you use them, it still may not be apparent what they do. So — in the name of completeness — let's address them here.

The Num Lock key, which you learned to turn off without knowing what it does earlier in the chapter, locks your numeric keypad into Numbers mode. When the Num Lock light is shining, you can only get numbers out of that numeric keypad. This is a great thing when you're entering a column of numbers into an Excel spreadsheet and you really don't want to be moving the cell pointer all over creation when you mean to be entering numbers. When you turn the Num Lock light off, by pressing the Num Lock key again (it's a toggle), you can press the keys on the numeric keypad to move the pointer around on the screen as needed.

The Scroll Lock key is a different animal that works in a similar way. Scroll Lock keeps the screen output (something we saw commonly back in the days of DOS rule) from scrolling off the screen. In Windows, it doesn't really do anything except use up a little more electricity to keep the light on.

The Pause key is another DOS leftover that won't make a hoot of difference to your Windows programs. Picture this: You've just entered a command that is going to display on your screen a list of all the students who graduated with you at your alma mater. Long list, right? It's going to go flying by on the screen so fast you won't be able to soak it all in. You start the command and press Pause. Ah! The list stops. When you're ready to get moving again, press Pause again.

So much for the usefulness of *that* key.

In some programs, the Print Scrn key is said to print whatever your screen happens to be showing at the time you press it. In Windows it takes a picture of whatever is on the screen; then it's up to you to paste the picture in a document. In any case, using Print Scrn depends to a huge degree on which program you're running and the printer you've got set up. But hey, you may love it.

Specialty Keys

All around the QWERTY keys you see a variety of keys with different words and symbols. Some you might recognize from your typewriter days: Tab, Shift, and Caps Lock. Others, like Ctrl, Alt, and Esc seem a bit cryptic. Table 7-2 gives you a quick overview of what these different keys do.

TABLE 7-2 Special Keys on the PC Keyboard

Key	Function
[ESC]	Cancels an operation
[Tab]	Moves the cursor forward
[CAPSLOCK]	Makes all typed letters CAPITALS WHEN TOGGLED ON
[SHIFT]	Used with letter or number keys to produce Uppercase Letters
[CTRL]	Used with other keys to carry out commands or select options
[ALT]	Used with other keys to carry out special operations
[BACKSPACE]	Moves the cursor one character to the left and erases what's there
[INS]	Turns Insert mode on, so any character typed will be inserted at the cursor position (pressing Ins again turns Insert mode off, so any characters you type will overwrite existing characters)
[HOME]	In most word-processing applications, moves cursor to the beginning of the current line
[PGDN]	Scrolls the screen down one page
[PGUP]	Scrolls the screen up one page
[DEL]	Deletes highlighted information or character at the cursor position

Key	Function
[END]	In most word-processing applications, moves cursor to the end of the current line
[\]	Used commonly in DOS to separate directories in path names (such as C:\WORD)

TIP Some software manufacturers offer programs that change the way a standard keyboard functions. This is called *remapping the keyboard.* If you are a single-handed typist, for example, or have some other idea about the way you want your keyboard keys arranged, you can alter the key placement and function to suit your needs.

Escape! Escape!

The Escape key is one of the most helpful keys you've got on that keyboard. When a program looks like it's locking up, Escape may unfreeze it. When you've started an operation you want to cancel, opened a dialog box you want closed, or done something else you want to stop midstream, Esc is your key.

The worst thing you can do with the Escape key? Push it too much. What will happen? Nothing. That's my kind of key.

Healthy Keyboard Practices

There are two parts to healthy keyboard ownership. First, you've got to take care of your keyboard. Second, you've got to take care of yourself while using your keyboard.

Keyboard Care

In general, keyboards don't like the following natural elements:

* Melted Reeses Pieces
* Spilled coffee or soft drinks
* Pet hair (or even your own)
* Cigarette ashes
* Paper clips

Common sense, maybe, but it bears saying: the keyboard is electronic equipment. And just like anything electronic, it doesn't like water or any reasonable facsimiles. And gooey things like melted candy or gum. Coke spills aren't good for its mechanical or electronic workings, either. And the too-much-pressure issue — well, who *does* work well under too much pressure? — isn't good for the keys themselves.

A Keyboard in the Hands Is Hard on the Wrists

The dawn of the computer age has brought with it new hazards. Today thousands of computer users are suffering from carpal tunnel syndrome, a disorder that results from stress and strain on the hands and wrists.

Notice how you type at your computer keyboard. Are your hands straight so your fingers can type in a relaxed reach, or do your wrists bend upward so you type at an uncomfortable angle? If it's the latter, you may be setting yourself up for wrist injury.

Carpal tunnel syndrome is sometimes pooh-poohed as one of those complaints that's easy to claim and hard to prove; however, if you've ever suffered from it, you know the pain can be extremely intense and that it can seriously affect your work.

To take good care of your hands and wrist — and your keyboard in the process — follow these general guidelines:

- Make sure your chair is tall enough to enable you to work with your wrists straight.
- Use a wrist pad to cushion your wrists and the palms of your hands as you type.
- Practice good wrist posture. Make sure your hands are straight as you type and your wrists aren't bent as your fingers reach for the keys.
- Take a break every 30 minutes or so to get the pressure off your wrists.
- Do finger-stretching exercises and rotate your wrists several times a day.
- If you suspect you have the beginning symptoms of carpal tunnel, have it checked out.
- Use a bandage or brace when you feel you need additional support (but check with your doctor first).
- Purchase one of the specially designed keyboards if you feel carpal tunnel may be a problem for you.

BONUS

Keyboard Add-ons

One of the easiest items you can add to your keyboard to help prevent wrist strain is a simple wrist support called a wrist rest. This is a long, narrow pad — similar in weight and texture to a mouse pad — that fits along the bottom edge of your keyboard, supporting your wrists. You can find wrist pads in all major department stores and in a variety of patterns (even Looney Tunes) and colors.

Summary

A little more impressed with the keyboard, aren't you? The keyboard is one of the most often used — and most often overlooked — components of your computer. You may not think about the ways those keys serve your every keypress, but the keyboard you use — and how happy you are with it — is a major factor in how comfortable you are with your PC.

The next chapter takes you up close and personal to your favorite rodent, the mouse. And you'll learn about some other pointing devices, too.

Some Web Sites to Hit

Typing Injury FAQ:
http://www.cs.princeton.edu/~dwallach/tifaq/keyboards.html

Lefthanded Computer Keyboard:
http://www.lefthanded.com/

Sejin America, Inc. (wireless keyboards):
http://www.sejin.com/

CHAPTER EIGHT

OF MICE AND OTHER POINTING DEVICES

IN THIS CHAPTER YOU LEARN THESE KEY SKILLS

MEET YOUR MOUSE   PAGE 98

LEARN BASIC MOUSE MOVES   PAGE 100

KNOW HOW TRACKBALLS AND TOUCHPADS WORK   PAGE 104

CHECK OUT MOUSE ADD-ONS   PAGE 107

It's hard to imagine life without the little rodent. The mouse—or the trackball or the touchpad — is such a common part of computer use these days that it seems unthinkable that at one point it didn't exist.

Pointing Devices: Why We Need 'Em

The mouse enables you to point at an item on the screen. You move the mouse and the pointer on the screen moves correspondingly. You click the mouse button and the item you're pointing at is selected. You use the mouse to start programs, open menus, select files, copy and move files and folders, and do all sorts of other things specific to the program you are using.

The mouse makes using the computer almost as easy as point-and-click. Your preschooler will be able to page through an electronic storybook as soon as he or she understands where to put the mouse pointer and how to push the mouse button. You will be able to start programs, play games, access the Internet, move from continent to continent, buy things, and balance your checkbook, all with a click or two.

Meet Your Mouse

Most mice are similar in size and shape. The mouse is a small, rounded object, curved a little to shape your hand. Figure 8-1 shows a typical mouse.

Figure 8-1 Your general, no-nonsense mouse

The mouse may have one, two, or three buttons, depending on the mouse. The mouse button always does the same thing, however; it carries out an operation in the program.

The mouse connects to the system unit of your computer through a cable. When you roll the mouse across your desk, the sensors in the mouse send signals through the cable to the mouse card in the system unit and to the processor. The action is then communicated to the program, and you see the movement on the screen.

Mouse Families: Serial and Bus

Two kinds of mice are available for PCs: bus mice and serial mice. These two mice work the same way. The only difference between them is the way they are connected to your computer.

If you are using a bus mouse, the mouse is connected through an opening in the back of your computer to a board that is plugged into one of the expansion slots (remember those?). If you are using a serial mouse, the mouse is connected to the serial port in the back of your computer.

The bus mouse connector looks different from the serial mouse connector. The serial mouse is a longer connector, rectangular in shape, with two rows of connector pins. By contrast, the bus mouse connector is a small round connector.

Deciding whether you should purchase a serial mouse or a bus mouse is probably out of your hands; most likely, the mouse came with the system when you bought it. If you find that you have to replace your mouse, just look at the connector of what you have now so you know the replacement mouse will fit the available port.

TIP Serial ports are called COM1, COM2, and so on. Most PCs have one or two. Your computer may have labels on the back of the system unit, showing you which port is which, but don't be surprised if there's no such label.

How Does the Mouse Work?

The secret to the way the mouse works is on the underside. When you turn the device over, you'll see a small, moveable ball. You can easily move this ball with your finger.

When you turn the mouse back over and push it across your desk, the ball rolls, pushing against one of four very sensitive electrodes inside the mouse. These movement sensors send information to your computer and to the program you're using, and the arrow on screen that represents the mouse position (called the mouse pointer) is moved to match the mouse's movement on the desk. This all happens in a fraction of a second, so the mouse pointer on screen appears to move the same instant your hand moves the mouse.

How Many Buttons Do You Need?

Many software programs make use of two mouse buttons. Windows 95, for example, builds in many right-click operations that wouldn't be available to you if you had a single-button mouse. Usually, the left mouse button is used for selecting, dragging, and activating items; the right mouse button often offers a pop-up menu that allows you to change the item you've just selected.

Your mouse comes with its own software. And it's probably loaded automatically, so you don't have to do anything with it unless you want to. If you feel like changing certain things about your mouse, such as the way the mouse buttons function, how slowly or quickly the mouse responds to your clicks, and what clicks and double-clicks do, you can use the mouse software to make the changes. Check out the manual that came with your computer to find out about the options available with your mouse.

Working with the Mouse

Now that you've got the lowdown on mouse basics, you can find out specifically how to use it. This section explains a couple of the most common mouse operations.

SIDE TRIP

MOUSE ACTION WORDS

* *Point* means to move the mouse pointer to an item on the screen.
* *Click* means to press and release the mouse button once quickly.
* *Double-click* means to press and release the mouse button twice quickly.
* *Drag* means to position the mouse on an item, press and hold the mouse button down while dragging the mouse in the direction you want to drag the item.

Moving the Mouse

Moving the mouse is as simple as moving your hand. You place your hand on the mouse (so the round back of the mouse fits against your palm). Your index finger should rest on the left mouse button. If you're left-handed, you'll probably adapt to the mouse in a way that's most comfortable for you. (You can also buy a left-handed mouse if you wish.)

When you push the mouse one or two inches on your desktop, the pointer on the screen moves as the mouse moves. When you move the mouse so that the pointer is positioned on something you want to select, you are doing what's known as *pointing*.

Clicking and Double-Clicking

You select items and carry out commands by *clicking* the mouse button. This is the mouse's "Do it!" key. A mouse click is technically a two-step process: press the mouse button and then release the mouse button. For example, the screen in Figure 8-2 shows an open File menu, which appeared on the screen after I moved the mouse pointer to the word File in the menu bar and clicked the mouse button once.

Some operations require that you *double-click* the mouse button. A double-click is simply—you guessed it—two quick clicks of the mouse button. In Windows 95, for example, you double-click an icon to open it into a window. Figure 8-3 shows the My Computer window after it was opened with a double-click.

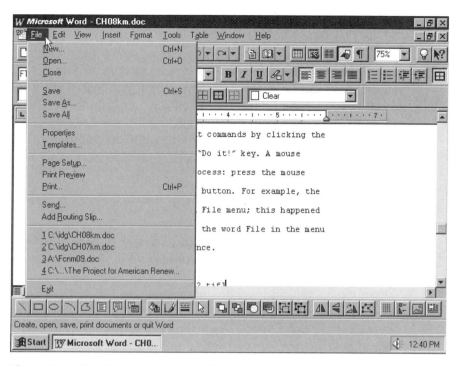

Figure 8-2 The File menu was opened with a click of the mouse.

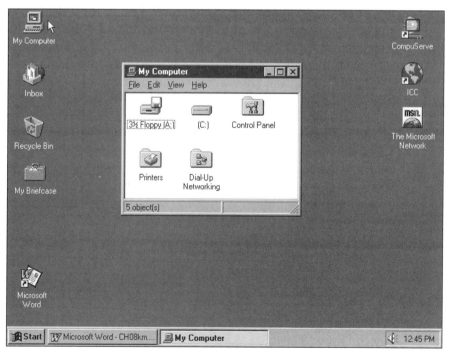

Figure 8-3 Double-clicking the My Computer icon opens it into a window.

Dragging Items

Yet another technique allows you to select and move items on the screen. This process is known as *dragging*. To drag an item, you first point to it; then press and hold the mouse button while moving the mouse. This drags the item in the direction you move the mouse. When the item is in the desired location, release the mouse button to let go of the item.

You might drag a file from one location to another, or from one window to another. Or you might drag a corner or edge of a window to make it larger or smaller.

Other Mouse Options

The typical mouse is not the only kind of mouse there is. In addition to the one- or two-button mouse, you may see ads for an optical mouse or a high-resolution mouse.

Unlike the typical mechanical mouse, which has the roller ball and the four movement-sensitive sensors, the optical mouse uses laser optics. You put the optical mouse on a special pad that has a wire grid inside; when you move the mouse, the mouse "sees" where it is going by bouncing a light beam off the wire grid.

A cousin of the optical mouse uses optical technology to keep track of its position on the mouse pad, but you don't need a wire grid as part of the deal. One such mouse is the MDS mouse, available from Marlow Data Systems for under $20. Proponents claim optical-mechanical encoding gives you more precise control over the way you position the mouse pointer on the screen; the rest of us are happy with our Microsoft, or look-alike, mice.

A high-resolution mouse is just an extremely sensitive mouse. The high-resolution mouse is very responsive to even the tiniest movement. This enables you to be more precise in the movements you make on the screen. Most mice offered today have a high-resolution capability, depending on how you set the responsiveness of the mouse. By using the mouse software included with the mouse, you can set the mouse from low responsiveness to high responsiveness. Some ads claim "high-res," which probably means the mouse is configured to work at a high-resolution so that you don't have to change the settings.

Cleaning Your Mouse

If you're the kind of person who takes his dog to be groomed, you may not be interested in cleaning your own mouse. Pet ownership is no picnic. But there are a few things you can do to keep that inexpensive but necessary little device pointing and clicking for a long time to come. Perhaps the most important thing you can do is to keep it clean.

SIDE TRIP

ABOUT THIS RESPONSIVENESS THING

Imagine a wire grid superimposed on your mouse pad. Each square on the grid is half-inch square. This is your mouse functioning at low-res; each time the mouse passes one of the wires on the grid, it sends a location signal to your PC, which relocates the mouse pointer on the monitor. Now turn up the responsiveness to high-res. The grid, instead of having half-inch squares, now has $1/8$-inch squares. The mouse has a shorter distance to travel before it sends a new location signal to the PC. You have a smaller distance to move your hand before the new position of the mouse is registered on the screen. The mouse pointer location on the screen therefore gets updated more frequently because of the increased responsiveness of the mouse.

Inside the mouse, as we've already established, is a little ball and four tiny sensors. As you move the mouse, the ball rolls against the sensors, sending a signal to the PC that the mouse is moving and indicating the direction in which it is headed. The pointer on the screen is moved accordingly.

You may be working happily enough when all of a sudden your mouse begins to do strange things. Your mouse may

* Stop and refuse to move any further.
* Only move up and down, not side to side, on the screen.
* Only move side to side, not up and down.
* Skip strangely from place to place as you move the device wildly on your desk.

If any of these events occurs, your mouse probably needs cleaning. (Actually, if your mouse stops where it is and refuses to move, check your mouse connection. The cable may be unplugged from the back of the computer.) Any weirdness in movement often means that environmental hazards such as dust, grime, and Doritos crumbs have wrapped themselves around the little sensors in the mouse and need to be removed.

TIP   The tools for mouse cleaning? Q-tips, rubbing alcohol, and a steady hand.

To clean your mouse, follow these steps:

1. Turn the mouse belly-up on your mouse pad.
2. Locate the round disc that keeps the ball in place. There should be two little arrows on the disc to show you which direction to turn it in order to open the mouse.
3. Turn the disc in the direction shown.
4. Remove the disc.
5. Remove the ball. (It should fall right out if you turn the mouse on its side.)
6. Dip a Q-tip in alcohol and gently wipe off each of the four sensors, making sure to get all sides of the rollers. You may see little pieces of lint or gummy substances on the rollers that guide the sensors. Make sure you remove them.
7. Wipe off the ball and replace it in the mouse casing.
8. Put the disc back on the mouse and turn it to lock it.

How often does a mouse need cleaning? That depends on your mouse, your desk, how often you use it, and the general state of your environment. My system needs a good mouse cleaning every three to four months, and I use my computer every day. (And I've also got three kids, two dogs, a cat, and canaries. They are the messy ones.)

Trackballs and Touchpads

One cousin of the mouse is the trackball. The Macintosh PowerBook was the first big-name computer to incorporate the trackball in the machine, and now all notebooks that are sold have either a trackball, a touchpad, or some other kind of pointing device.

Trackballs and touchpads are popular for desktop systems, as well. They attach to the system unit through a cable, similar to the mouse.

Why a Trackball Isn't a Mouse

A trackball works on the same basic principle as the mouse; the small ball moves, touching sensors that send movement information to the computer. However, instead of moving the entire device, you move only the ball, rolling it with your thumb or index finger. Figure 8-4 shows a typical trackball.

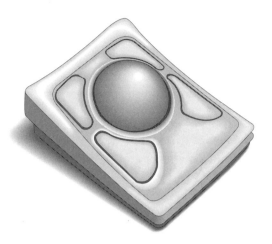

Figure 8-4 The trackball stays put on your desk, and you move the ball to move the pointer.

Trackballs may have two, three, or four buttons, and they remain stationary on your desk. Trackballs cost anywhere from $39 to $99 and are available from a variety of manufacturers.

Clip-on trackballs were the first pointing devices available for notebook computers, and they were slightly less than helpful. Sticking out from the edge of your notebook (they were clipped on to the edge), they were neither comfortable nor handy.

Today's notebooks include trackballs built right into the notebook itself, usually placed just below the keyboard. The trackball is set right where you need it, not off to the side. Problem solved? Maybe. Built-in trackballs are often sensitive creatures that are easily gummed up with oil from your fingers, lint from your desk, and crumbs from those cookies you had at lunch. Figure 8-5 shows a trackball included in a notebook.

TIP If you use your notebook computer for day-in, day-out operations, consider adding a regular mouse for those times when you're working at your desk. You can simply plug the mouse into the port in the back of your notebook. (You may have to disable the trackball, too. Consult your computer manual for specifics.) Using a regular mouse whenever you can saves wear and tear on the trackball so it will be ready, willing, and able when you *really* have laptop work to do.

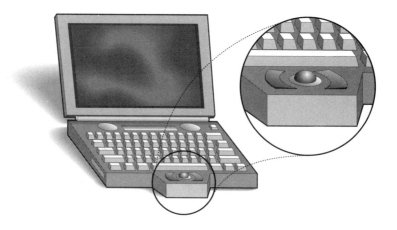

Figure 8-5 A trackball is often included as the pointing device in a notebook computer.

Touchy, Aren't You?

Touchpads, also called *trackpads*, are one of the new-fangled pointing devices literally taking the middleman (or, should I say, *middlemouse*) out of it and letting you physically point at the items you want on the screen and tap to select them. Touchpads have a touch-sensitive grid that sends an electronic pulse through the cable to the port. Touchpads are usually the size of business cards, or they may be smaller.

Some notebooks include touchpads in the place of trackballs. You can also purchase add-on touchpads as alternatives to the mouse. One such add-on touchpad is the Cirque GlidePoint Desktop.

A touchpad offers a sensible alternative to potential trackball frustrations. At least one notebook user and frequent traveler who has threatened on more than one occasion to throw his notebook out the window at 30,000 feet because of trackball frustrations has endorsed the touchpad as the "trackball that makes sense." No more moving parts. No more rolling balls. No little moving sensors that can be damaged or coated with foreign substances.

As with any computer device, however, certain common-sense guidelines apply. There are buttons on the touchpad, which means they can stick or get sticky. The pressure-sensitive screen is itself an input device that could be damaged by too much pressure or by things that don't belong on its surface, like ballpoint pens, paper clips, or perhaps even really sharpen fingernails.

BONUS

Mouse Add-ons

You need only one thing to make your mouse comfortable: a mouse pad. The mouse pad provides a number of functions. It gives the roller ball traction, so the movement sensors receive continual input — not jolts and jumps — and the mouse pointer moves smoothly on the screen.

The mouse pad also helps keep dust, crumbs, and other environmental hazards away from the roller ball and out of the internal workings of the mouse. It also keeps mouse scratches from marring your desk's fine mahogany finish.

Some people use their mouse only sporadically and like it out of the way when they're not using it. You can get a mouse pocket to hang on the side of your system unit; just tuck the mouse inside when you want to clear your desk.

And, if you're really in the mood to treat your mouse right, you can spring for a mouse suit. No kidding — a little furry mouse suit, ears and all. Not real practical, but maybe just the right thing for your rodent-loving sibling next Christmas. (Check out your local computer store, Software Etc., Egghead Software, or B. Dalton Booksellers to find them.)

Summary

The mouse on your system enables you to start programs, work with files and folders, navigate through applications, and play games. You open menus, choose commands, highlight text, click buttons, and more, all using the pointing device on your system. Instead of a mouse, you might use a trackball or a touchpad to accomplish the same tasks.

The next chapter moves from input (mouse, that is) to output, as in printing.

Some Web Sites to Hit

Polytel computer Products (touch pads):
http://www.danish.com/polytel/

Logitech Live:
http://www.logitech.com

Microsoft HomeMouse:
http://www.microsoft.com/products/hardware/homemouse.htm

CHAPTER NINE
POINTS ABOUT PRINTING

IN THIS CHAPTER YOU LEARN THESE KEY SKILLS

KNOW WHAT QUALITY OF PRINT YOU NEED   PAGE 109

IDENTIFY DIFFERENT PRINTERS   PAGE 110

LEARN ABOUT MULTIFUNCTION CENTERS   PAGE 118

KEEP YOUR PRINTER RUNNING WELL   PAGE 119

You may be tempted to underestimate the importance of your printer. Don't. At first you may not use it much — in fact, you may never use it a whole lot — but there *will* be times when you will be tempted to bang your head against the wall if you didn't go ahead and get one when you purchased your PC.

What will you do with a printer? Here are just a few of the things you can print:

Checks	Household budgets
Reports	Tax-documents
Letters	Book reports
Greeting cards	E-mail
Recipes	Songs
Mailing lists	Kids' artwork
Mailing labels	Photographs
Financial reports	Newsletters

109

Checking out Printer Types

The way your printer prints has everything to do with what kind of printer it is. There are a number of different printers available and happily in use today, ranging in cost from minuscule to enormous.

Some computer setups are sold today with a relatively inexpensive printer included, usually a dot-matrix or an inkjet printer. Both are midrange in terms of quality, the inkjet being slightly better than the dot-matrix, and they run between $100 and $300. (You'll pay more for better quality and color potential.) In many cases, printers are add-on items, above and beyond the cost of the basic system.

Thermal printers are popular for notebook computers and, in the price category, they weigh in on the light end of the scale. Laser printers produce high-quality output — better, clearer-looking print than dot-matrix, inkjet, or thermal printers — but also come with a higher price tag. At the top of the scale, you'll find PostScript printers, a type of printer that uses a language of its own to produce the highest quality print. PostScript printers are often several thousand dollars, compared to the few hundred dollar investment of a good inkjet printer.

The following sections give you an idea of how the different printers work so you can decide which one is right for you (or learn more about the one you already have).

TIP Many people have more than one printer: an inexpensive one that produces low-quality output that they use for notes, internal memos and letters, and printouts; and an expensive, high-quality one they use for letterhead, financial reports, or professional documents.

When a Cheapo Printer Will Do

So you can see that printers range in cost from $100 or so to upwards of $10,000 (but that's for a really good, high-quality, high-speed PostScript color laser printer). You can get a good-quality laser printer that gives your documents a professional look for under $1,000. But how do you know whether you need an "okay" printer or a "great" printer? Think about how you'll use it.

Consider the kinds of things you'll be printing on your PC. Checkbook registers? Letters to the editor? Book reports? Mailing labels? A printout of the e-mail message to Aunt Edna hardly needs an expensive piece of equipment (see Figure 9-1).

```
To: edna@in.net
From: julianne@iquest.net
Date: 09-16-96
Re: Party!
    Yes, I can be there at 3:00. You aren't
bringing Uncle Harold, are you? Don't forget
what he did last time!
    See you there,
    Julianne
```

Figure 9-1 A printout of an e-mail message doesn't need a fancy printer.

If you use your PC primarily for household uses and the documents you print are for your own use, the type of printer you need is probably one that will simply produce readable text. If you are running a small business from your home or are investing in computer equipment as part of your work and your printed materials will be going to clients, coworkers, and employees, the quality of the printer may be more of a consideration (see Figure 9-2).

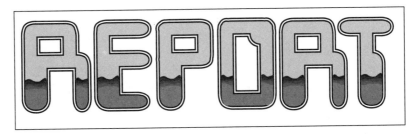

Figure 9-2 If you are creating a corporate report for a client or a flyer for your own company, you want the highest-quality print you can get.

TIP The inkjet is quickly emerging as the "do-everything" printer of choice. It's inexpensive. It's relatively fast. The text is clear and you can get color for printing charts, presentations, and logos without investing thousands of dollars. The downside of the inkjet is the cost of the print cartridges, how quickly these printers go through print cartridges, and the slow-dry effect of the pages.

When You Need a Good-Quality Printer

You'll know when you need a high-end printer because it will have something to do with why you bought the computer in the first place. If you are creating annual reports for companies, you need a printer that can print good-quality text and graphics and create special text effects like wrapping, rotating, and twisting. If you are working with desktop publishing applications, you will be concerned with more than good-looking text; you'll need to be able to print artwork, photos, and other graphics items.

NOTE Remember that "professional quality" and "good quality" are two different things. If your business is to provide professional-quality reports and newsletters and marketing materials to other companies, you either need a professional-quality printer or you need to be able to send your files to one for printing. If you are interested only in sending out nicely printed letters to clients, however, you can get the job done with a good-quality laser or inkjet printer.

How Does It Print?

When you print a file — whether it's a letter, a shopping list, a book report, or a check — it is sent from the system unit to the printer. The data travels via the printer cable, which is connected on one end to the system unit and on the other end to your printer.

The data travels into the printer and is stored for a brief moment (which depends on the size of the file being printed and the capability of your printer) in your printer's own memory while the printer is activated. *How* the image on the screen is printed is the variable part; different printers handle the process in different ways, and the image is output as the result of the file sent to the printer.

Dot-Matrix Printers

The dot-matrix printer is the dinosaur of the low-cost printers (see Figure 9-3). Around for eons (as far as PCs are concerned), the dot-matrix printer gets the job done with little fuss and fanfare. It doesn't take up a lot of room on your desk, and supplies for the dot-matrix printer — ribbons and paper — are generally inexpensive.

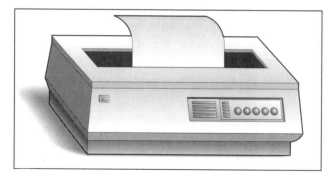

Figure 9-3 The dot-matrix printer is low-cost and low-maintenance and provides quality that's in the ballpark for most routine printing jobs.

SIDE TRIP

WHAT'S IMPORTANT?

Different people get bugged about different things, but in general these are the most important issues to consider in a printer:

* **Print quality.** No matter how fast, no matter how cheap, if you aren't happy with the way it prints, you're sunk. It's the print resolution that controls the quality of the type — how many dots per square inch are used to print the letters or graphics. Like screen resolution, the more dots, the better the resolution.
* **Cost.** Don't pay for more printer than you need, but don't buy less printer than you want. Weigh the cost against the need/want factor before you buy.
* **Print speed.** Some people demand a printer that cranks out pages fast. Others use the time to go get a Coke and chat a while in the cafeteria. If speed is your issue, make sure you get a printer that can keep up with your expectations. The speed of your printer is measured in "ppm," or pages per minute.
* **Ease of use.** Not all printers are easy to load. Some dot-matrix printers are a challenge paper-wise; other printers, like some laser printers, use cartridges and downloadable fonts so you can get the type styles you like. Make sure you find out how easy your printer will be to use before it officially becomes "your" printer.
* **Cost of upkeep and maintenance.** Although you'll only pay for the body of the printer once, you'll continue to pay for the supplies. The print ribbon for your dot-matrix is inexpensive but, depending on the number of pages you print, you may go through a lot of them. A print cartridge is more expensive than a ribbon, and a toner cartridge (for laser printers) is more expensive still.

The dot-matrix printer gets its name from the way it prints characters and graphics on the page. As the information comes through the printer cable (from the microprocessor), the printer receives the data and forms a character by firing certain pins in a mechanism called the *print head*. Which pins are used depends on which character is being formed (for example, the letter *A* would use different pins than the letter *L*).

The print head then pushes the pins through a printer ribbon, leaving the imprint of the character on the page. The character looks like a pattern of dots, which it is. No matter how you look at it, a dot-matrix printer produces dots.

NOTE Once upon a time, dot-matrix printers were called "impact printers" because the print head struck the printer ribbon, which pressed the ink onto the page. Because of this impact technology, dot-matrix printers are the only printers you can use with carbon forms.

Some of the features dot-matrix printers offer include smoothing features that blend the dots together and make the characters look cleaner. Some dot-matrix printers also have color capability and extremely fast print times.

The speed of the dot-matrix printer makes it a great printer for printing rough drafts. You might want to use your dot-matrix printer for documents you need around the house or your office — memos, reports, letters, budgets, and so on — because you can print them quickly and then stick them in a filing cabinet. The dot-matrix provides a quick print for editing and saves money and time in the process.

The only real trouble with the dot-matrix printer is the inescapable fact that everything it prints has a usually visible pattern of dots. No matter what you do, the quality produced on that printer will be less than the quality available on a laser printer. Another common complaint is that noisy dot-matrix printers are as loud as typewriters, making that clackety sound reminiscent of typing class.

Inkjets

Inkjet printers create the printed page by spraying characters and graphics in a pattern of ink dots. The printer uses ink cartridges instead of a ribbon or toner, which means you can easily swap different colors in and out if you have a printer that is capable of printing only in one color. You can also get color inkjet printers, such as the Hewlett-Packard 550C, which enable you to print in black

---

SIDE TRIP

SEVEN WAYS TO STAY HAPPY WITH YOUR DOT-MATRIX PRINTER

1. Make sure your ribbon is dark; change it as soon as you notice some of the characters fading.

2. Check the paper tension to make sure the page is secure.

3. Get "perfect" perforated paper so the edges tear away without a trace.

4. Make sure your printer has little rubber feet to cut down on noise.

5. Close the paper cover to cut down on clatter from the print head.

6. Get or create a paper tray to hold long documents so the printed pages don't interfere with the paper in the paper feed.

7. Use a tractor feed mechanism to keep the pages feeding accurately; this helps you avoid paper jams.

and in color (combinations of red, green, and blue). This means you can print slides, photos, graphics, and multicolored text at a reasonably low cost. The resolution of inkjets is high — some claim "better than laser" output. Again, the speed of the output is not as high as a dot-matrix printer could offer, but the inkjet is easier on the ears.

Inkjets are small, taking up only a fraction of the desktop space a normal dot-matrix printer would, and much less cumbersome than your average laser printer (see Figure 9-4). The printer uses laser printer paper, which is similar to copier paper, and when the printed sheet is done, the ink is still drying.

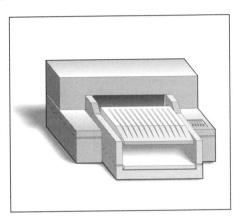

Figure 9-4 The inkjet printer takes up only a small amount of room on your desktop and can provide great print quality for your money.

SIDE TRIP

WHAT DOES MY INKJET WANT FROM ME?

* Inkjets use print cartridges. Ordinarily, cartridges don't run out gradually. All of a sudden, they're empty. Best advice? Keep an extra print cartridge on hand. And when you use it, go out and get another one right away.

* If your printer is a color inkjet, like the HP 550C, keep two cartridges on hand for backups — one black and one color.

* Get good-quality laser printer paper for your inkjet. If you buy the cheap stuff, it might get jammed inside the printer, which can be really frustrating when it happens fourteen times in the same afternoon.

* Don't grab the pages out of the printer as soon as they print, no matter what kind of a rush you're in. Part of being printed by an inkjet means that the ink has to dry before it's completely set on the page. Picking it up too soon may smear the print, and you'll wind up printing the document all over again.

* Be careful with the paper feed mechanisms. Inkjets aren't exactly delicate, but some are more temperamental than their dot-matrix cousins. Load paper carefully and watch the little levers and tray releases as you do so.

Laser Printers

Laser technology made it possible to really get things done on the desktop. No more rushing off to Dr. QuickPrint to have them typeset that brochure — now you can do it on your PC at home. The logo you designed for your new window washing business could be done right there on your laser printer. See? Already you're saving money working for yourself.

The laser printer itself is not a small-footprint item. It takes up considerable desk space (see Figure 9-5).

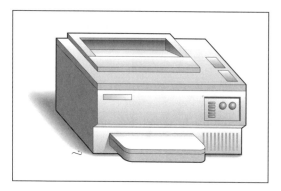

Figure 9-5 The laser printer is the largest of the lot. It gives you the highest-quality text and graphics printout.

Quality is the best thing the laser printer can offer you. It offers a high standard of *resolution* — that's the greatest number of dots in the smallest space — which produces clear, clean printouts. But, like everything else related to computers, you still have additional choices to make.

Laser printers are available in two varieties: regular laser printers and PostScript laser printers.

SIDE TRIP

WHAT'S THAT LASER DOING IN THERE?

The laser printer works by receiving the information from the microprocessor through the print cable. The information then goes to the image processor, which translates the data into the laser instructions or the PostScript language. The printer then fires up the laser, which strikes a rotating mirror and is reflected into the toner cartridge where it strikes the drum, which is coated with a light-sensitive substance. The drum rolls past a cartridge full of toner and picks up the toner on its magnetically charged surface. Then the toner is transferred to the paper, and the paper rolls out of the printer.

YOUR RUN-OF-THE-MILL LASER PRINTER

The regular laser printer will drain your checkbook of $800 to $1,200 and give you thousands of pages of clear, readable text — in different fonts, sizes, and styles — and good-quality graphics.

Most laser printers print somewhere around eight pages per minute, unless they are printing some heavy-duty graphics, in which case you may be waiting several minutes on a single image.

POSTSCRIPT LASER PRINTERS

A PostScript laser printer is different in that it uses a *page description language,* or a set of print instructions, to explain the way text and graphics are to be printed on the page. The PostScript laser printer offers you a high degree of control over your output. Characters and graphics are communicated to the printer not as a pattern of dots, like the dot-matrix and inkjet printers, but as mathematical equations. This means that when you stretch an image, the dots that make up the original size of that image aren't stretched as they would be on a regular printer; the image itself is recalculated to accommodate the stretch. There's no loss of clarity and no distortion. Such is the benefit of the PostScript printer over the regular laser printer.

The regular, non-PostScript laser printer uses a different page-description language known as PCL to communicate the text and graphics to the printer. PCL printers can give you high quality but not the flexibility of PostScript.

For this added benefit, you'll write a bigger check. Most PostScript printers cost upwards of $2,500. And color PostScript hit the highest mark with price tags in the $10,000 range.

SIDE TRIP

LIFE WITH LASERS

* The laser uses a toner cartridge to get the print on the page. A toner cartridge usually lasts for several thousand pages, which may translate to a year or more for you, depending on how often you use it. You can tell when the toner is running out because the pages are not uniformly dark; some lines of text look lighter than others. When you see that lightening effect, it's time to get a new toner.

* You place laser paper in the tray and slide the tray into the laser printer; the printer does the rest. But sometimes paper can jam inside the machine and you'll have to open it and see what's what. Ordinarily it's cheap paper or paper inserted crooked that causes a jam. Get the good stuff and put the paper in the tray carefully to avoid scrunched pages.

(continued)

SIDE TRIP

LIFE WITH LASERS (continued)

* Every 10,000 miles or so, open the hood and blow the dust bunnies out. Or, if you have dust allergies, take your printer to your local computer tech once a year for a ten-minute checkup.

* Avoid dropping, shaking, or throwing your laser printer. This makes them very unhappy. (One coworker, who had been trying to print to a network printer for over an hour, stomped down the hall, picked up the poor HP laser printer, and threw it on the floor. It didn't make the thing print any faster and didn't help the rest of us much, either. Lucky he was the boss.)

Thermal Printers

Thermal transfer printers create characters and graphics by melting a wax-based ink off a ribbon and pressing it onto the page. These characters are still dot-based; they are simply placed very close together to give the illusion of a solid character. The thermal printer provides good resolution, quiet printing, and cool effects — like blending, shadowing, and blocking — for color printing.

Thermal printers also come in very small sizes; you can easily get a little thermal printer for your notebook computer. It fits right inside the notebook satchel, and you just plug it in and print.

Multifunction Centers

Well, okay, it's not a very exciting name, but *multifunction centers* may be the printers of tomorrow. Beloved by small business owners worldwide, the multifunction center may be the hottest new peripheral around.

What is it? It's a device that does it all: prints like a laser printer, makes copies, scans documents, functions as a fax, and serves as a messaging center. This rather bulky machine resembles something akin to a laser printer with a fax machine growing out of the side (see Figure 9-6).

Multifunction centers are especially popular for small businesses and home offices because they wrap a number of functions into one device, thereby reducing the number of cables you've got strung all over the place and taking up less accumulated space. These centers can also be cost-effective, weighing in at $269 to $999, depending on the number of features, amount of memory, and so on.

Figure 9-6 Multifunction centers require less desk space and wrap a lot of functionality into one relatively inexpensive piece of equipment.

The printer part of the multifunction center varies depending on the quality of the system you buy. Low-end centers offer 200 × 400 dpi, while higher-end printers offer 600 × 600 dpi, which is laser-quality output. The speed is another aspect you'll pay for, although the higher-quality multifunction centers can produce printouts at a rate of six pages per minute.

Things to Worry about When You Use a Printer

Having a printer isn't a difficult thing. Learn a few basics and you're set.

Paper

The type of paper you use in your printer depends to some degree on the type of paper you have. A dot-matrix printer can use continuous-feed paper, which means the sheets are connected and there are holes for the tractor feed mechanism to guide the paper through the printer. You can use regular laser printer paper in a dot-matrix printer; however, you need to have a paper tray to keep the pages straight and to feed the paper in at the right time.

If you use an inkjet printer or a laser printer, you can use regular 8 1/2-by-11-inch paper. The quality of paper will be important, however. Paper is available in a variety of weights; the heavier the paper, the better it will hold the ink or toner, and the nicer your printout will look. As usual, though, the heavier the paper, the more you'll pay for it. For day-to-day use, a medium-weight paper is fine — not so lightweight that it gets jammed in your printer, but not so heavy that it puts you out of business.

TIP You can get specialty paper that has borders, backgrounds, or special designs. Specialty paper costs more than traditional white paper, but it can really spruce up a report or brochure.

Ribbons, Cartridges, and Toner

Another cost you'll find yourself repeating is the outlay for things like ribbons, cartridges, and toner. These items are the parts that supply the ink to the page. So you can be guaranteed you'll need them as long as you need your printer.

The cost for each of the items is dramatically different. Dot-matrix ribbons are inexpensive; print cartridges for inkjets are more expensive (black is less than color); and toner cartridges weigh in at the top at $80 to $120.

Switching from One Printer to Another

If you're one of those people who use different printers for different tasks, how do you switch back and forth between them?

Some people simply change the cable hooked up to the port on the back of the system unit. (That's what I do.) When I want to use the inkjet, I leave the regular cable connected. When I need to use the laser printer, I disconnect the inkjet's cable and connect the laser printer.

For about $12.95, you can come up with a better way if you get tired of unscrewing thumbtabs on your printers' cables. A *switch box* enables you to plug both printers' cables into the box; then the box plugs into the printer port on the back of your system unit. You can then choose the printer you want by simply flipping the switch to the one you want to use.

BONUS

Do-It-Yourself Business Cards

One of the expensive parts about being in business for yourself is the initial investment in business cards, stationery, envelopes, and so forth. Easy-to-use publishing programs (like Microsoft Publisher) allow you to create and print your own business cards, letterhead, or whatever, on any type of printer you have.

You can purchase predesigned and precut business cards at your office supply store, which means you can print out a few business cards for that meeting while investing only a few dollars and a few minutes of your time. Likewise, you can get enveloped, three-fold pages for brochures and all kinds of other items to help you do it yourself as you start up your new business or continue your existing one.

Summary

Printing may or may not be a regular part of your computing routine. Nevertheless, you can be sure that someday you'll be glad you've got a printer. Whether it's dot-matrix, inkjet, thermal, or laser, having the ability to print the items you create is an option you can't do without. As one friend put it, "Walking across the street to use your neighbor's printer one time is okay. Twice is annoying. The third time it's time to write the check."

Some Web Sites to Hit

Panasonic (printers):

http://www.panasonic.com

***PC World* article on "Top 10 Personal Printers" (February, 1997):**

http://www.pcworld.com/hardware/printers/articles
/feb97/1502p213.html

NEC Computer:

http://www.nec.com

CHAPTER TEN
MODEMS, MODEMS

IN THIS CHAPTER YOU LEARN THESE KEY SKILLS

DISCOVER WHAT A MODEM IS   PAGE 123

FIND OUT HOW PEOPLE ARE USING
    MODEMS   PAGE 125

LEARN ABOUT THE MODEM TYPES   PAGE 128

GET THAT MODEM CONNECTED   PAGE 131

Many computers sold today are sold without modems. I can't figure out why. Who, when given a choice, wouldn't be interested in trying out the Information Superhighway? Who, when faced with the options of saving $100 bucks or splurging and getting a PC already wired for telecommunications, wouldn't take the dive?

I wasn't always such an easy sale. For years I had a modem I never used. And then I discovered CompuServe. And then America Online, The Microsoft Network, and the Internet.

Okay, so I'm hooked.

A modem gives you a terrific advantage if you're into instant communication. Whether you're sending an e-mail to Cousin Charles in England, faxing materials to a client in Japan, or chatting with a coworker in a cyberspace conference room, the modem — and the software that controls it — makes it all possible.

What's a Modem?

A modem is an electronic device that allows you to use the phone lines to send and receive data to and from other computers. You can connect to a computer in another office, another city, or another country. You can link

123

up with a single person at a single computer tucked away in the corner of the den, or you can access a huge computer that runs hundreds of programs and services the needs of thousands of computer users every day.

The word *modem* is short for modulator/demodulator, which is what the modem does to make the data sendable through the phone lines. First it changes the data into audio signals (that's *modulation*). Then the data signals are sent through the phone lines to the other computer, where the data is turned back into electronic data (*demodulation*). Both computers communicating must have modems, of course, in order for the communication to happen.

Think of modulation and demodulation as computer chitchat: modems give computers a mouth to speak with and a language to speak in.

> **SIDE TRIP**
>
> ## A Modem Glossary
>
> **Baud rate.** The speed at which data can be sent and received with your modem.
>
> **Chat room.** A meeting place where computer users gather to "talk" to each other in a live discussion by exchanging written messages.
>
> **Cyberspace.** The buzz word meaning "Information Superhighway" or Internet, cyberspace is that imaginary nowheresville in which seamless communication is a not-so-far-off possibility.
>
> **Download.** The term used to describe the process of copying a file from a remote computer to your own via a modem. The computer you're copying files from might be a PC in another room or a mainframe computer in another part of the world.
>
> **E-mail.** Electronic mail.
>
> **Information service.** A super-large computer (or collection of computers) that provides a number of services for a subscription fee. CompuServe, America Online, Prodigy, and The Microsoft Network are examples of popular information services.
>
> **Modem.** The computer device that makes communications between computers possible.
>
> **Newsgroup.** A discussion group that trades messages, articles, and whatnot about a specific topic.
>
> **Upload.** The process of copying a file from your computer to a remote computer via a modem. Often "uploads," or files that have been uploaded, are stored in a library of files so that other computer users can download the files as needed.
>
> **Virtual conferencing.** Meeting in a cyberspace chat room with clients, friends, relatives, or whomever. Nowadays you can even bring your video camera and see whom you're talking to (and let others know whom *they* are talking to).

What Can You Do with a Modem?

Oh, lots of things. Talk to people who aren't there next to you. Play with games you haven't got on your computer. Search for esoteric files miles away. Send proposals to clients. Sell your product. Fall in love and argue with others.

Just the fun side of using a modem could take up an entire book (and already has). In addition to the chat potential, you can use your modem to do the following things:

* **Send files back and forth.** You can send a report to a prospective client in Benton Harbor from your work-at-home office in Louisville.

* **Leave messages in an electronic mailbox.** Join the e-mail revolution. Don't return the call — e-mail 'em. What do you gain? Instant documentation, quick responses, and easy answers. Meet your deadlines right on time by turning in that bid, completing that paper, or submitting that proposal electronically.

A Modem and Then What?

The modem is the hardware that allows the computer to talk over the phone, but you also need software to make everything work properly. When you purchase a modem, it comes with a program that enables you to get online. Which program it is depends on which modem brand you buy. But when you purchase that system and if it has a modem installed, rest assured you've got a program on there that will help you get online. You may need more software, depending on what you want to do with your modem. But you'll have enough to get you started. Unfortunately, bare-bones documentation for most modems is primitive at best, often written in the same strange English we've grown accustomed to in household appliance manuals.

NOTE For more information on different types of communications software and what you'll do with them, see the section "The Software Difference" later in this chapter.

Essential E-mail

Perhaps the biggest craze — or the first wave of the craze that's bound to get you — is e-mail. E-mail is the electronic equivalent of the paper letter. Except that you can send it right now. And get an answer in ten minutes. So much for the postal system.

And you know that family reunion you are planning? Instead of calling your dad in Michigan, your Aunt Flo in Austin, and your brother in Oregon, you can send them each an e-mail message free, except for the charges you pay your service provider (see Figure 10-1). So much for the long-distance phone company — provided your family is all hooked up to e-mail.

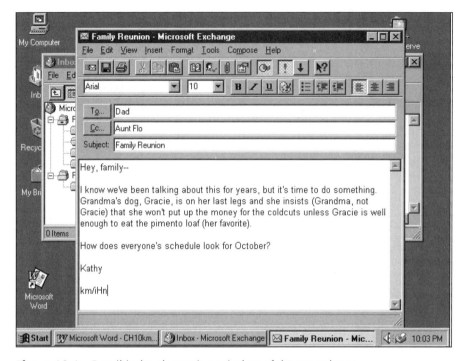

Figure 10-1 E-mail is the electronic equivalent of the paper letter.

New Worlds to Explore — Through the Phone Line?

Another addicting aspect of modem use is the information service, which is also called the online communications service. An information service like CompuServe offers literally hundreds of discussion groups (known as *forums*) with e-mail, files, libraries of articles and other documents, and live discussions related to the topic you're interested in. Whether you want to find out about business, travel, computers, home, and family, or you want to go shopping online, you can find items of interest. Figure 10-2 shows the opening screen of WinCIM, one of the programs you can use to connect with CompuServe.

Another information service that has gained popularity recently is The Microsoft Network, or MSN. Packaged with Windows 95, MSN is available to all Windows 95 users. You have all the basic categories of interest represented, and many more besides. Although there are still substantially more people out there in the world using CompuServe than MSN, the new service is doing remarkably well for an information service technically still in its infancy. Figure 10-3 shows the opening screen of MSN. (It'll look different when you see it, since the screen is changed daily.)

Figure 10-2 WinCIM shows you the different categories you can explore. There are dozens of forums in each category group.

Internet Mania

Ah, but is this the Internet? It could be. All information services now have Internet access, so you can search for files and programs using the Internet and get started on the World Wide Web.

The Internet is a truly amazing, potentially unlimited resource for any kind of interest or avocation you may have. Do you have only four hours to research a term paper? If you've got Internet access, you can do it. Through your phone line, you can access reference works in the best universities in the world. Want to find the best price for your flight to Europe? Buy a car? Find out about the latest federal legislation? Download cool games from all over the world?

Exploring the Internet doesn't have to be an isolating experience. You can join newsgroups, which keep you in touch with people via online exchanges about topics you're interested in. You can get involved in global chat sessions, trade e-mail, and play games online.

Figure 10-3 You can register all your Windows 95 programs online and access technical support forums on MSN, a relatively new information service.

The World Wide Web provides a unique way to get around on the Internet; you can click highlighted text and icons (called *links*) to move from one page of information to another. You'll notice all sorts of people and companies making their presence known on the Web — and you can stop by their *Web page* on your journey through links in cyberspace. A Web page is a page of graphics and text and tells the visitor something about the person or company. The IDG Books home page, for example, includes information about the newest ... For Dummies books. (see Figure 10-4).

Even though you can get to the Internet through a commercial service like CompuServe, you may instead prefer to set up your own Internet account with an Internet service provider (ISP). This may help you bypass long-distance charges and give you a number of Internet tools above and beyond those offered by information services.

Checking out Modem Types

So the first thing to do if you're sold on a modem is to get one. You may have already invested in one as part of your new PC. If not, you've got a purchase to make.

First you need to know a little about what's out there.

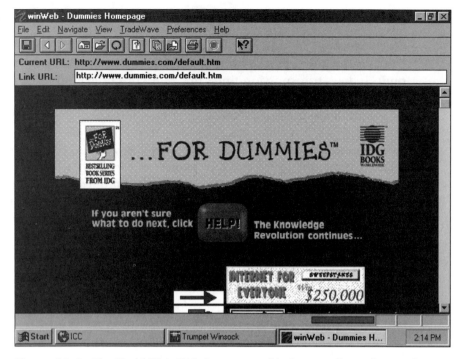

Figure 10-4 The World Wide Web features graphical "pages" from all sorts of people, organizations, companies, and the like.

External and Internal

Two kinds of modems are available: external and internal. An *external* modem sits outside the system unit of your computer and is connected to the PC via a cable and to the wall phone jack with a standard telephone line. The external modem looks like a small rectangular box with red lights (or one red and one green) on the front.

The *internal* modem fits inside the system unit of your computer and plugs into the motherboard. You won't see the modem — no lights or anything — but on the back of the system unit you will see the phone jack as part of the modem port. The phone jack is part of the modem and extends from the back of the system unit in an internal modem or from the back of the device on an external modem. Rather than plugging the phone line into the wall, you plug the phone line directly into your computer.

> **NOTE** If you are working on a notebook computer that comes with PCMCIA slots, you can easily upgrade your modem by buying a faster modem that comes on a PCMCIA card. (A PCMCIA slot is a special port in notebook computers that enables you to plug in peripherals not built into the system.)

How Important Is Speed?

Modems come in different speeds. The first modems pumped information through the phone lines at a molasses-like speed of 300 bps (that's bits per second). Today's transmission times are 28.8 Kbps or even higher, at 33.6 Kbps. As a general rule, get the fastest modem you can afford.

What difference does it make? Not much, if all you're sending are simple e-mail messages. But when you start to do things like trade files or browse through Web pages on the World Wide Web, the wait will make you crazy. In order for your computer to display the Web page you're visiting, the information from the site about how to create the page must be communicated to your computer. This information travels through the phone line to your modem and your PC's microprocessor. How fast does the information travel? As quickly — or as slowly — as your modem allows. A slow modem will leave you waiting while your computer struggles to draw the Web page on your monitor. A fast modem — together with plenty of RAM, which you'll need to get full advantage of the Web — will have you surfing the Net with less wait and fewer worries.

Here's another reason to get a fast modem. There will be times when you want to copy a program from an information service or the Internet to your computer (called downloading). Some programs can take 45 minutes or longer to download on a fairly swift modem. Can you imagine what that wait would be like with a slow modem?

TIP Read the fax/modem ads carefully. Some modems transmit regular modem transmission — e-mail and files — at the full advertised speed, but send and receive faxes at a slower rate, sometimes at half the rate.

The Software Difference

The type of software you use with your modem depends on what came with the modem and what your personal preferences are. There are many different kinds of software programs available. For example, mail programs enable you to send and receive e-mail (and sometimes faxes). Microsoft Exchange, Microsoft Mail, Eudora Light, and CIS:Mail are a few examples of mail programs.

Web browsers are programs that help you navigate the World Wide Web and perform other tasks, as well. Mosiac was one of the first popular Web browsers, overtaken by Netscape Navigator. Microsoft is making a big splash with its Internet Explorer. Your ISP can give you a browser. Online services (such as America Online) come packaged with their own browser.

Connecting a Modem

The trickiest part of setting up your modem is plugging in the phone line. Pretty difficult, eh? On the software side, however, you may have a bit of a challenge as you figure out which port your modem is using and instruct the software to work with that port so you've got data coming and going at the right point.

If you use Windows 95, you're in luck: The plug-and-play component of Windows 95 will automatically sense the type of modem you're using and the port it's occupying. That data will then be communicated to the software automatically.

If you are using a version of Windows pre-95, check in the Modems group of the Control Panel to see whether your modem is recognized by the program. If you are using a DOS program, consult the modem manual for instructions on installing the communications software and getting ready to go online.

The best advice on modem installation? Let someone who knows do it. If you're not comfortable popping the lid off the system unit, don't expect to install an internal modem. Take it down to your local computer store and let Bob do it for you. Setting up the modem involves knowing things like the COM port, the IRQ, and things like protocol and parity settings.

When you — or the person you've hired — have the modem and the software ready to roll, simply plug that phone line into the back of your system unit (or external modem) and then into the wall. Then . . . ready, set, dial!

NOTE If you have call-waiting on your phone, disable that feature (press *70) so calls coming in won't lock up your computer while you're online. If you prefer, you can add it to the number your modem dials out. Simply add *70 before the phone number in your communication software and save the settings — for instance, *70,123-4567 (the comma means a pause before dialing the actual number).

BONUS

Modem Extras

This is the age of bundling, after all. We don't just want a modem, we want a fax/modem. And we don't just want a fax/modem that sends e-mail and receives faxes; they tell us we want one with Caller ID, a headset for hands-free listening, PBX adapters, and security features.

Today, modems come with all kinds of bells and whistles. The Supra Sonic 288, for example, offers this package for $279:

- 28.8 Kbps
- Voice-mail, fax, Internet, and file transfer capability
- Remote access for fax and voice messages
- Hands-free headset
- Caller ID
- Cables included

If that's too rich for your blood, the Boca On-Line Express is a 28.8 Kbps fax/modem, Windows 95 ready, with setup fax and communications software, and free trials for major online services and the Internet — all for $109.

The moral? Check around. The modem you want is out there — with all the add-on gadgets you could ever want — at a price you'll find impossible to resist.

Summary

Modems are as standard as printers. Today, we're missing out if we can't get online to find the latest in news, stocks, weather, gossip, and more. We're missing an opportunity if we can't research on the Web or e-mail at will. A modem is a small-cost item that has big potential for your future PC happiness. When in doubt, buy. (I'd never make it on the stock market!)

The next chapter is a grab bag of additional items you may never have thought about (graphics tablets, scanners, digital cameras, and more!) but may decide you've got to have before you're finished.

Some Web Sites to Hit

U.S. Robotics (33.6 modem information):

http://www.usr.com

Cardinal Communications:

http://www.cardtech.com

PC World article on "Top 10 Modems (March, 1997):

http://www.pcworld.com/hardware/communications/articles/mar97
 /1503p239.html

CHAPTER ELEVEN

ADD-ONS YOU CAN OWN AND LOVE

IN THIS CHAPTER YOU LEARN THESE KEY SKILLS

LEARN WHAT A SCANNER DOES   PAGE 134

INVESTIGATE DIGITAL CAMERAS   PAGE 136

TAKE A LOOK AT A QUICKCAM   PAGE 137

CONSIDER GRAPHICS TABLETS   PAGE 137

STOP AND HEAR THE MIDI MUSIC   PAGE 138

At first you may be happy with your basic PC system. Nothing fancy, just the system unit, monitor, keyboard, mouse, and printer. Learning to handle all these items is enough of a challenge, after all.

But once you get the hang of using your computer for whatever purpose you bought it, you will raise your head and look around. What other things are out there? How else could you use your computer? What haven't you thought of? What new gadget is the computer press hyping?

This chapter explores some additional uses—and devices—you may be interested in, which take you above and beyond basic computing tasks. Indeed, these devices in many ways allow you to plug your traditional outlets of creativity—music, photography, and drawing—into the computer, so that you can use it as a tool for further expression.

Who says the computer should only do office work?

Scanners: Not Just Sci-fi Stuff

This may sound obvious, but computers cannot read. Reading a printed page is easy for you, but if you want to take that text or image and work with it on your computer, you have to somehow get it *into* your computer. That's where scanners come in. The basic function of the scanner is to convert something that's already printed into an electronic file you can work with on your PC. If you've ever heard the word "digitize," that's what it means.

Scanners are available in different sizes and price ranges. A hand-held scanner is a small device you (surprise, surprise) hold in your hand (see Figure 11-1). They cost around $100. You move the scanner down the page (the 4-inch width of the scanner enables you to scan one-half the page with each pass) and the image or text is sent through the scanner cable to the scanning program.

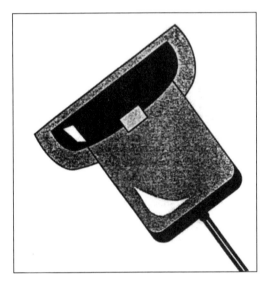

Figure 11-1 A hand-held scanner is fine for scanning small images.

A hand-held scanner is fine for scanning logos, special designs, and other small items. If you are attempting to scan an entire page, however, you'll have a challenge trying to get the two sides of the page to match up. For full-page scanning, a flat-bed or desktop scanner is a better bet.

A flat-bed scanner is like a photocopier in its approach to scanning. You simply open up the top of the scanner and lay the page inside (see Figure 11-2). The quality of the scan is very high. No fuzzy edges. But they're pricey: $500 and up.

The scanning software scans the page and converts the document or graphic into various file formats in high resolution. Some color flat-bed scanners are capable of scanning over 16 million colors.

Figure 11-2 A flat-bed scanner gives you the best resolution, several scanning options, and terrific color capability.

> **TIP** Dots-per-inch, or *dpi*, is an important number for scanners. Low-end resolution is 200 or 400 dpi. 1200 dpi is better, and 2400 dpi is tops.

Another type of scanner—the desktop scanner—falls into the mid-range in terms of its capabilities and resolution quality. Desktop scanners, like the HP ScanJet, take up only a small amount of room on your desk and feed the pages through. (It works like a fax machine.) The resolution on a ScanJet is less than the resolution on a flat-bed scanner, but the ScanJet gives you the option of saving the file in several formats. And the price offsets the loss of resolution, which may be a worthwhile trade-off if the scanning you need doesn't demand high quality. Desktop scanners start at $300.

SIDE TRIP

A FEW POPULAR SCANNERS

- Artec ViewScan (hand-held scanner)
- Epson ES-1000C (flat-bed scanner)
- Hewlett-Packard ScanJet 4p (flat-bed scanner)
- Hewlett-Packard ScanJet 4s (desktop scanner)
- Microtek ScanMaker E3 (desktop scanner)
- Xres PageScan Color (desktop scanner)

Scanners convert text and images into a digitized image, simply dots on a page. This is fine if you're scanning photos, artwork, or logos that you want to use as-is in your documents. But what if you've got a 25-page document and simply want a fast way to turn all that text into an electronic file? If you've got the right kind of software, you can use your scanner as an input device for scanning documents, memos, newsletters, and more to your heart's content.

The software you need is called OCR, or optical character recognition software. As the document is scanned, the OCR software "reads" the characters, turning them into real text you can edit, format, and enhance with fonts, colors, and more—just as though you'd typed it all in by hand. Popular OCR programs include OmniPage LE OCR, WordLinx OCR, and Xerox TextBridge OCR.

Here's Looking at You, Kid: Digital Cameras

A fairly recent addition to the peripheral game is the digital camera. So much for that 35mm film. Now you can point and shoot pictures—up to 96 of them—and store them in your camera until you're ready to send them to your PC. Because the photo is an electronic file, you can play with it in any way you like, changing colors, moving images, and creating special effects, backgrounds, or whatever.

The digital camera resembles a traditional camera, but the internal workings of the device are different. The digital camera captures the image you're pointing at and saves it in an electronic file. Different cameras offer different resolutions, and all fall in the $500 to $1,000 range.

Most digital cameras offer over 16 million colors and connect directly to the serial port of your PC. Some place the viewfinder at the back of the camera as a screen, just as on some camcorders.

Why get a digital camera when you could just scan a photograph? For one thing, a digital camera enables you to replace two peripherals with one. If you don't have a digital camera, you snap a few shots with your traditional camera and then send out your film to be developed. A few hours (or days) later, you pick up the pictures and take them home. You choose the shot you want to scan, run it through your scanner, and save it as a file in your computer.

By comparison, with a digital camera, you take the photos, take the camera home, plug it into your PC, and save the photos you want directly as files on your hard disk.

> **SIDE TRIP**
>
> ### POPULAR DIGITAL CAMERAS
>
> - Casio's QV-30, with two lenses and viewfinder
> - Epson PhotoPCColor Digital Camera
> - Kodak's Digital Science DC40, with add-on lenses and room for 48 photos

Smile, You're on QuickCam

People are finding that the ability to send and receive video is making the impersonal world of PCs more personable. Useful for video conferences with clients, chat rooms with coworkers, or online conversations with relatives, video cameras are putting a face on an online voice.

One of the most popular and inexpensive video cameras available right now is the QuickCam, a little ball-like camera that perches inconspicuously on your PC. The QuickCam is available in both black and white and color. The grayscale model carries an approximate $85 price tag; the color model is around $200.

Another popular video camera looks more like a microphone than a camera. It's a tall, goosenecked device you can angle any way you need—even in normal room lighting—to get a good picture. CCD-PCI makes one such video camera that retails for about $450.

Connectix VideoPhone is a QuickCam software combination package that enables you to see whom you're talking to on the World Wide Web, assuming, of course, the other user also has a QuickCam video camera. (CU-SeeMe is another such product.) You can project and receive live video to go along with your PC communications. And the cost isn't too lofty: around $150 for the whole shebang. Now you just have to decide whether you want the world to see you in your Bart Simpson T-shirt and Tigers baseball cap.

P.C. Escher: Graphics Tablets

Are you a doodler? Do you like to sketch out your ideas before you try to create them on the screen? Do you need to modify photos you've saved on disk? If you like to do your own artwork or design your own logos, you'll like using a graphics tablet. A graphics tablet gives you an open space for drawing and a pen (also called a *stylus*) to draw with (see Figure 11-3).

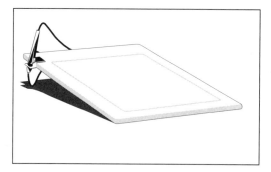

Figure 11-3 You can create, edit, or enhance graphics easily with a graphics tablet.

You simply draw on the pressure-sensitive surface of the tablet, and your marks are recorded on the screen. The graphics tablet plugs into the mouse port on the back of your system unit. Most graphics tablets costs just a few hundred dollars; small tablets come with a smaller price tag, and larger tablets have correspondingly larger price tags.

Even neater, some software packages like Fractal Design Painter recognize the pressure sensitivity of the pen so that you can create realistic-looking brush strokes and special shading effects.

SIDE TRIP

POPULAR GRAPHICS TABLETS

- ArtPad II, 4" x 5"
- ArtPad II, 6" x 8"
- DrawingSlate II, 4" x 5"
- DrawingSlate II, 6" x 9"

Do Re MIDI

If your gift is music, you can turn your PC into a sound studio, capturing and arranging music and playing it back in various voices, instruments, or styles. You'll need two things for certain: a MIDI-equipped sound board (check your PC manual or sound board information) and a MIDI instrument.

What's a MIDI? It stands for *Musical Instrument Digital Interface* and it turns the musical output into computer input. When you play a MIDI instrument plugged into your PC, your computer becomes an extension of that instrument and can capture the music as an electronic file ready for editing or playback. A MIDI instrument has a special output jack that sends the digitized music to your PC.

What kind of instrument? Today, many different instruments are available with MIDI capability. Keyboards are the most popular, but other instruments are available as well: guitars, drum sets, even violins. Synthesizers combine the sounds of hundreds of instruments, percussion pieces, or choir voices. Samplers store real recorded samples of hundreds of different sounds, including sound effects of all sorts.

What do you need in order to make music with your PC? A sound board with MIDI capability, a MIDI instrument, and software capable of recording, editing, and manipulating sound. Windows 3.1 and Windows 95 have built-in sound capabilities in Media Player and Sound Recorder so you can experiment with your MIDI equipment before you invest in a full-blown music editor.

TIP One MIDI keyboard that sells for a low price of $139 comes with 49 keys, a SoundBlaster MIDI-compatible interface, a sustain pedal, and composition software. Other keyboard manufacturers, like Yamaha, Ensonic, and Roland, all make top-quality MIDI keyboards that work with various music programs.

BONUS

Joysticks and Game Gear

Gaming is big business, and add-ons that make games more exciting, more fun, or more interactive are extremely popular. A number of different styles, sizes, and control levels await you as you begin to explore the world of games and action-oriented and flight-simulation programs.

Those of us who don't have as much time on our hands as we'd like to play games still use the mouse—or even the keyboard arrow keys—to play Pinball, 3D Arcade, or Myst. But when you begin exploring programs like Microsoft Flight Simulator, your friend the rodent simply won't do—you're ready for a joystick.

A joystick is a device that follows the pilot's approach to gaming. The control stick lets you control the direction, altitude, and balance of your aircraft; buttons on the joystick enable you to shoot attacking aliens. The joystick plugs into your PC through the mouse port.

A game pad is a device similar to the ones you'll find hooked up to the Super Nintendo game in your family room. Directional buttons on the left enable you to move Mario and Luigi (or the characters in Dr. Brain) through various worlds;

buttons on the right give you the lift you need for jumping over mushrooms, picking up puzzle pieces, and more. The game pad plugs into the mouse port. Prices range from about $20 to $50.

SIDE TRIP

POPULAR JOYSTICK AND GAME PADS

- Fighter Series Control Stick (joystick)
- Thunderstick OTC (joystick)
- Wingman Extreme (joystick)
- Gravis PC GamePad (game pad)
- PC ProPad (game pad)

Summary

As you can see, there are any number of add-ons that broaden your PC horizons. As you begin to explore more ways you can use your PC, you'll find more and more peripherals available to help you go electronic with your hobbies, your interests, and your talents.

Some Web Sites to Hit

WEB PATH

Yamaha (digital keyboards):
http://www.yamaha.com

Microtek (scanner information):
http://www.mteklab.com/

Connectix QuickCam:
http://www.connectix.com/

PART THREE

ON THE ROAD TO PC PRODUCTIVITY

THIS PART CONTAINS THE FOLLOWING CHAPTERS

CHAPTER **12** SETTING UP YOUR SPACE

CHAPTER **13** STARTING OUT WITH THE OPERATING SYSTEM

CHAPTER **14** PROGRAMS! PROGRAMS! READ ALL ABOUT 'EM

CHAPTER **15** TRAVELING WITH YOUR COMPUTER

CHAPTER **16** GETTING ON THE INTERNET

Now that you've found out what your PC can do (that was Part One) and learned how the PC does it (that was Part Two), you're ready to discover what you can do with your PC. This part introduces you to the operating system of your computer, the programs you will use, and more. Don't think that you're stuck at your desk just because you use a computer. If you've got a laptop computer, you can travel across town or across the world and not lose a day's work. When you're traveling, your PC becomes a link with the office; whether you're at home or abroad, you can easily send e-mail to clients in Ecuador or surf your way across continents on the World Wide Web.

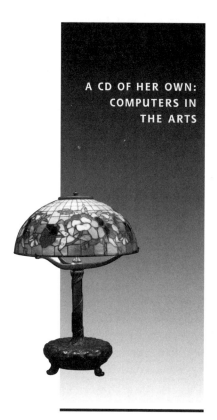

A CD OF HER OWN: COMPUTERS IN THE ARTS

Julianne Williams is a musician who was tired of relying on producers at the sound studios to get things done. With a PC, a music program, a MIDI keyboard, and a four-track recording system, Julianne can create her own demo tapes in a recording room in her home.

"I decided to learn how to do this after a sound studio lost an entire side of a tape I'd recorded," she said. She looked into what she needed to add to her 486 computer: more RAM, a better sound board, and a music composition and sequencing program called CakeWalk Home Studio. With the help of a MIDI cable, she hooks the keyboard directly to a port on the back of her PC; then she prepares the program to record the music and starts playing. CakeWalk records the music she plays and even writes it in score-arrangement style.

Once the music is captured in the computer, Julianne can play back the music through the MIDI keyboard. The music travels through the keyboard to the four-track recorder, which records in high-quality sound. She then does a voice-over to the musical track, and, voilà — a music demo tape.

The hardest thing for Julianne was finding out what options were out there as she was trying to put the system together. And then things didn't work right at first — the MIDI cable output on the first cable she got didn't work correctly, and the settings in CakeWalk were difficult to figure out. But once the system worked, Julianne was able cut out the middleman and use her PC for unusual and creative work, right in her own home studio.

CHAPTER TWELVE

SETTING UP YOUR SPACE

IN THIS CHAPTER YOU LEARN THESE KEY SKILLS

CHOOSE YOUR SPACE   PAGE 144

PLAN YOUR WORK AREA   PAGE 144

RATE THE USABILITY OF YOUR WORKSPACE   PAGE 149

Whether you organize your workspace in a corner of the living room, on the bar, in your office, or on the veranda overlooking the Pacific Ocean (wouldn't that be nice?), the way in which you set up your system has a lot to do with whether you use it on a regular basis and how comfortable you are while you're using it. This chapter helps you set up the system so you—and it—are safe from traffic, dust, and other environmental hazards.

NOTE For the most part, we're talking desktop systems in this chapter. After all, you don't need to assemble a notebook computer—you just take it out of the box and use it. You might use what's known as a *docking station* with your notebook (that's a component similar to a system unit in which you "dock" the notebook as though it were a full-sized system), in which case the basic information about positioning your PC still applies. For most on-the-road notebook computers, however, you don't need to choose a work area and worry about lighting, office traffic, etc., because you'll be taking it with you and using it in airplanes, bus terminals, rest areas, and so on.

Choose Your Space

One of the biggest steps in setting up a good workspace involves choosing the right area. By the window or in the corner? Behind cubicle walls, where the temptation to daydream is minimized, or right out in the open, where everyone passing by will stop to chat? Do you need to be stuck back in the corner of the basement where you won't be interrupted, or do you need to be in the family room so you can keep an eye on your kids while you work?

Making that initial decision—Do I want my office in here or in there? Upstairs or down? In sight or out of view?—is an important one. Everything else just helps you turn your selected workspace into a comfortable and productive one.

When you are choosing the room for the computer, make sure the room has plenty of office resources—a phone line that can be reached easily, direct or indirect lighting (whichever you prefer), and plenty of electrical outlets. And don't forget the basics like room for a desk, a filing cabinet or two, a chair, and maybe a bookshelf of some sort.

Plan Your Work Area

Once you've decided where your office is going to be, you've got to decide what you're going to do with it. How will you place the system? On which side of the desk? Facing what and turned away from what? If it has a modem, you need easy access to the phone line. And if your computer is at all typical, it ought to be near an outlet, preferably with an Uninterruptible Power Supply between it and the wall.

Even if you're working with a limited space, you need to plan out the best place for your computer. And then, once you choose the general arrangement, you need to place the components so they are easy to reach and comfortable for you to use.

SIDE TRIP

OFFICE POSSIBILITIES

The possibilities for creating your own office are limited only by your imagination. Here's where you can get really creative. Try these locations for your office: in the basement, in the attic, in an extra bedroom, in a portion of the family room, on the kitchen table, in rented office space, in a shared cubicle, or in a heated pole barn (that's not just something we do in the Midwest, is it?).

TIP Initially, short computer cables may control the design of your office more than anything else. But don't let that stop you if you've got something different in mind—longer cables are available from retail and mail-order computer companies.

In your chosen work area, ask yourself the following questions:

* **Where will I put the desk?** Make sure you are within reach of electrical outlets and a phone jack. And remember that lighting—what type and from where—is important, as is your vantage point if you are working with or for others you need to be able to see.

* **Is the desk big enough?** Make sure that your desk is big—and sturdy—enough to support your computer and other peripherals. Working on a wobbly desk won't make you feel very secure.

* **How will I position the other furnishings?** Think about your office chair. How much room does it take up? Will you be using a filing cabinet often? If so, will the chair have rollers so you can easily roll from the PC to the file cabinet?

* **How do I want the system placed on the desk?** Are you left-handed or right-handed? Your answer will determine where you should place the system unit and the mouse. If you are right-handed, you will want to leave room for the mouse pad and writing space to the right of the system unit. If you are left-handed, you need extra space on the left side of the PC.

SIDE TRIP

ODE TO THE CHAIR

One of the most underappreciated pieces of office equipment is the office chair. A good chair helps you stay more attentive and focused on your work. A good chair also helps your posture (comfortably), helps you relax, and makes it easy for you to look your monitor in the eye.

Different chair types appeal to different people. Fast typists often like chairs with small armrests or no armrests at all; others like things such as lumbar support, height adjustment capability, or back tilt control. Different chairs (often called *task chairs* in office supply catalogs) have different support and seat shapes; you'll find a variety of colors and styles, as well. Prices range from $30 to $250 and up. Best advice? Sit on it and think awhile. Imagine yourself spending hours in that seat. After you've tried out a dozen chairs or so, choose the one that fits you best.

Setup 101

Now that you've chosen your office and considered where you'll put what in your workspace, you are ready to set up the PC. PCs generally come to you in boxes—several boxes, in fact. The monitor in one, the system unit in another, the keyboard in another, and the mouse is perhaps enclosed in a see-through plastic package. You'll have other stacks of stuff: software, extra disks, computer manuals, and perhaps computer paper for the printer.

Make a List

Before you take anything out of the box, make a list of everything you've purchased. If you purchased everything from the same company, you may have an invoice that lists the individual items. If not, make sure you write everything down. Include important things like serial number, warranty, and manufacturer information. An example is shown in Table 12-1.

TABLE 12-1   Sample List of Items Purchased

Item	Serial #	Warranty	Tech Support #
Sager 486Pro	WM454-122 1	1 year on-site	(800) 433-4777
Colida CD-ROM	33345A	1 year	(213) 555-3222
Toshiba V28	VMKH4545	1 year parts	(800) 555-1212
Okidata 2412	919KV	1 year parts	(800) 323-9851

TIP Is anything missing? If so, contact your dealer (or mail-order company) immediately. Don't assume that a certain piece was backordered and will arrive eventually—take the initiative and find that missing piece. Don't do what I did and discover, six months after you begin using the PC, that it has eight fewer megabytes of RAM than you ordered!

Get the System Unit Right

Choosing the first spot is the biggest step. The first PC component you'll position is the system unit. Here are a few things to remember:

* Place the unit so that you can get disks in and out of the drives easily.
* Place the system unit so that the power switch is on the side you reach most easily.

- Make sure there's room for the CD-ROM drive drawer to open.
- Keep an eye on the computer's reset button. Is it in a place where you could bump it easily or little fingers could reach it at the wrong time?
- Where's the power outlet? Near enough to reach without stringing wires precariously across paths of heavy foot traffic?

TIP Most systems, with their system unit, monitor, and printer, have more power cords than a single electrical outlet can handle. A surge protector takes care of this problem. A surge protector is a specially designed strip of outlets that absorbs any surges or spikes in electrical power, protecting your plugged-in computer. Most surge protectors have at least seven outlets, giving you plenty of space to plug in your computer components as well as several other office necessities like the lights, answering machine, and copier.

Eyeing the Monitor

The primary portion of your PC experience will be spent gazing (or grimacing) into your monitor. When you are getting ready to set up the monitor as part of your system, you need to think about a few important considerations:

- Will the monitor catch the glare of the morning or afternoon sun?
- Does your desk lamp reflect on your computer monitor?
- Make sure the lighting is good for reading and manual work but not too bright for the PC.
- Is the monitor positioned so it will be at eye-level for you?
- Is the monitor in a place where air can circulate around it? Similar to the PC, the monitor can generate a little heat. Make sure that the ventilation grid (usually on the top or back of the monitor) isn't blocked by being pushed up against a shelf or wall.
- Is the monitor positioned securely so it won't be knocked off the system unit when your daughter and her soccer teammates come through after practice?
- If your desk or table is too short or too tall and you can't look directly into your monitor, don't get the hammer and saw—there are other options. You can buy items that will bring your monitor more in line with your eye. Monitor stands can raise up screens that are too low; swivel and angle stands can let you tilt the monitor so that it is easy to see. In addition, you can get anti-glare screens to fit over monitor faces that are not treated with an anti-glare surface. And, if all else fails, you can get an adjustable height chair to help you rise to the PC occasion.

Proper Printer Positioning

You may have a little more latitude about where you put your printer. Depending on the length of the cable, you might be able to put it on the other side of your desk or even on the other side of your office. If you print continually throughout the day and want to have the printer nearby so you don't have to get up to get the printout, put that on your list of setup considerations. Here are a few more things you can weigh out when you go to set up your printer:

- Watch that cable—don't stretch it or run it in such a way that others might trip over it.
- Make sure wherever you place the printer you can load it with paper easily.
- If the paper is continuous-feed paper for a dot-matrix printer, make sure the paper can move freely through the printer.
- If the printer is noisy, move it as far away as you can without making it a burden to get to.
- If the printer is not too noisy, can you reach the paper output tray easily or do you have to get up, walk around the desk, and lean over to get the letter you just printed?

Cables, Cables Everywhere

Once you've got the major parts positioned, you're ready to connect everything. Your PC will have an instruction manual that should diagram everything out for you very nicely, thank you very much. But in the event that such a thing is missing, simply take your time, look at each individual cable, and plug it in where it fits.

> **NOTE** Each cable matches the shape of a certain port. If you were good at shape sorting in kindergarten, you won't have any trouble hooking up the cables.

Some cables have little thumbscrews that you turn to tighten the cable into place. Others have little metal handles that snap the cable into place. Some need a little twist of the screwdriver to secure them in place. In any event, this is not a complicated task, and it has taken me a lot longer to explain it here than it will take you to do it. Although it may be a pain, tighten them so that they won't loosen accidentally and fall off.

Cable ties (the plastic things you can get at Radio Shack for a dollar or so per package) are useful for keeping control of your cables, especially when you want to route them unobtrusively around the room.

How Usable Is Your System?

Now that you've got everything together and positioned, take this little test. For each question, answer 1 (oops) to 5 (great!), depending on how usable your system is.

____ Walk into you workspace and sit down in front of the computer. How easy was it to get to your desk?

____ Reach around to the power switch. How easy was that?

____ Look into the monitor. Is it the right height? Are you the right height? How easy will it be to work with that monitor all day?

____ Place your hands on the keyboard and type something. Are your arms at a comfortable height? Are your wrists straight and relaxed? How easy will it be to type for long periods of time?

____ Reach over to the printer, first to the power switch and then to the paper output tray. Will you be able to get to the printer without getting up from your desk? How easy will your printer be to use as you work?

Scoring:

20–25: Highly usable.

15–19: Pretty comfortable, but revise a little.

10-14: There are some things you can do to make your workspace better.

0–9: You'd better reread this chapter!

BONUS

Let's Talk About Desks

If you are purchasing or have just purchased your first computer system, you are very aware of the expense. You may be tempted to scrimp on furniture. After all, a card table will hold a computer, right? Maybe even a TV tray, although they definitely come up short in the sturdiness department. How important is the desk you put all this expensive computer equipment on?

For the short term, you may be happy working with whatever you've got handy. But at some point in your computer life, if you haven't already done so, you're going to investigate the possibility of purchasing a desk. A real desk. With drawers and maybe a rolltop.

Before you go to the traditional furniture store and try to find something that fits your PC, take a look at your local office supply store. Thumb through a few catalogs. Lots of computer desk manufacturers have designed what they call *workstations* that will help you get everything set up properly.

A workstation is actually a multifaceted group of furniture. The desk is the centerpiece (or one part of the L shape) and often has a keyboard shelf that slides away out of sight so your keyboard is protected and hidden while you are working on other things. Workstations also may include bookshelves, built-in filing drawers, and all kinds of cool, scratch-resistant surfaces for your writing and research work. You can find them in mahogany or maple; pressboard or graphite.

The best thing about a workstation is that it's designed to do exactly what you need it to do—create a PC workspace that is comfortable, well-organized, and easy to use. Anything else is just a desk.

> **NOTE** Some people feel that the best computer desks are the simplest. One friend got two low (27") file cabinets and a full-height (8'6") solid door. Putting the door across the cabinets, he has a great desk that's sturdy enough to stand on and wide enough for two people to work at comfortably. And it only cost about $40 for the whole thing—used cabinets and used door.

Summary

You want to be comfortable using your computer. A PC that makes you miserable is not a good addition to your family. A monitor that gives you headaches or a chair that gives you leg cramps is not going to help you be more productive on the job. This chapter has encouraged you to take a look at the way you're planning on setting up your computer so you can get right off to a happy, healthy start.

The next chapter discusses your computer's operating system, the basic brains of your PC.

Some Web Sites to Hit

New England Computer Supply (ergonomic PC furniture):
http://emanate.com/necs/

Workstation Environments (ergonomic workstations):
http://www.workenv.com/

CHAPTER THIRTEEN

STARTING OUT WITH THE OPERATING SYSTEM

IN THIS CHAPTER YOU LEARN THESE KEY SKILLS

FLIP THE SWITCH!   PAGE 152

LEARN THE USE OF THE OPERATING SYSTEM   PAGE 154

MEET THE DIFFERENT OPERATING SYSTEMS   PAGE 156

INSTALL OR UPGRADE THE OPERATING SYSTEM   PAGE 161

FOLLOW SOME FRIENDLY OPERATING TIPS   PAGE 162

The term *operating system* sounds important. Boring, but important. In fact, the operating system of your computer is so important that you couldn't get anything done without it. You could still turn on the power to the PC, and you could still type at the keyboard, but your computer would just sit there and say "Huh?" while you were waiting for it to carry out your commands. The operating system is the software that enables the other programs on the PC to work. It provides the *shell,* or interface, that you use to interact with your computer.

Knowing what the operating system is and what it is not is *not* something you need to know to use your PC on a daily basis. It's like driving your car without knowing exactly what makes it go. However, the more you know about your operating system, the more you'll be able to use your computer effectively and solve problems on your own. (This applies to your car, too, you know.)

In this chapter, you'll fire up your PC and learn the basic functions of the operating system. Different operating systems have different personalities, and this chapter helps you discover common features about them and learn how you can keep your operating system happy.

Flip the Switch!

If you've just finished setting up your computer, you are ready to let the juice flow. Take a quick look around, making sure all the cables are connected at the proper places and the computer is plugged into the wall outlet or power strip.

When you flip the switch, electricity floods in and your computer comes to life. It's not apparent right away, but your operating system plays a role in there, communicating with your computer's BIOS and parceling out the memory everything needs to run smoothly.

What Happens During Startup?

In Chapter 4 you learned about the BIOS of your computer—its Basic Input/Output System. Much of what happens right after power-up involves the BIOS of your machine. The BIOS is a set of programs that is burned onto the ROM chips on your computer, which means that, power outage or not, that information isn't going anywhere. Information burned onto ROM is stored there permanently—and it's a good thing, because your computer couldn't start without it. Your operating system works with the BIOS, gathering information about any peripherals that may be attached, where they are, and what types they are.

System Checks and Other Automated Events

A good portion of the testing the BIOS does at startup is just making sure that everything is running properly. (If you're really into acronyms, you can call this test the *POST*—that's short for *power on self-test*—but chances are no one else will know what you're talking about.)

After the startup text appears on the screen, your computer begins to load special software called *device drivers* that enable it to communicate with hardware such as the mouse, CD-ROM drive, tape drive, and sound card.

Any programs you use that load automatically at startup are also started during this time. You might use a compression utility, antivirus software, or a screen saver that automatically loads itself during the startup phase (also called the *boot process*), along with the device drivers.

> **SIDE TRIP**
>
> *FINDING OUT WHAT STARTS UP AUTOMATICALLY*
>
> If you purchased your computer *preassembled* and *preinstalled*, which means everything was basically done for you before you bought it, how do you know what programs are loaded automatically? First, watch your screen carefully during power-up. You should see some sign—a file name, a descriptive line, a company name, that could help you identify the loading product.
>
> *(continued)*

SIDE TRIP

FINDING OUT WHAT STARTS UP AUTOMATICALLY (continued)

If you use DOS as your operating system, you can check in your computer's CONFIG.SYS or AUTOEXEC.BAT file to see what loads when. (Be forewarned, however—this is not for the fainthearted or the foolhardy. See "A Note About DOS" later in this chapter for more information.)

If you use Windows, you can check your StartUp window (in Windows 3.1) or the StartUp folder (in Windows 95) to see what's being slipped into your PC's RAM without you knowing it. Check out "Windows's Likes and Dislikes" for details on how to find and investigate the StartUp folder.

After the initial testing is done and your system passes, the operating system kicks in and displays its user interface. Depending on which operating system you're running, this could be a graphical user interface such as the one you see with Windows 3.1 and Windows 95, or a command-line interface like the one MS-DOS provides. Figure 13-1 shows the Windows 95 desktop; Figure 13-2 shows the DOS command-line interface.

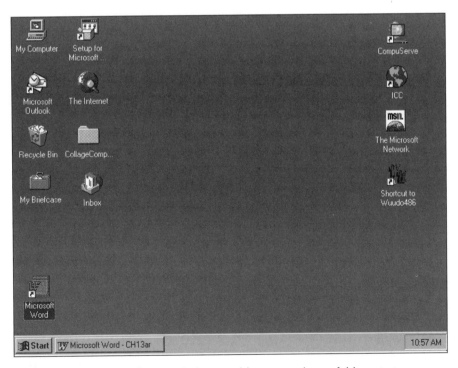

Figure 13-1 The Windows 95 desktop enables you to choose folders, start programs, and more by clicking the icons on the screen.

If you're using Microsoft Windows, or if you've seen it loaded, you know what this looks like. The Windows logo appears on the screen, accompanied by a chime, bell, or some other sound that some clever person has assigned to the startup event.

Figure 13-2 The DOS command line requires that you enter operating system commands by typing them directly at the prompt.

NOTE Some things about your operating system are subject to change, such as the startup sound that plays when Windows loads. Other things, such as the commands you choose to save a file or the steps you take to exit a program, are built-in features that you are stuck with.

What Is the Operating System Good For?

Your PC's operating system is the interpreter between you and your computer hardware. The operating system is *software,* instead of the you-can-knock-on-it hardware of your computer's system unit, monitor, printer, and so on.

But the operating system is not software like the programs you use to create things on your computer: letters, spreadsheets, drawings, music, whatever. That type of software is known as *application software* because you use it for a specific application (see Chapter 14).

A Millisecond in the Life of Your Operating System

The operating system works in layers, from the basic data processing that happens beyond your reach (the *lowest layer*) to the human processing you control when you enter data and select commands (the *highest layer*). As illustrated in Figure 13-3, the actual data crunching takes place in the microprocessor chip of your computer, the lowest layer. The next level up is the BIOS, which translates input into code that the microprocessor can understand and act on. The next level up is the operating system, which interacts with both the BIOS and your PC's software (the next layer), which interacts with you (the highest layer). More confused than ever? Let's put it in practical terms.

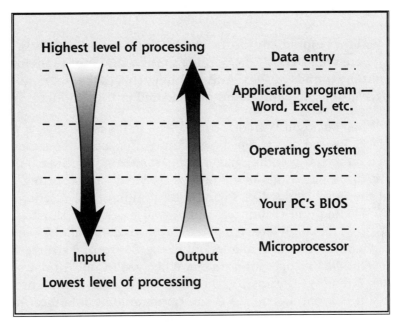

Figure 13-3 The operating system works with both the highest and lowest levels of processing in your PC.

You're sitting at your computer and you decide that you need to answer a coworker's e-mail before you dig back into work for the afternoon. Your computer is still on, and the friendly Windows 95 user interface gleams patiently, awaiting your selection. You move the mouse pointer on the screen to the Microsoft Exchange icon (that's what you use for e-mail) and then —

As soon as you began to move that mouse, Microsoft Windows 95, which is an operating system in its own right, sent the information to the BIOS, which went then to the microprocessor. Faster than you could notice, information sped back from the microprocessor to the BIOS to the operating system and showed the mouse pointer moving on the screen. (Gee, Mister Wizard. Show me more!)

The System Versus Environment Issue

Don't get confused when we talk about Microsoft Windows as an operating system. Windows can be either an operating system or environment, depending on which version of Windows you use. All versions of Windows up to 3.1 are operating environments. Windows 95 is an operating system.

Here's the difference. Windows 3.1 put a friendly face on DOS, which was the operating system. DOS (short for Disk Operating System) has been alternately blasted and hailed for being cryptic and difficult to remember and use. With DOS, you have to type commands at a prompt, such as **REN** (for Rename) when you want to rename a file, or **DEL** (for Delete). Not really difficult, but not nearly as exciting as Windows.

> **NOTE** Another ingredient for the mush: There are different kinds of DOS. There's MS-DOS, PC DOS, and Compaq DOS, not to mention other less visible brands of DOS. And within each DOS camp, new versions (such as 5.0, 6.0, 6.2, and so on) are released as the product is improved.

When Microsoft Windows came along in the mid-1980s, it put a happy face on DOS. Instead of dry, typed commands, users had little pictures on the screen and a mouse for pointing and clicking, something Macintosh users had had for a long time. But Windows still needed DOS to do the basic interacting with BIOS and the CPU. Things like saving files, printing files, deleting and organizing files, opening and closing programs, and more were still the true domain of DOS, even though it looked like Windows was doing all the work.

Windows 95 took Windows out of the OS-wannabe category and turned it into a full-fledged operating system. When you install Windows 95 on your computer, it removes DOS as your primary operating system. (The DOS commands are still on your system, as is the command-line interface, just tucked away where they won't interfere with Windows's greatness.)

Know Your Operating Systems

Different operating systems work on different types of setups. In this book, we're focusing primarily on SOHO (jazzy 1990's word for small office/home office) setups, which use two basic operating systems: Windows and MS-DOS. You'll discover other operating systems, too, for different machines and more specialized applications, including OS/2 and UNIX.

Microsoft Windows

As you learned in the last section, Windows is available in several incarnations. Windows 95 is the most recent, but since we're already into 1997, we can expect a new release anytime. Different versions of Windows are available for multiuser systems as well (Windows NT and Windows for Workgroups), so you can use Windows as your operating environment of choice, even on networks.

Windows 3.1

The benefits of Windows include its friendly user interface and the easy point-and-click method of opening and closing programs, working with files, selecting menus and commands, and performing routine operations.

Figure 13-4 shows a screen from Windows 3.1 (that version of Windows that relies on DOS for the basic operational stuff). The small on-screen icons open into windows (hence the name, I suppose), making everything easy to see and use.

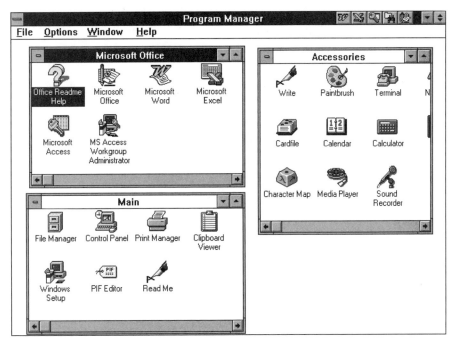

Figure 13-4 Microsoft Windows 3.1 puts a friendly face on DOS and makes PC operations easier.

Windows 95

Windows 95 includes additional cool features like plug-and-play (which enables you to add other devices like printers, modems, and whatnot to your computer without all the headaches and hassles you might suffer if you used DOS), multimedia support, almost seamless Internet access, the availability of MSN (Microsoft's online information service), and a number of built-in programs and accessories that can make computing easier.

Microsoft Windows 95 changes the look and feel of earlier Windows but sticks with the same ease-of-use philosophy. You can create shortcuts on the desktop to quickly launch the programs you use most often. The Taskbar at the bottom of the screen makes it easy for you to switch between open programs, as illustrated back in Figure 13-1.

DOS

The first operating system created for the personal computer was DOS. Microsoft produced its version, called MS-DOS, and IBM produced a similar but slightly different version of its own, called PC DOS. Both types of DOS did the same basic things: They interacted with the BIOS, allowed you to perform disk and file maintenance operations, and enabled you to launch and work with programs. Other DOS versions you might see include DR-DOS and Novell DOS.

> **NOTE** Humble moment: Okay, so you can tell how bored I get when I talk about DOS. It just doesn't do anything for me. With our age of visual everything, looking at a single line of bare letters doesn't give much spark to the imagination. It does, however, get the job done, and many power users prefer entering DOS commands for those tedious-but-necessary disk and file maintenance operations.

Here's an example of a DOS command:

```
DIR
```

Pretty exciting, huh? DIR is short for DIRectory, which gives you a listing of the contents of the disk you're currently using. For example, if I wanted to see what files I have stored on the disk in drive A, I would type the following line at the DOS prompt:

```
DIR A:
```

Your computer then takes a quick look at the disk and displays the results of the search on the screen. Figure 13-5 shows what the directory for my disk looks like.

THE DOS SHELL

Once Windows had made its impact on DOS, the makers of DOS looked into ways to make their *interface* friendlier. The DOS Shell was born. With MS-DOS version 6.0, users could now use a mouse to open menus, choose commands, work with files, and so on. Users could also do things like edit *batch files* (miniprograms users created to perform specific tasks, like print many files at once, autoformat disks, and so on). Figure 13-6 gives you an idea of the appeal of the DOS Shell.

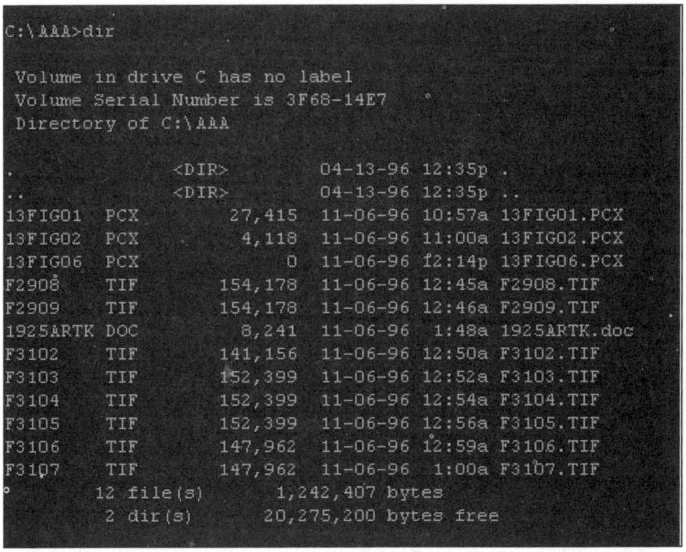

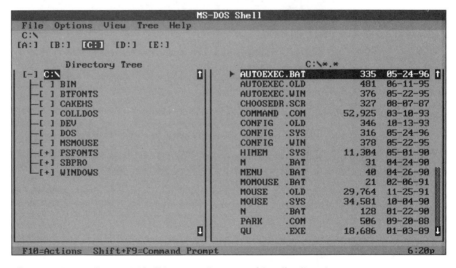

Figure 13-5 The results of the DIR command are straightforward.

Figure 13-6 The DOS Shell is a step in a user-friendly direction.

DOS IN THE WINDOW(S)

You may be able to tell from this example that DOS offers a streamlined approach for those people who aren't particularly impressed with little pictures, colors, and desktop metaphors. For some procedures, such as zipping files, doing mass copying, and locating files, I prefer the old DOS command line. If you're not so quick with your fingers or don't yet know the appropriate DOS commands, you'll prefer using the graphical method.

Luckily, all versions of Windows have a built-in MS-DOS Prompt selection, as illustrated in Figure 13-7, so you can display a window and work with DOS command lines if you prefer. When you're finished, you can type **EXIT** and return to your Windows work session.

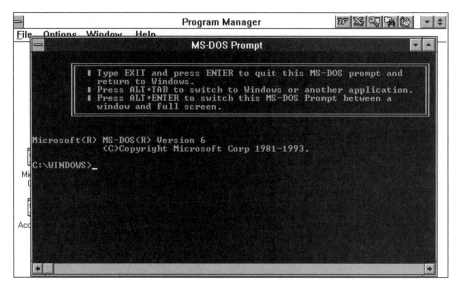

Figure 13-7   From within Windows, you can work with DOS in an MS-DOS window.

OS/2

OS/2, short for Operating System/2, was expected to take the operating system market by storm. IBM and Microsoft, which had worked together on the new system, expected nothing short of overnight success.

The public wasn't so sure. OS/2 demanded a powerful PC, which put the operating system out of the reach of most SOHO users. Developers were slow to write programs for OS/2, which meant there weren't a lot of supported application to run on it. Today OS/2 is still around, but the enthusiasm is a mere trickle amidst the Windows flood.

UNIX

Unless you're seriously into programming or you're working on a network, you may never need to know what UNIX is. Designed primarily for engineers and programmers, UNIX is great for multitasking and multiuser applications and has great security features. It is a bit high-end for the needs of most users.

Installing or Upgrading Your Operating System

You were probably not — or will not be — responsible for installing your operating system. New computers ordinarily come with the operating system already installed. In fact, if you are new to PCs, paying an extra $20 to have someone in technical support do it for you is a great deal. Let the experts install it, test it out, and show you how it works. Then if something didn't install correctly, they see it before it leaves the shop. It's money well spent.

But operating systems upgrade just like computer programs. Each year, it seems, brings a new crop of features. The last big harvest was actually a new program. Microsoft Windows 95 was the highly publicized sequel to Windows 3.1, and it was met with terrific success.

What do you do if you want to install a new version of your operating system? Here are a few pointers:

* Investigate the options carefully.
* Before you buy the upgrade, read the box.
* How much memory does it have?
* Does it require a CD-ROM to install it?
* What about storage space?
* Make sure your system meets all the hardware and software requirements for running the operating system before you make the purchase.
* Back up your computer before you change anything. Make copies of all important files—data files, program files, and system files. See Table 13-1 for a list of critical files that you need to make sure you back up.
* Know the answers to questions that the installation program may ask you. What type of microprocessor does your system have? How much RAM? How much disk storage? And so on.
* Read everything in the upgrade kit before you install anything.
* Have the technical support number handy and be prepared to use it.
* Follow the instructions carefully and slowly.

TABLE 1-1 Important OS Files to Back Up Before Upgrading

MS-DOS	Windows 3.1	Windows 95
AUTOEXEC.BAT	WIN.INI	USER.DAT
CONFIG.SYS	SYSTEM.INI	SYSTEM.DAT

TIP Most likely, everything will go smoothly, but it's better to anticipate problems and not have them. Do the installation during normal work hours so you can be sure to reach a technical support person if you need one. Having your computer hang up during the installation at 1:00 a.m. is a lot more traumatic than hitting a glitch at 1:00 p.m., when technical support is just a phone call away.

Friendly Operating Tips

Your operating system doesn't get a lot of glory. Day in and day out it performs those *disk and file maintenance operations* faithfully, carrying data back and forth and giving you a friendly environment in which to work. There are a few things you can do to keep your operating system happy, whether you are using Windows, DOS, or a combination of the two.

Windows's Likes and Dislikes

Windows becomes grumpiest about a lack of RAM. All the graphics, colors, and sounds you see on the screen come at a cost, paid in memory. Windows 3.1 needs 4MB to run comfortably, Windows 95 squeaks by with 8MB (but does much better with 12MB or 16MB), and Windows NT, UNIX, and OS/2 prefer 32MB or more. If you want to be happy while you're using Windows, don't scrimp in the RAM department.

One way to keep an eye on how the RAM in your system is used is to make sure you know which programs are being loaded automatically. In Windows 3.1, you can double-click the StartUp icon to open the window and see what's in there, as shown in Figure 13-8. Anything in the StartUp window will load automatically each time you start Windows, thereby eating up your PC's RAM.

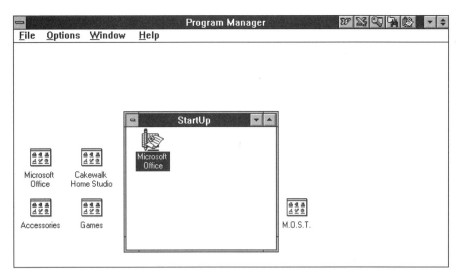

Figure 13-8 In Windows 3.1, check the StartUp window to see what programs are loaded automatically when you start the software.

If you use Windows 95, you can easily check what's automatically loading by clicking the Start menu button, choosing Programs, and pointing to the StartUp choice in the cascading menu that appears, as shown in Figure 13-9.

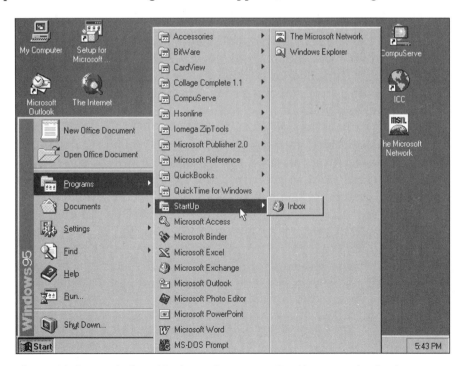

Figure 13-9 In Windows 95, choose Programs→StartUp to see what loads automatically.

A Note About DOS

DOS is more limited than Windows in the way it deals with available RAM. Later versions of DOS are better at making use of more memory than older versions, but all you need to do is:

- Make sure you purchase software that will work with your version of DOS with the amount of RAM you have installed.
- Keep backup copies of DOS's two main files in the event you have a system crash and lose your configuration files.

NOTE Losing the configuration files is more of an inconvenience than a tragedy; you can re-enter all the information in your AUTOEXEC.BAT and CONFIG.SYS files if you need to—and your computer will run without them—but you may find it running less efficiently and giving you more trouble after the crash if you don't have the latest copies of those files.

The two semi-sacred files you need to protect when you're working with DOS are AUTOEXEC.BAT and CONFIG.SYS.

CONFIG.SYS runs as soon as your computer's BIOS check is complete. This file contains important information that DOS needs in order to know its parameters. CONFIG.SYS tells DOS how many files it can have open at one time, how much memory is allowed for the files, and so on.

AUTOEXEC.BAT is an *auto-execute* or *batch* file that runs as soon as CONFIG.SYS is finished. In this file are the commands that run all the auto-loading programs, such as your mouse and print drivers, and important information about how you want the prompt and your screen to appear, where your CD-ROM drive is connected and what type it is, and how your computer should access the memory you have installed. When you install programs, such as Microsoft Word for DOS, the program's installation utility puts a line in AUTOEXEC.BAT so you can start the program simply by typing **WORD** at the DOS prompt. Not an earthshaking issue, but a convenience nonetheless.

You can display these files at the DOS prompt by entering **TYPE AUTOEXEC.BAT** or by displaying it from the MS-DOS Editor, seen in Figure 13-10, by typing **EDIT AUTOEXEC.BAT**. The MS-DOS Editor is a simple editor available with versions of MS-DOS 5.0 and later. The Editor displays a window in which you can easily review, edit, save, and print DOS files.

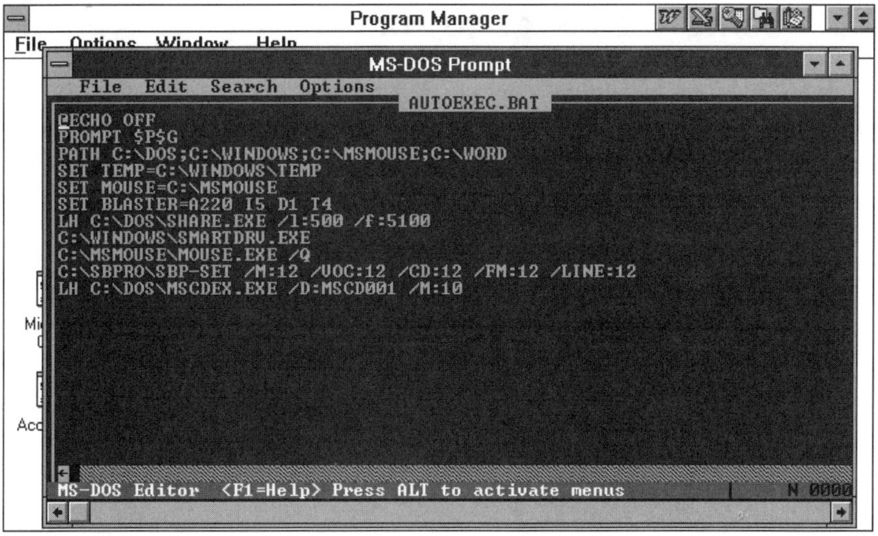

Figure 13-10 The MS-DOS Editor gives you an easy way to view and modify DOS files.

BONUS

Options, Options

If you're having a serious problem making a decision for or against a certain operating system, you can purchase a program called System Commander that enables you to use more than one operating system on your computer. You can only use one at a time, of course, but System Commander gives you the option of having up to 100 (!) operating systems on one PC. It's available at PC Connection for around $65. You can call them at (800) 800-5555.

Summary

This chapter has introduced you to your PC's unsung hero—the operating system. Chances are that you won't have to make a decision about your OS or install it yourself, but knowing what it is, what it does, and what you can do to help it puts you at an advantage. The next chapter moves to the next layer up in the processing chain by giving you a whirlwind tour of the types of application programs available today.

Some Web Sites to Hit

 Microsoft Corporation:
http://www.microsoft.com

ZDNet information on Windows 95/NT and add-ons:
http://www.hotfiles.com/win95.html

IBM Personal Computing:
http://www.pc.ibm.com

CHAPTER FOURTEEN

PROGRAMS! PROGRAMS! READ ALL ABOUT 'EM!

IN THIS CHAPTER YOU LEARN THESE KEY SKILLS

KNOW WHY THEY CALL IT SOFTWARE   PAGE 167

CHECK OUT DIFFERENT SOFTWARE TYPES   PAGE 168

LEARN WHERE AND HOW TO GET SOFTWARE   PAGE 185

INSTALLING AND STARTING PROGRAMS   PAGE 187

FINDING AND USING TECHNICAL SUPPORT   PAGE 190

This chapter gives you the scoop on software. What is software and where do you get it? What kinds of programs are available for your chosen system? How does software work with your operating system and your computer to accomplish the tasks you dictate? Find out about the different types of programs—on disk and on CD-ROM—and explore the possibilities they open up to you. (Integration! Communication! Games! Multimedia!)

Why Do They Call It Software?

We understand what a program is. We've all heard about school hot lunch programs. We've picked up a program just as we walk in to watch the Broadway production of *Cats*.

No, wait. Wrong program.

The program that you use on your PC is a piece of software—instructions your computer uses to help you accomplish specific tasks. The program you use to write letters, print envelopes, compose newsletters, even write books is called a word-processing program. The program you use to create a budget, track your investments, plan your mortgage, or calculate household improvement costs is known as a *spreadsheet program*.

When we're talking about programs generically ("What kind of programs do you use?"), we often use the term *software* instead ("What kind of software do you use?"). It means the same thing. Programs are software and software is a collection of programs or a single program by itself.

Some people think we call programs *software* because they used to come on floppy disks that you could bend (although they could hardly be called *soft*). Others think *software* got its name from what it's not: hardware. The rest of us try not to ponder such deep thoughts.

Building Your Own Software Library

You may be lucky enough to have purchased a PC with all the right programs installed. Everything you want and need is already installed on your hard disk and you don't have to do anything else.

That would be wonderful.

Most of us settle for some programs we don't really need (which eat up valuable storage space) and still must add programs we really wanted and didn't get in the original package. Knowing what you need and want, and then finding and installing those programs, is the straightest road through this jungle of software choices.

SIDE TRIP

EVERYTHING BUT THE KITCHEN SINK

If you haven't purchased your computer yet or are considering getting another one, look at all the complete systems you can find before you decide. Many manufacturers and retailers offer PC setups that include a whopping array of programs included in the deal. One PC offered by a leading computer manufacturer offers the following free pre-installed software (which means they do it for you):

Lotus SmartSuite 96	Clip Art Library
Quicken SE 96	Visio Home
EasyPhoto	City Streets
PhotoStudio SE	TripMaker SE
Tyrian	

(continued)

SIDE TRIP

EVERYTHING BUT THE KITCHEN SINK (continued)

In short, this computer gives you a suite of application programs: a word processor, database, and spreadsheet; a financial program to help you balance your checkbook, pay taxes, and more; and specialty programs with clip art, graphics scanning and editing features, maps, and games.

Word Processing

Everybody needs a word processor for something. If you type words at your computer—whether those words are part of a dissertation, a grocery list, or something in-between— you'll use a word-processing program to accomplish that task. Popular word-processing programs include Microsoft Word for Windows, Corel WordPerfect, and Lotus Word Pro.

TIP Sometimes you'll find a word processor you like that is part of another program. Both ClarisWorks 4.0 and Microsoft Works for Windows 95 include word processors that offer many good features and are easy to use. Both products retail for less than $100 and include other programs as well that handle spreadsheet, database, and communications tasks.

JUST THE BASICS

A word-processing program enables you to type information and save it in a file. You can edit the file however you want to, copying, moving, and deleting text quickly and almost effortlessly. You can use a spelling utility to check your work automatically and offer suggestions when you misspell something. When you've got the document the way you want it, you can print it, simply and painlessly.

WORD-PROCESSING WONDERS: FORMATTING AND ENHANCING

Word-processing programs offer these features and others that go beyond the basic text entry and editing tasks. You can control the way the text is formatted on the page. Some word processors let you create columns, newspaper style; all let you set margins, control indents, and set tabs so the text in your file is lined up the way you want it. You can create tables easily and, in some programs, even import tables you've created in other programs.

Word-processing programs also enable you to enhance the text you enter by changing the look, size, and style of the text. You can easily change the *font* (the typeface, size, and style of the text) and create a different tone or effect for your work. Take a look at Figure 14-1, in which the headline "You don't want to miss this!" is shown in different fonts. Each look conveys a different feeling.

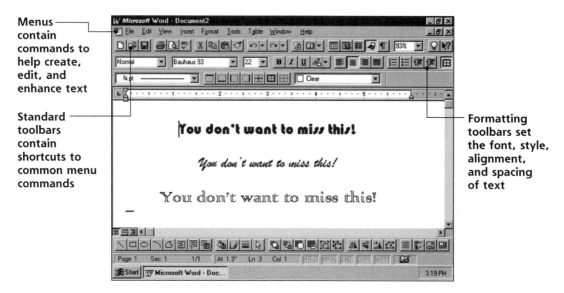

Figure 14-1 With word processing, you can change the tone and personality of your words.

One of the biggest benefits of the word processor is that you're in easy reach of all kinds of tools that make your document better and make formatting and enhancing text simpler. Menus contain the commands you use to open, view, edit, enhance, save, and print documents. Toolbars give you the tools you need to copy, cut, and paste text; insert tables and spreadsheets; specify columns, draw shapes and lines; and more.

SPECIAL WORD-PROCESSING CAPABILITIES

Most word processors also let you create what's known as a *style sheet,* which is a file of "memorized" formats that you can apply to text by choosing the style you want from a list. A style can specify the format of the text, including the line spacing, character spacing, and paragraph spacing, as well as the font, size, and style of the text itself. Using styles saves you time and trouble deciding how you want things to look; you can simply assign the text a certain style and let the word processor take care of it for you.

Not only can you make your letters look more inviting than a typewriter-written letter, but you can do things far beyond the reach of your Smith-Corona. You can design and print newsletters, business cards, résumés, fax cover pages, and more. You can write memos, books, faxes, and even design Web pages. With some word processors, you can insert clip art, photos, music, and even add audio notes that you record and attach to your written documents.

Word processors range in cost from $79 for a low-end program to upwards of $500 for top-of-the-line word-processing power. All programs go through regular upgrades—some as often as one a year—so purchase the most recent version that runs on your PC.

A WORD ABOUT TEXT EDITORS

A text editor, as compared to a word processor, is a program that works strictly with text. You can enter text and edit text and that's it. No slick enhancement features; no special formatting tricks like doing columns or funky features like voice-over notes. You would use a text editor simply if you don't have another word processor to use and you need to prepare text for use in another program or when you're working on something like programming code that is text but requires no special formatting or text enhancement techniques.

Text editors are often built into other programs or are available as shareware, often packaged on those 100-shareware-programs-for-$10 CDs, or found on the Internet for free downloading. Windows 95 includes both Notepad and WordPad. Notepad is a simple text editor; it doesn't include formatting, enhancement, and layout features, as seen in Figure 14-2. WordPad is a "light" word processor, with toolbars, menus, and special formatting and enhancement features, shown in Figure 14-3. If your word-processing needs are pretty straightforward, WordPad may be all you need.

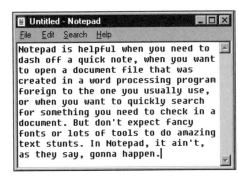

Figure 14-2 Notepad is a simple text editor with limited features, but for typing a quick note, it's fast and easy.

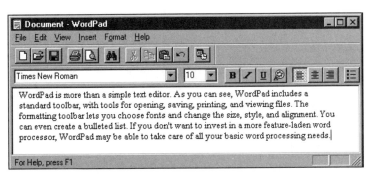

Figure 14-3 With WordPad, you have access to full word-processing features; nothing fancy, but enough to get the look and arrangement you want for your text.

Spreadsheets

A spreadsheet program does for numbers what a word-processing program does for words. It gives you a forum for entering and arranging them. A spreadsheet program enables you to perform calculations (correctly, too!) and keep all the data you enter in an electronic file. When you want to review, edit, print, or otherwise enhance the spreadsheet you have created, you can simply open the file and work with it. No more accountant's pads or calculators.

Reusable data is a big benefit, especially when it's part of your job or your life to enter long columns of numbers and calculate them. Once you get the numbers in there—accurately—you can move them, copy them, format them, and use them in other calculations. You don't have to worry about mistyping figures or transposing numbers. You can save the file and use it in documents, reports, balance sheets, whatever.

Spreadsheet programs include built-in formulas called *functions* that enable you to carry out sometimes complex calculations quickly. That is, they do the math so you don't have to. Want to know the average rate you paid Dr. Quick Print last year? You can use the Average function to figure it for you. You don't have to be a math major—you don't even have to like math—to use spreadsheet tools to your advantage.

High-end spreadsheet programs include features beyond those that let you work with numbers. You can create reports of all types, design and incorporate charts, and even add clip art in your spreadsheets. You may be able to use the data you enter in your spreadsheet program in other programs as well.

One of the most popular spreadsheet programs today is Microsoft Excel, which is shown in Figure 14-4. You'll notice that the spreadsheet offers its own set of toolbars for working with files and formatting purposes. Excel allows you to group worksheets together in workbooks, so you can put worksheets related to specific projects in one workbook. Excel is just one example of a spreadsheet program. Lotus 1-2-3 and Quattro Pro are other popular choices. Again, integrated packages like Microsoft Works and ClarisWorks include their own spreadsheet programs as well.

SIDE TRIP

SPREADSHEET TERMS TO KNOW AND LOVE

- *Spreadsheet file:* the file in which you save the data you enter, format, and enhance
- *Worksheet:* one "page" in the spreadsheet file
- *Workbook:* a grouping of several worksheets

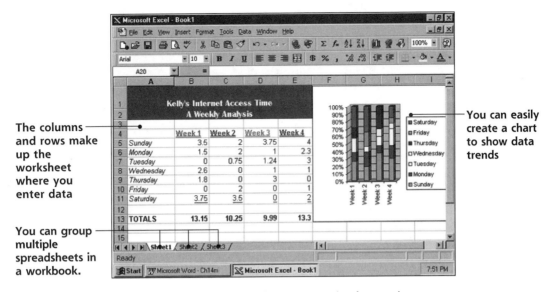

Figure 14-4 Microsoft Excel is one example of a popular spreadsheet program.

Costs range from under $100 to upwards of $495. The higher the cost, the greater the number of features. But if you need good, reliable spreadsheet functions with the possibility of some high-end data analysis and fancy reporting capabilities, you'll like the power of a high-end spreadsheet program.

Databases

Database programs are the organizers of data. Whether you need to keep track of your CD collection, your household inventory, your client list, or the names and addresses of all the kids in your 4-H group, a database program will help you enter, arrange, sort, and search through all the data you store.

There are a number of database programs ranging in complexity from simple mailing-label utilities to huge, sophisticated programs that enable you to build your own data-entry forms, create your own user interface, and fine-tune elaborate reports generated automatically based on the settings you enter. Popular database programs include Microsoft Access, Paradox for Windows, Approach, dBASE, and FileMaker Pro. The programs enable you to create data-entry forms, enter data in tables, query (question) the database for items you want to see, sort data in just about any order you can think of, and print reports of various sizes, shapes, and styles.

SIDE TRIP

KNOW THE LINGO, MAN

Database programs come with their own set of buzzwords. You need to know these before you start managing data in bulk:

* *Database:* the file in which you save all records related to one particular subject. You might have a database of names and addresses of friends and relatives, for example.
* *Field:* one single category of data, such as all first names or phone numbers in your friends-and-relatives database.
* *Record:* one collection of fields related to a particular item. For example, one record would store the information about a single person in the friends-and-relatives database.

The database program you use will help you enter and organize data. You can then sort and print the data however you need to: mailing labels, client lists, inventories, and more. You can keep track of your business's ordering system, know when projects are due, follow up on contacts with suppliers, update the names and addresses of your garden club members, and keep track of just about anything that's important to you.

Database programs offer a full range of menus and views that enable you to look at your data in various ways, according to criteria you have set. Figure 14-5 shows an example of a data table in Microsoft Access. You have the option of entering the data directly in the table or entering information on a data-entry form you design. Figure 14-6 shows a data-entry form in Access.

Games!

As long as there have been computer programs, there have been games. You'll find games to suit every personality — from fast-action, 3D adventures to brain teasers to solitaire. Windows 3.1 included two popular games, Solitaire and Minesweeper. (Watch out — they're both addictive!)

Figure 14-5 This is an example of a data table in Microsoft Access. Database programs give you the means to store, arrange, and report on your data in a variety of ways.

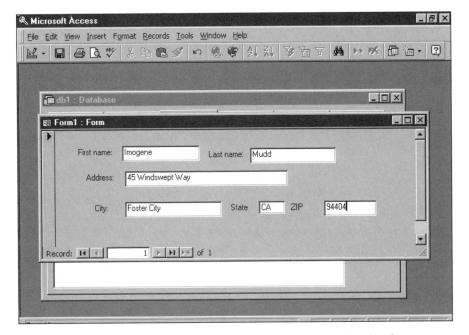

Figure 14-6 A data-entry form gives you an easy way to enter the data for your database.

What types of games are out there? Here are a few of the more popular ones:

- **Zork Nemesis (by Activision):** an award-winning 3D game that incorporates Hollywood actors in action video and lets you explore worlds in an underground empire.
- **MechWarrior 2 (by Activision):** a 3D experience that enables you to put on huge, directable combat armor and fight battle missions in the 31st century.
- **Myst (by Cyan):** an award-winning, role-playing adventure game with stunning graphics and a captivating storyline.
- **3D Pinball (by Microsoft):** a test of hand-eye coordination (and, okay, a little skill).

Communications Software

Communications software enables you to use your modem to link up with the outside world. It provides your modem with a brain. You can get communications software in many places and in many formats. Integrated packages, such as Microsoft Works for Windows, include a Communications module so you can send e-mail and files from within the program. Windows 95 comes with both Microsoft Exchange, an e-mail utility, and Microsoft Fax, a faxing program. Other stand-alone programs, such as Eudora, offer Internet e-mail features, and still others, like the much-touted Netscape, offer Web browsing and Internet navigation tools.

SIDE TRIP

INTERNET AND COMMUNICATIONS SOFTWARE JARGON

- E-mail program: a type of communications program that enables you to send and receive e-mail.
- Web browser: communications software that enables you to access, view, and browse Web pages on the World Wide Web.
- Internet tools: a collection of software utilities for navigating the Internet, usually provided by your Internet service provider. A set of tools might include an e-mail program, a Web browser, a global chat utility, search tools, and more.

Here are a few of the communications programs you'll run into as you begin exploring the world beyond your four walls:

- **Em@iler,** by Claris, helps you automatically sort and respond to messages.
- **Microsoft Exchange,** built into Windows 95, is your mail utility liaison with online services, networks, and Internet mail.
- **Microsoft Mail,** included with Windows 95 and available as part of the Microsoft Office Professional package, is your mail server for networked systems.
- **Smartcom,** by Hayes, a full-featured communications package that includes a messaging center, supports two phone lines, and gives you the option of setting up voice mailboxes.
- **WebTalk,** by Quarterdeck, gives you the choice of voice communications along with your Web browsing.
- **Internet Phone** enables you to hear whom you're conversing with on the Internet and cut down on long-distance phone bills at the same time.
- **FocalPoint,** a communications control center that helps you control e-mail, faxes, and voice mail from within Windows.
- **Internet Explorer,** a Web browser available free-of-charge from Microsoft (you must use Windows 95 in order to use Internet Explorer).
- **Netscape Navigator,** a Web browser that has taken the Web by storm and includes a number of Internet navigation tools and customizable features.
- **WinWeb,** a shareware Web browser that works within Windows and enables you to surf the World Wide Web.

TIP When you subscribe to an online service, you are given access to their software. CompuServe uses the program WinCIM, and America Online sends its own software with which you can access their service. The Microsoft Network, or MSN, is available to all Windows 95 users—it is included free as part of the Windows 95 package.

Web Page Design Programs

Not long ago, we were just figuring out how to *find* Web pages; now we're thinking about creating our own. Much to the surprise of code-phobic people, designing a Web page is really a simple matter if you have the right tools. Here's a list of some of the tools you can use to generate your own Web page:

* **Spectacular 3D Web Workshop** is a Web page design tool that gives you more than one thousand 3D images to use in your own page, along with instructions for creating the effects you want without learning a new language.
* **Corel/WEB.DESIGNER** is a Web page design tool that lets you turn a text file into a Web page by using templates, bookmarks, links, and more.
* **Microsoft FrontPage** is a Web page creation program that walks you through the process of creating a Web page without any coding at all.
* **SoftQuad HoTMetaL PRO** is another Web page creation product that provides an easy-to-use graphical environment for designing Web pages.

Graphics Programs

Graphics programs are programs you use to add art to your documents, spreadsheets, Web pages, and more. Many types of graphics programs are available, each focusing on a different aspect of artistic endeavor. Table 14-1 gives you an overview of some.

TABLE 14-1   All Kinds of Graphics Programs

Program Type	What It Does	An Example or Two
PAINTING PROGRAM	Paints individual pixels the screen; allows dot-by-dot editing	WindowsPaint, Fractal Design on Painter
CLIP ART PROGRAM	A collection of professional art and photo images ready for your use, usually packaged on CD	Corel Graphics Pack, PhotoDisc
DRAWING PROGRAM	Draws images from a series of shapes, not dots, based on calculations; images are manipulated as objects	Microsoft Draw, Adobe Illustrator
PRESENTATION GRAPHICS PROGRAM	Enables you to create slides for presentation or printing, complete with text, graphics, charts, animation, and more	Freelance Graphics for Windows, Microsoft PowerPoint

Program Type	What It Does	An Example or Two
CAD (COMPUTER AIDED DESIGN) PROGRAM	Enables you to create precise drawings such as schematics, blueprints, and other documents that demand technical precision	AutoCAD, GenericCAD
PHOTO AND IMAGE EDITING PROGRAM	Enables you to scan, mask, edit, alter, and enhance photos and images you capture	Adobe Photoshop, Collage Image Manager
SPECIAL EFFECTS PROGRAM	Enables you to bend, turn, morph, and create special effects with graphics; creates 2D and 3D versions of imported images	Adobe After Effects, Final Effects AP
FONT MANIPULATION	Helps you create your own fonts, alter existing fonts, create special font effects, and manage the fonts you use	Adobe Type Manager, Adobe Type on Call
MULTIMEDIA GENERATION PROGRAM	Enables you to create multimedia documents, Web pages, training materials and more, using graphics, sound, text, animation, and video	Macromedia Director, Strata Virtual Studio

No matter what type of graphics program you're working with, you are provided with a set of tools to use. If you are using a paint program, you have a paint palette complete with color choices, brush sizes, and more. If you are using a drawing program, you have a set of drawing tools in various shapes, line thickness, fill colors and patterns, and so on. Figure 14-7 shows the simple paint program, Windows Paint, which is included with Windows 95. Figure 14-8 shows a screen from Microsoft PowerPoint, a presentation graphics program that enables you to create slides for presenting purposes.

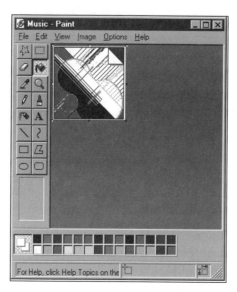

Figure 14-7 Windows Paint is a simple paint program you can use to enhance photos and artwork you create or import.

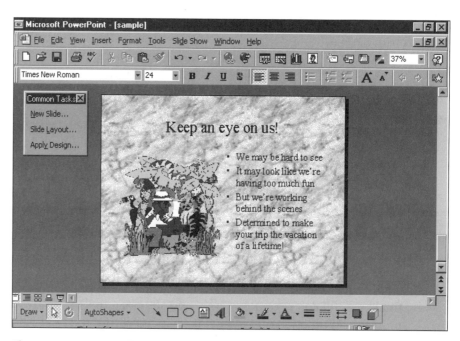

Figure 14-8 Microsoft PowerPoint is a presentation graphics program that includes a good set of drawing tools and comes with its own set of clip art.

Desktop Publishing Programs

Desktop publishing programs enable you to publish all sorts of materials—books, newsletters, flyers, brochures, business cards, and more—right from your desktop PC. Several publishing programs are available, with a wide range of features and costs.

One of the biggest benefits desktop publishing offers individuals and companies is the time-saving facet of doing your own print work. And the money-saving aspect is nothing to sneeze at, either. If you are creating a brochure for your small business, you might sketch out a few ideas and then take it to a printing company. You'd have to wait for the designer to come up with a rough draft of the brochure, which you then need to approve. That's one set of charges and perhaps a few days' wait. Then the typesetter sets the type for the brochure. There's another set of charges and another day or two spent. By the time you get your brochures back, you've invested quite a bit of time waiting for other people to make your project their priority and you've spent a good chunk of change, too.

If you are publishing your own brochure, you sit down at the PC with your desktop publishing programs, brainstorm a few ideas on screen, print the ideas, revise, and come up with your final brochure, perhaps in a single afternoon. You then take it to the printer, if you like, and have it copied—you don't have to wait for anyone else to do their job and you save the expense of having done the design and layout yourself.

Low-end and high-end desktop publishing programs are available. Those on the lower end are used for things like garden club newsletters, mailers advertising the school chili supper, and business cards and stationery for your small business. High-end desktop publishing programs are used by corporations and individuals for high-quality print and Internet publishing. A high percentage of the books printed today (and this book is one of them) are put together using desktop publishing software. Here are some of the DTP programs you'll find in PC catalogs:

- **QuarkXPress** is a the top-of-the-line desktop publishing program used by large and small companies alike.
- **Adobe PageMaker** is available for both the PC and the Macintosh and is another high-end standard used in professional publishing.
- **Adobe FrameMaker** is a document publishing program for long or complicated documents.
- **Microsoft Publisher** is an easy-to-use, friendly, and fun publishing program that doesn't rival professional DTP programs, but gives simple documents, newsletters, and brochures a professional look for a fraction of the cost of using a high-end package.
- **Print Shop Deluxe II** is a simple print kit that enables you to create cards, letterhead, banners, calendars, and posters.

PIMs and Schedulers

Ever heard of a PIM? It's an acronym for personal information manager. Keep track of those appointments. Make those phone calls. Prioritize that to-do list.

PIMs are a form of electronic assistant that help you keep track of the details you juggle during your work week. Most PIMs have scheduling utilities built into them, but some programs focus only on scheduling your projects.

Here are two basic guidelines to remember. First, no two PIMs offer the same set of functions. Second, people tend to get fanatical about them—they'll defend their choice rather fiercely, so look carefully before you select. Don't simply take someone else's word for it. Here are a few examples of PIMs and schedulers:

- **Day-Timer Organizer 2.0** is an electronic approach to your favorite personal scheduler. Keep track of your schedule, your to-do lists, addresses, expenses, and phone calls. The Deluxe version offers time-management tips, a restaurant guide, and CompuServe access.
- **Now Up-to-Date** is a scheduler and contact manager that helps you keep track of important addresses—both traditional and e-mail—and enables you to keep Web page addresses by simply dragging them to your address book.
- **ECCO Pro 3.0** is a PIM that keeps track of your contacts, deadlines, project segments and more. You can use the calendar to remind you of upcoming events and the to-do list to help you prioritize your plans.
- **Sidekick** is a pop-up utility included with Corel's WordPerfect 7 suite that helps you keep track of notes, appointments, to-do lists, addresses, phone numbers, and more.
- **FastTrack Schedule** is a scheduling program that enables you to create timeline schedules for presentation purposes.

Money Managers

Other programs take care of financial matters. Although you can use a spreadsheet program to do your number crunching and data analyses, having a financial program that understands how to balance a checkbook, print a profit-and-loss report, and build an income statement is a real help, especially when you don't like to do those things yourself. Here are a few programs that are created specifically to help you keep track of financial matters at home or in your small business:

- **Quicken** is one of the most popular money managers out there, and at a low cost, too. Quicken is simple to learn and use, an electronic version of your checkbook, with built-in register and check-writing capabilities.
- **Microsoft Money** helps you set up your personal or small business finances and get control of your income and outgo. Microsoft Money works with all other Windows products and is part of the Microsoft Home Essentials pack.

- **QuickBooks,** also by Quicken, is a more full-featured version of the popular financial software, ideal for small businesses. QuickBooks helps you set up income and expense accounts and maintain your records so everything is smooth at tax time.
- **MYOB Accounting** is another small business accounting program that offers a full range of features—general ledger, check writing, invoicing—and even packages in video and CD multimedia help.
- **Timeslips Deluxe** helps you keep track of all your billable hours, making invoicing a breeze.

Utilities

Utilities cover all kinds of tasks. Generally they are add-on features, fill-in-the-gap kinds of programs that make PC life a little easier. They help you protect your PC from viruses, run backup programs, give you troubleshooting tools, compress files, uninstall programs, and enhance the other features of your system. Here are a few examples of utility programs you'll see:

- **Norton Utilities** is one of the first and still the most popular utility collections, including programs for unerasing and unformatting files, recovering damaged data files, repairing bad disks. Norton also makes Anti-Virus, a utility that protects your PC against viruses, and Norton Navigator, a set of tools that enhance the features of Windows 95.
- **Uninstaller for Windows 95** removes programs that you've previously installed much more efficiently than you could do manually.
- **PowerDesk** enhances Windows 95 Explorer features and adds a toolbar to help you get your desktop organized.
- **Zip-It,** from Vertisoft, is a file compression utility that enables you to easily zip and unzip files from within Windows. WinZip is another such program. Vertisoft also publishes two other utilities: Remove-It, which uninstalls programs, and Name-It, which enables you to use long filenames (supported in Windows 95) with Windows 3.1 programs.
- **Conversions Plus for Windows** enables you to open Mac files on your PC.
- **MacLink Plus/Easy Open** helps Mac users open PC files.

Educational Software

You will find all kinds of educational software from all kinds of sources. Programs abound for kids of all ages—no reading required. Many, but by no means all, educational titles come packaged on CD-ROM; often the titles that are multimedia-ready and include video, sound, or interactive tests are

CD-ROM titles. But many educational programs run right from the floppy disk, use whatever monitor you've got, and don't demand much memory. In other words, if you've got a PC and you've got kids, get out there and get some educational software!

Educational programs usually focus on a particular topic or skill and use several methods of reinforcing the learning of that skill. Programs for the younger set (preschool through age 7) rely on the point-and-click method or perhaps the pressing of a few simple keys. Readers will be interested in educational programs with more of a story line and perhaps interactive testing that scores them on the number of correct responses or enables them to move ahead in the game to the next level after they master the current one.

Many educational titles make great use of multimedia capabilities, incorporating video clips, talking-head interviews, interesting music, and demos of various concepts. These educational programs are usually packaged on CD-ROM and will not run unless the CD is in the drive.

Here is a sampling of a few popular educational titles for different age groups. Rest assured that there are thousands more out there in the marketplace awaiting your review:

* **Kid Phonics CD,** for kids 4 to 7, is a reading program that incorporates music and animation to reinforce reading skills.
* **MathBlaster: In Search of Spot,** is a program for kids 6 to 12 that relies on graphics, sound, music, and an interactive story to teach basic math concepts.
* **The Learning Advantage, Library 1 and 2,** for kids 3 to 7, offers a collection of award-winning programs that build basic math, reading, geography, art, and creative skills.

Fun Stuff and Edutainment Titles

Multimedia—the mixing of sound, video, graphics, and text to create an interactive experience—has brought a new age of enjoyment to PC use. Yes, that's right, I said *enjoyment.* You might enjoy playing games and you might enjoy writing a really good report, but *edutainment* software is a new, fun approach to using your PC for perhaps it's best purpose of all: learning about something new you're interested in. Have you wondered how you might plan out the perfect garden? Want to learn about all the greatest composers? Perhaps you've never walked through the Louvre but always wanted to know what's in there.

Edutainment is your answer.

Edutainment titles mix entertainment and education. You're having a good time learning about something you're interested in. There's no real "productivity" purpose here; you're just expanding your horizons. Here are a few examples of edutainment software:

- **Golf Tips: Breaking 100** for beginning golfers includes more than 20 hours of instruction from real golf pros.
- **Planet Earth: Explore the Worlds Within** is a guide to cultures, lands, and peoples of the world.
- **Better Photography: Learning to See Creatively** teaches you the basics of putting together a good photograph and offers workshop information on better photography.
- **Passage to Vietnam** takes you on an interactive journey through Vietnam accompanied by award-winning photojournalists and writers.
- **FLOWERscape** helps you identify and plan the garden just right for your geographic location and personal preference.
- **Everything Weather** tells you everything you want to know about weather around the world, complete with weather maps, video footage, and Internet access for weather trackers.
- **Poetry in Motion** is an interactive poetry experience lead by poets such as Tom Waits and Amiri Baraka.

> **NOTE** The software examples listed in this chapter are meant to give you a sample of some of the wide range of choices available. You'll find programs of all types, sizes, and capabilities. Some cost several hundred dollars, some are free, and most are somewhere in between. Be sure to explore, explore, explore, and find the incredible array of software awaiting you. New programs appear every day.

Finding Software

So when you've identified what kind of software you want, where do you find it? Major discount stores like Wal-Mart, Target, and Kmart have gotten into the software business. Although their supply may be limited, you can't beat them for convenience. More technical catch-all stores like Best Buys and Incredible Universe carry a hefty supply of software choices. Some bookstores also carry CD-ROM titles, as do all computer retail stores and even some used computer outlets.

> **TIP** Get an idea of what type of software you want—and know the names of a few possible candidates—before you make that trip to the computer store or pick up the phone to call the mail-order house. Check out recent copies of popular computer magazines and read the reviews of the programs you're considering.

Some stores focus primarily on selling software. Places like Egghead Software and Software, Etc. earn their living keeping up on the latest software, making sure it's in stock, and carrying a representative selection of the best-selling programs in all the software categories.

TIP If you are considering several programs and don't know which ones to buy, go to a store that sells software and compare the titles, box to box. Read about the system requirements, find out what the manufacturer thinks the best selling points of the program are (that's the stuff they put on the back of the box). If you're in a place where there's a computer handy, ask if you can see the program demonstrated. You should see the software in action before you make the investment, especially if you are spending several hundred dollars on it.

Many people buy software through mail-order houses like PC Connection. This is generally a fine practice and speedy, too, since most mail-order places guarantee overnight shipping for no extra charge. The only problem with purchasing a program sight unseen is that until you've seen it in action you can't really be sure it will do what you want it to do or that you'll be comfortable using it. If you purchase a program from a mail order catalog, ask what the return policy is. What if you don't like it? What if it doesn't do what you need it to do? The person on the other end of the order line will be able to fill you in on the company's return policies.

The safest way to buy a program is to go to a store and see it demonstrated. Try it out. Point and click. See if it will do what you want. Ask questions. When you're satisfied with the answers you get, ask about return or refund policies, and then write the check.

The Internet is a great source for programs—both those you pay for and those you do not. All software companies worth their salt these days have a Web site of their own. As part of educating yourself about the software you plan to buy, visit the company's Web site.

 WEB PATH If you are thinking about buying Microsoft Word for Windows, for example, check out

http://www.microsoft.com

and see what you can find about Word. If you want to check out Lotus SmartSuite 96, go to

http://www.lotus.com

You can also find thousands of shareware and freeware programs on the Internet, just there for the picking. How do you find them? If you know the name of the program you want, you can use one of the Internet search tools to find it. If you have run across the name of a specific Web site with a crop of shareware or freeware programs, you can access that with your Web browser. (For more information on using Internet tools, see Chapter 16.)

One of the big problems with downloading programs from the Internet is the risk of viruses. A virus is a mean-spirited program that infects your hard drive and wreaks havoc with your data files, perhaps rendering them unusable. To protect against viruses, make sure you use an anti-virus utility such as Norton Anti-Virus to check all files you download or receive from any source other than a shrink-wrapped box.

SIDE TRIP

How Do You Know a Good Program from a Not-So-Good One?

Hundreds of programs are available to help you master that particular task you need to accomplish. As you think about which programs you want to purchase, answer each of these questions for yourself:

1. Will the program be easy to learn?
2. Will the program be easy to use?
3. Does the program share features with other programs? A Windows program, for example, shares basic tasks such as file copying, opening and closing files, moving text, and so on. So many of the basic procedures you learn in other Windows programs will carry over to the new Windows program.
4. Does the program offer enough flexibility and advanced features so that you can do everything you want to do, and more? (In other words, you won't grow out of it.)
5. Do software reviewers report that it is a robust product? That is, does it stand up to daily use without crashing?

Installation Issues

Until you've done it once or twice, installation sounds like a fearsome task. Installation is simply the process of copying the program files to your hard disk so you can run the program. If you are using a program that runs from a CD-ROM, installation may take just a minute or two, while the installation program copies the startup files to a place on your hard disk. If you are installing a program on your hard disk—a large program, like Microsoft Office—it may take 30 or 40 minutes while the install program copies files, prompts you to change discs, and gets the right settings entered.

There are two important steps in installing any program:

1. Back up your important data files.

2. Follow the installation instructions.

You need to make a backup of important files just in case something squirrelly happens and you can't get into your data files after you install the new program. This is not likely to happen, but it's better to be safe than sorry.

NOTE In Windows 95, you can install and uninstall all programs using the Add/Remove Programs icon in the Control Panel window. Using this procedure makes sure that programs are installed correctly, and when you decide to uninstall the program, Add/Remove Programs checks to see that all program files for that program are removed and no stray files are left on your system.

Starting Programs

Once the program is installed on your computer, you're ready to use it. Starting a program is a simple task, which, depending on your operating system, includes one of these three procedures:

* In Windows 95, you click the Start menu, point to Programs, and select the program you want from the cascading menu. Figure 14-9 shows Microsoft PowerPoint being started in Windows 95.

* In Windows 3.1, you start Windows, display the Program Manager, find the group window icon that represents the program you want to start. Double-click it. Inside, find the program icon for the program, as shown in Figure 14-10. Double-click the program icon, and the program starts.

* From DOS, change to the directory of the program you want to start. (For example, to change to the WORD directory of drive C, you would type **CD C:\WORD** and press Enter.) Then type the name of the program and press Enter.

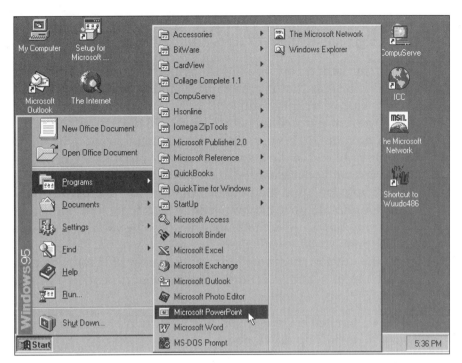

Figure 14-9 To start a program in Windows 95, you begin with the Start button in the lower-left corner of the screen.

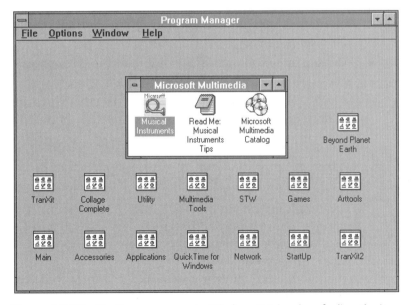

Figure 14-10 Starting a program in Windows 3.1 involves finding the icon that represents the program you want and double-clicking it.

Getting Help When You Need It

The second best reason for buying a legal copy of a program (the first, of course, is that it's the right thing to do) is that you are entitled to some kind of technical support.

The first place to turn for help should always be the help system built into your program. In Windows programs, help is always available in the Help menu at the right end of the menu bar. In other programs, you can press F1 to display a screen with advice related to the task you are trying to accomplish.

If you don't find the solution you need in the program's help system, look in the manual. I know, I know. Nobody likes to look in the manual. But someday you may run across something that will solve your problem and save you beaucoup phone time.

If neither of those solutions has the answer for you, you can contact the software manufacturer's technical support department. You may find one or all of these options available:

* Limited call-in support. It may be a toll-free number or you might have to pick up the charge.
* Fee-based call-in support. This could mean that after a certain number of minutes you are charged on a per-minute rate, or you pay a yearly subscription rate that entitles you to a prescribed amount of service.
* Fax information line.
* Automated help and answer line with recordings of solutions to common problems.
* Web site or e-mail address for online technical support.
* A forum on one of the information services, such as CompuServe, AOL, or MSN, where you can trade stories with other users, get technical support, and find out about the latest releases of the software.

To Upgrade or Not to Upgrade

Okay, let's jump ahead into the future. You've been using your PC for six months. You're happy with it and you've settled into your programs just fine. You are using your computer for all sorts of things, both in your small business and for home use.

And then you get a notice in the mail. New, improved version of your software! Upgrade now for only $79!

Should you do it? The answer depends on several things.

First, do you need to? If you use Word 6 at home, for example, and they are upgrading at the office to Word 7, you might need to upgrade if you plan to take work home.

SIDE TRIP

THINGS TO HAVE READY WHEN YOU CALL

The friendly technical support people at the other end of the phone line need to know certain things about your program and your computer before they can offer any solutions to your problem. Have the following information ready:

- The version of the program you are using
- The registration number of the program
- The type of system you have (know the microprocessor, how much RAM you have, how much disk storage, and, if it's a communications problem, what speed your modem is)
- A clear description of the problem
- What you've tried

Make sure you are sitting at the computer when you call because the technical support person may suggest you try various ways of solving the problem. You may also want to have a notebook handy so you can write down any commands or steps you receive so you can repeat the process on your own if the situation ever arises again.

Second, are the new features worth it? Software manufacturers continually make their programs better, faster, more powerful, and it's not just a customer-service issue. They want your business, and to keep getting your business they need to keep adding things or revising things in their software. But are the changes the ones you really want, or are they just an enhancement for enhancement's sake?

Third, will you be as happy with the upgrade as you are with the current version? That's the $20,000 question and the one that keeps most people watching and waiting before they upgrade. Unless you absolutely have to jump on the bandwagon when a new version of your software is released, wait a while. Watch what the PC magazines write about the upgrade. Find out whether it stands up to their barrage of tests. Talk to other people who have used it. Give the product some time to get a thumbs-up or thumbs-down from the industry before you buy.

BONUS

Keeping Your Programs Straight (and Safe)

So now you have all these programs. You have a word processor and a spreadsheet. You keep track of your friends and relatives in a database and you use an e-mail program for e-mail and a Web browser to while away the hours on the World Wide Web.

Your kids have made their own mark on the family PC. They have educational software, edutainment software, and games, games, games. One day you turn on the computer and find their paint files in your word processing folders. One day the icon for your spreadsheet is just gone, deleted mysteriously from the Windows 95 desktop.

"Who blew away my spreadsheet program?" you call into the family room.

"Not me!"

"Not me!"

Your spouse looks around the corner at you, sitting there at the computer desk, miffed. "Well, *I* didn't do it!"

When you have a *multi-user PC*—that is, a PC that many pairs of hands have access to—how do you make sure that the things that are important to you stay where you want them?

One solution is to create additional desktops. You can do this with Norton Navigator 95, written specifically for use with Windows 95. With Norton Navigator, you can create several desktops and switch among them at will. This means you could keep all your applications on one desktop and all your kids' programs on another. If there are applications you all share, you could create a family desktop that displays only those programs. You can customize the different desktops so they are different colors, have different background patterns, and so on. For a small investment, you can save yourself the time and trouble of finding that missing Excel icon or weeding out KidPix files from your Word documents. Now, if only they had something similar to protect the family car . . .

Summary

In this chapter you learned about the software aspect of working with your PC. You learned what software is and found out about the different types available. You also discovered where to get software, what to do with it once you get it, and whom to yell for when you need help. The next chapter takes you out into the world, traveling with your PC.

Some Web Sites to Hit

WEB PATH →

Happy Puppy (resource for games):
http://happypuppy.com

ZDNet Software Library:
http://www.hotfiles.com

Microsoft Small Business Resource:
http://www.microsoft.com/smallbiz/

CHAPTER FIFTEEN

TRAVELING WITH YOUR COMPUTER

IN THIS CHAPTER YOU LEARN THESE KEY SKILLS

DEFINE YOUR NEEDS   PAGE 196

GET WHAT YOU NEED FOR PC TRAVEL   PAGE 198

PREPARE YOUR PC   PAGE 200

INTERNATIONAL TRAVEL WITH YOUR PC   PAGE 201

Not a traveler? Maybe not today, but tomorrow, who knows? If you stay home because you can't afford the time off, maybe you can take your work with you on a notebook PC. Go ahead, have lunch at the beach. Spend that weekend away in the Rockies. With a portable computer—one small enough to lug around easily—you have the benefit of your office right there with you.

Today the virtual office is a real possibility—pack up your notebook computer, travel around the world, and still get your report in on time. Whether you're a hobbyist who doesn't want to leave the computer at home or a business user who needs to stay connected no matter how far you roam, this chapter focuses on the possibilities for the computer user on the move. Find out about e-mail and online services, provided to help you stay in touch through the use of the nearest phone line.

What Is a Virtual Office?

The term *virtual office* is used to describe what's quickly becoming the office of the '90s, not a specific place with four walls, a door, and a fern, but a cyberplace that can change locations as often as you do. The bottom line is that in a virtual office, the work is getting done, and employees are often happier and more productive than their walled-in counterparts.

If your job takes you on the road, your office might be your briefcase. Or the trunk of your car. Or the phone booth on the corner. (Hey, don't knock it—it worked for Superman!) Today's virtual office can happen because of the expansion of communications technology. Now, if you have a modem, you can be at the client meeting online. You can return messages and faxes just as though you were at your desk. You can log in to your network or your standalone PC and have access to files you would work on at your desk.

 To find out more about portable computers, see Chapter 3.

A Traveler's Guide to Computing

First things first. If you're thinking about traveling with your computer, what will you need?

Number one: A good reason to take the PC along. A notebook computer is a great thing, but like anything else, it's extra luggage if you take it along when you don't need it. If all you plan to do is introduce yourself to a potential new client and drop off some literature about your small business, you don't really need to take your PC, unless you're going to show the client an animated presentation that demonstrates the highlights of your company. For that, you need your PC, your favorite presentation graphics program, and your ready presentation.

The second thing you need when you're considering hitting the road with your PC is a good notebook or laptop computer. Let's distinguish between these terms. A laptop is generally between 9 and 12 pounds and is approximately the size of a briefcase. A notebook is the laptop's smaller cousin, usually weighing in at around 7 pounds (or less). Both are convenient for traveling, but your shoulder will appreciate the lighter of the two PCs.

Next, you need the software to accomplish what you're planning on the road. You might need only the programs you think you'll work with away from home. You might need those programs, plus communications software that enables you to link into your PC at the office and get into files there on your primary PC. The real difference is in whether you will be calling in to another computer or simply using what you've got on the notebook.

What you need to do depends on what type of PC traveler you are: the occasional traveler or the mobile computerist.

The Occasional PC Traveler

If you're an occasional PC traveler, you need to be able to take your computer along once in a while on family journeys, trips to the library, meetings at a client's office, or other in-and-out travels. What you want is a computer similar to the one you use at your desk at home (or in the office) but portable. You want to be able to get into your word-processing program, your spreadsheet, or perhaps your financial manager (especially if you're visiting your accountant).

The notebook computer you need is one that gives you the speed, storage space, and display quality that's comparable to the PC you use most of the time. You need to install your favorite programs on the notebook, if they are not already installed, and make copies of the files you need to take. In addition, you need a battery pack—charged up and ready to use—so that when your notebook starts to beep (a universal cry, translating into "I'm running out of power!") you can save your file and change your PC batteries.

NOTE If you're preparing to travel for your company, make sure you've got the legal go-ahead to create another copy of your programs. Check with your company's PC support person to find out for sure. Most large companies purchase site licenses that allow for a certain number of copies—usually for notebook or backup use. If you have purchased your own software, you can create a copy for your laptop—for your own use—without violating your license agreement.

The Mobile Computerist

The mobile computerist is a different sort of animal, one that makes a living in an ever-changing set of circumstances. Your job takes you all over the city, the country, the globe, and you couldn't do it without your PC. For you, communications hardware and software—the fastest fax/modem around and powerful messaging and connectivity software—is key to accomplishing your business goals. You keep track of your daily schedule, record notes, send e-mail, hold online conferences, check sales reports, and do inventory checks with your PC plugged into the whatever phone jack is handy. You're the one in the airplane with the notebook open on your pop-down tray when everyone else is eating the airline food. You use your PC to stay in touch with everyone, from Mom to the boss to the hotel reservation clerk in Zürich—provided they're as Internet-savvy as you are!

The most important difference between the mobile computerist and the occasional traveler is the need for communications. If you work primarily on the road like the mobile computerist, being able to link up with other computers and send and receive e-mail is the lifeblood of your computer work. If you travel only occasionally, communications is not as vitally important. Simply equip your notebook with the programs you need to be effective while you are away from the office, but don't worry about having a complete PC system that handles all your computing needs on the road.

What Do You Need for PC Travel?

Thinking ahead and planning out your road trip will help you make sure you've got everything you need. You don't want to set up that presentation in Toledo and realize you've left your laser pointer home. Make sure you think through everything you need before you leave.

The Hardware

The best bet is to make a list of everything you need to take. Your list should include the following items:

* Your notebook computer, of course, with case
* An extra battery pack or two (already charged)
* A power cord
* Your modem cable if it's a PCMCIA card
* Extra disks (in case you have to mail something home)
* A boot disk you can use to start your PC if necessary
* A backup of important files

One item unique to notebook computers is the battery pack. You can buy backup packs and keep them charged—the normal charge holds for four to six hours of continual use. The case also is important. Get one that's easy to use. It should be simple to put the notebook in and take it out, the pockets should be secure but easy to open (maybe Velcro), and the strap should be comfortable and wide enough to support the computer's weight comfortably on your shoulder.

> **TIP** A product that can make your life easier as you're transferring files and programs from your desktop PC to your notebook PC is Laplink by Traveling Software. You can easily move programs and data among different computer systems, even if those PCs are running on different operating systems.

The Software

If you plan to be calling back to the office, you have another consideration. Software. You need to be able to dial in and have your PC answer the call so you can get to the files you need from the remote site. Microsoft Exchange, which is included with Windows 95, can take care of that part of the preparation for you. You simply set your desktop PC to answer the phone and then dial in when you're on the road to get to the files you need.

Most people who rely on their portable PCs to help keep their businesses organized use personal information management software (PIMs) to help them enter, arrange, and print out information on clients, products, projects, whatever. You may also need messaging software to access your e-mail and fax messages periodically while you're away.

> **TIP** If you're doing the "remote computer" thing, first try it out close to home. Set up the receiving PC to answer your call and take the modem down the hall to someone else's office (or across the street to the neighbor's house) and attempt to call in to the PC using your notebook. That way, if something's amiss, you can go tinker with settings and fix the problem. Finding out that your PC in Boise won't answer when you're in Brazil isn't going to make your day.

The Other Stuff

The computer ads would have you think that portability means tucking your notebook computer under your arm and heading happily out the door. It's not exactly that easy. For really short, easy jobs—like a trip to the library when you're just going to type in a few notes—you may be able to just grab the PC and run. Most journeys, however, require a little more thought and a few more items.

Depending on how far you need to go and what you need to do with your computer when you get to your destination, you may need cables, disks, a battery pack or power cord, and you'll need the case to put everything in, as well. And while you're at it, throw in a small PC toolkit in case a disk gets stuck in the drive or you face some other such challenge. PC toolkits are small, take-along sets of tools, which include a miniature Phillips screwdriver, a straight slot screwdriver, tweezers, and more. They don't take up much room (about 4" by 5") and are an inexpensive precaution, too (around $10).

SIDE TRIP

WILL SOMEBODY PLEASE EXPLAIN CELLULAR PHONES TO ME?

Okay, so I'm behind the times. I've been wandering around my office for a year thinking I had a cellular phone. I don't. I have a portable phone. A cellular phone is a phone that uses no phone cord or no phone cord connected to the base unit. Instead, the communication bounces off satellites to get to its destination. Like a cellular phone, a cellular fax/modem transmits data via the airwaves instead of the phone lines.

So this brings up a question: Can you travel internationally with cellular phones? The answer is yes, but you're not supposed to use them on airplanes while taking off or landing. Likewise, you're not supposed to use a cellular fax/modem while you're taking off or landing. Modem hookups are provided on the plane (if not at every seat, at least in every row of seats) so you can plug in and send your messages and faxes without interfering with communications on the aircraft. But be forewarned: These calls can be expensive ($15 per call, no matter what the duration) and can really rack up a bill if your modem keeps disconnecting because of a bad connection at 35,000 feet.

Preparing Your Computer

Now that you've identified the hardware and software you need, you need to get everything ready. First, make sure you've removed everything you *don't* need from the notebook you're taking on your journey. Then use the following utilities (or something like them if you don't have the following ones) to make sure your PC is healthy and ready to roll.

First, run ScanDisk. Whether you use Windows 95, an earlier system, or a DOS system, ScanDisk is available to you. (ScanDisk is not available if your computer uses a version of DOS prior to 6.0.) ScanDisk looks for ominous things like bad clusters and file fragments that can take up portions of your hard disk that you need and identifies any trouble spots you may run across at an inopportune moment.

Running Disk Defragmenter is also a good idea. Sometimes when your operating system saves a file to disk, it doesn't put it all in one block of storage space; the file may get divided into several different clusters, as space permits. Disk Defragmenter pulls files together wherever possible and organizes the way in which your disk storage is used. This gives you a cleaner hard disk and minimizes your chances of having disk storage troubles on the road.

While you're preparing things, format a few floppies in case you need to copy files to disk while you're away. Also create a bootable floppy so that in case your computer acts strange and won't start up properly, you can still start it up and retrieve your files before taking it in for repairs. Finally, scan your computer for viruses to make sure it's free of them before you take it out of the office.

> **TIP** A few before-you-go tips: First, test the *actual* life of your batteries before you leave on a trip. Experience shows that they don't last as long as they're supposed to (this applies to video camera batteries, too). Second, if possible, use your notebook solely for a couple of days before you leave to make sure you haven't forgotten a little, but important, file here and there.

The International PC

Depending on your location, it's probably easier to get to the art museum in your town than it is to get to the Louvre in Paris. Mix that distance with the added challenge of taking a PC along and using it in a land with different phone connections and power standards, and you've got a few things to think about.

Is Your PC AC/DC?

Different countries have different voltage standards. In America, the standard is 110. ("It's about 117 coming out the wall," my expert tells me. Whatever *that* means.) In most of Europe, it's 220. But in the United Kingdom it's 240, and in Italy it varies considerably from 125 to 220. That's quite a difference, and your PC needs to have the converter to be able to handle the downshifting to 110.

Many notebook computers sold today have what's called *world current voltage*, which means the power system of the PC can adapt to the voltage standards worldwide. Both NEC and IBM have world current voltage. How do you tell if your computer can adapt to worldwide current? Check the AC adapter you use to plug the PC into the wall. On the adapter itself, you should see printed the range of voltages your computer can accept.

> **NOTE** If you don't have a notebook capable of taking in various voltages, you can get a converter to handle the change for you. You'll find voltage converters in travel stores, electronics specialty stores, and in some airports. One company that specializes in items used in international travel is Appliances Overseas, based in New York City. Call them at (212) 545-8001.

Can You Plug a Square Peg into a Round Hole?

Another difference you'll find in countries outside the U.S. is the basic shape of the wall plug. Sound silly? It's not if you've traveled thousands of miles with everything you need and then your computing plans are sunk because you need a plug with *round* prongs.

What you need is an adapter so your power cord can plug into the wall outlet. Travel stores should carry them or you may be able to find one in your destination spot. But I wouldn't recommend waiting until then; Radio Shack stores aren't everywhere, you know!

Où Est le Téléphone?

This is a hard one for most people to believe, but in some places, it's hard to find a téléphone . . . er, telephone. In a small town in Spain, for example, on a recent trip, one friend of mine had to wait over an hour to check his e-mail in the States because it took that long just to get an international telephone line. Different countries, and different cities within those countries, can have limited international telephone access. On a trip to Greece, a fellow traveler had to spend an afternoon outside a public building waiting to use a pay phone, which was only available during certain hours.

> **TIP** Check your ISP or online service about how to access your American e-mail account and the Internet from overseas. For instance, CompuServe has international access numbers, so you may not have to make a long-distance call to log in to the service, and AOL has European versions you can dial up.

In most places frequented by business travelers, you'll find modem access lines and plenty of opportunity for connectivity. You shouldn't have trouble in larger cities, but if you plan to go exploring on the road less traveled, you'd do well to invest in a *cellular* fax/modem. As with cellular phones, however, don't expect the service to come cheap.

> **TIP** One of the joys of traveling throughout the world is that there are places where your modem needs to be registered with the local constabulary to avoid running afoul of local statutes. Make sure you know the regulations before you go. Also, make sure your modem understands the local dial tone; it's not the same everywhere, and you can't count on most PC card modems to know that. So if you're planning international travel, look for a modem that guarantees it can handle phone systems from the United States to Chile—now *there's* an interesting dial tone for you (higher pitched and sounds "bursty")—to India, to wherever.

(Almost) Online and Ready

The final consideration you've got to worry about as a traveler in a new land is the process of connecting. Here, we simply do whatever we want to do and dial. Plug in the computer, turn it on, plug in the modem, in whatever order we see fit. In some countries, however, the order in which you do these things matters.

Why does it make a difference? Because in some countries, phone lines carry currents up to 70 volts, which is enough to perm your hair and fry some of your data. The order in which you do what (plug the computer in first? plug the modem in first?) may vary from country to country, so check with someone who knows before you hook up for the first time to make sure you don't get zapped.

TIP You can also get special devices that plug into a phone line to test whether it is digital or analog — or something that was just invented by Telefonik Obscuratio or whoever else runs the local loop. They typically cost $50 or so, but if they save your $250 modem from certain death they're worth it. Also, you can get acoustic couplers from Konexx that give you a reasonable connection without actually having to deal with the local dial tone; all you do is manually dial and hook the coupler up to the phone and you're connected. That kind of thing is useful when you're in the back country.

Once you're hooked up, you simply need to dial in and make the connection as you would from any other location. When you're traveling out of the country, however, you first need to dial the international direct dialing access code (0011), followed by the U.S. (or Canada) country code (1), before you can dial the familiar area code and access number of your ISP.

BONUS

Leaving a Paper Trail

As you romp around the world, you'll learn that taking your laser printer with you isn't all that practical. So what do you do when you need to print out something that you're working on, but you're on the road? Various printer manufacturers make laptop printers — from tiny-sized to book-sized, in capabilities ranging from draft-quality black-and-white to full-color "photo quality" printing. If you need to print while on the road, don't think it's impossible — check out Canon, HP, and Epson to see who's got the most perfect portable printer around.

Summary

In this chapter, you've learned about the issues involved in traveling with PCs. You've got to think about where you're going (we'll leave the "why" to you) and what you need. You need to gather together your hardware and software and prepare your system for the big trip. Once you and your PC are ready, you can take the show on the road, or the sea, or the plane.

Some Web Sites to Hit

Power-One (power conversion products):
http://www.power-one.com/

Northwest Airlines:
http://www.nwa.com

Appliances Overseas:
http://www.best.com/~applover/about.html

CHAPTER SIXTEEN

GETTING ON THE INTERNET

IN THIS CHAPTER YOU LEARN THESE KEY SKILLS

LEARN WHAT THE INTERNET IS   PAGE 205

GET ONLINE   PAGE 207

USE THE INTERNET   PAGE 211

DISCOVER THE WORLD WIDE WEB   PAGE 215

Unless you've had your fingers in your ears for the last two years, you've heard about the Internet. Now you can take the on-ramp to the information superhighway at your own speed. Learn what the Internet is and what it has to offer you; learn how it is used today and how it may be used tomorrow. This chapter shows you the basics of the Internet and introduces you to the World Wide Web and the browsing method of gathering information.

What Is the Internet (Am I the Last Person on Earth to Know)?

The Internet is a system of networks, joined together all over the globe. Tens of millions of users are already surfing the Internet, and thousands more try it every day. Most people find it's less intimidating than they thought. A great number of people are getting hooked—discovering how simple it is to search for and find up-to-the-minute information on the topics most important to them, how easy it is to send and receive e-mail, and how fun (and addictive) it can be to chat with people across the world.

You should know, however, that all information on the Internet is not created equal. While it's possible to find late-breaking news and so forth, it's also possible to find completely useless trash. The Internet increases the quantity of information available, but it's still largely up to you to determine the quality.

The networks that comprise the ever-changing, ever-expanding worldwide Internet network are not all the same. Some are large corporate-run networks, others are small points of contact. Individual users, with the right software, can get on the Internet without becoming part of a smaller network at all.

Confused? Let's tackle the network issue first.

What Exactly Is a Network?

A *network* is a system of linked computers that can share files. Suppose you have three computers in your office. You use one to create presentations; another keeps track of all the client and vendor data for your small business. Your part-time bookkeeper uses the third to track company expenses and do payroll.

You're working with the Small Business Administration, applying for a loan so you can expand your operation. They need a report that shows your client base (income) and your financial information (outgo). You've got all the information you need, but the information is in three different places—on three different computers.

If your computers are standalone PCs, you'll spend the better part of the morning walking from machine to machine, copying this data file to that computer and this financial file to that computer, and so on. It's a lot of walking and a lot of hassle. However, if your computers were networked, you could stay at one computer and get right into the files on the other computers. And you could not only access the files in the different computers but you could share software and run a program that isn't even loaded on your computer.

There are networks large and small on the Internet. The Internet itself is one huge interrelated network of networks, giving you the ability to share files and programs with computers all over the world.

NOTE You'll see the acronyms LAN and WAN when you read about networks. *LAN* is an acronym for Local Area Network, a network of computers in an office or in a local area. *WAN* is an acronym for Wide Area Network, a larger-scale network of LANs.

SIDE TRIP

INTERNET TIME TEST

Once upon a time, in the early days of the PC, the personal computer was an isolated machine. Unless it was a terminal on a network (which doesn't qualify it as a PC but rather as what we lovingly refer to as a "dumb terminal"), the system had to rely on its own power and resources to complete the job you asked of it. Programs you ran had to be stored on that machine. Files you created were saved on that machine. If you needed to give a copy of the report you just wrote to your partner three states over, you had to save the file to a disk, put the disk in a cardboard envelope, mail it, and hope for the best. Once the file reached its destination, your partner had to open the envelope, put the disk in the slot, and copy the file to his or her PC. The whole process may have taken anywhere from three to five days.

With the Internet, in the time it took you to read that paragraph, the file could be on your partner's PC. You create an e-mail message, attach the report, and send it surging through the phone lines. Your Internet provider sends the message and file to your partner's Internet provider and it goes into his or her mailbox, just like that. When he or she checks the mail after their morning coffee, the report is there waiting.

A Little Internet Evolution

The Internet began as a government project, back in the late '60s. Researchers were looking for the most secure way possible to communicate military information. The original project was called ARPANET, and it focused on a method of sending information in small packets, each of which traveled a different route through different networks. This ensured a means of communication, even in the event of war.

Almost twenty years later, ARPANET split in two; MILNET become the network used specifically for the military, and ARPANET was used for civilian research. ARPANET became DARPANET, the Defense Advanced Projects Research Agency Net, and the two networks continued to communicate with each other. The Internet was sparked in that connection.

How Do I Get There?

Getting on the Internet is much easier today than it was two years ago. You can get on the Internet directly from any online service, such as America Online, CompuServe, The Microsoft Network, and others. You can link up with an Internet service providers (ISPs) in your area or, if one isn't available locally, you can subscribe to a national provider.

First Things First: The Speed Issue

Let's talk about hardware. What do you need to access the Internet? First, you need a modem. The faster, the better. The "fast" modem of last year is this year's slow modem. A 28,800 baud modem (written *28.8*) or a V3.4 fax/modem is the fastest you can currently buy. There's also a new crop of asymmetrical 56K download, 33.6 upload modems being released by U.S. Robotics and Rockwell. (Having a birthday sometime soon?)

The speed of the modem, obviously, affects the speed with which you can send or receive information. The speed controls things such as how quickly the images appear on your screen, how quickly you jump from one place to another, how fast files are downloaded to your computer, and how quickly you see your comments in a chat room.

Using a Commercial Service to Get on the Internet

If you have an account with an online service, such as CompuServe, you can access the Internet within that service. Figure 16-1 shows WinCIM, a program used to access the CompuServe information service, and the button you click to get to the Internet.

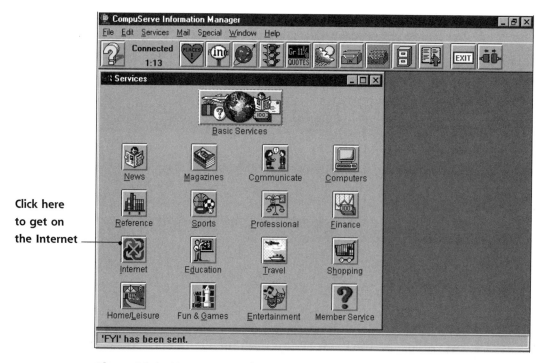

Click here to get on the Internet

Figure 16-1 You can get to the Internet on CompuServe by clicking the Internet button.

No matter what service you use, accessing the Internet is a simple matter of clicking a button, opening a window, or selecting a program icon.

Once you're on the Internet, you can perform searches, play games, download files, chat with other users, and use the Internet as you normally would.

Accessing with an Internet Service Provider

An Internet Service Provider is a company that offers you Internet access for a monthly fee. You probably have an ISP in your area (you can find them by looking in the yellow pages, calling a local computer store, or asking your local librarian). If there is no ISP in your immediate area, you can contact a national ISP and participate in their services.

For a standard monthly fee, the ISP gives you a range of services. One local provider in my area charges $19.99 a month for 300 hours of Internet access time and gives you a full suite of Internet utilities, including programs for e-mail, searches, Web browsing, newsgroups, and global chats. Some providers offer even better deals, such as unlimited access time for $20 a month. Figure 16-2 shows the set of buttons you use to access different Internet features with one local ISP.

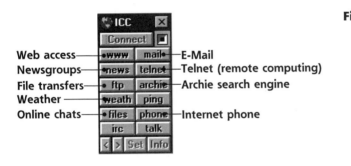

Figure 16-2 One Internet Service Provider provides a set of utilities that help you perform Internet searches, send e-mail, access the Web, and more.

The benefit of an ISP is you have a direct high-speed link to the Internet, a substantially lower cost than online commercial providers (CompuServe, for example, charges a $9.99 month fee plus $2.50 per hour for every hour over the first 10 spent online each month). Another benefit is you can access the Internet by dialing a local number, which saves you long-distance charges that might be necessary for you to reach your online services. Even if you subscribe to a national ISP, you can get access through an 800 number.

SIDE TRIP

A FEW NATIONAL SERVICE PROVIDERS

AT&T WorldNet
1800 Perimeter Park Drive West, Suite 100
Morrisville, NC 27560
(800) 967-5363

CERFNET
P.O. Box 85608
San Diego, CA 92186
(800) 876-2373

IDT
294 State Street
Hackensack, NJ 07601
(800) 245-8000

JvNCnet
3 Independence Way
Princeton, NY 98540
(609) 897-7300

Netcom
Two North Second Street, Plaza A
San Jose, CA 95113
(800) 638-2661

Northwest Nexus
P.O. Box 40597
Bellview, WA 98015
(800) 539-3505

What should you consider when thinking of joining an Internet service provider? Remember that even the best ISPs can have spotty local access success. If you sign up and then later don't like your service, check out another ISP. Before you join with anyone, however, here are a few basic questions you should ask:

* What's your monthly fee?
* How many hours does that cover?
* What is your charge for hours over that amount?
* Are there any "set-up" charges? What are they?
* How many subscribers do you have?
* How long have you been business?
* Will the access number be a toll-free call? Do you have access numbers across the country for when I travel?
* Do you provide a Web browser as part of your software package?
* Do you provide a free home page for subscribers?
* Do you offer technical support, training, and manual(s) with the software?

How Will I Use the Internet?

Once you get on the Internet, what will you do with it? The following sections give you an idea of how users are working with the Internet at home, at the office, and at school.

The World's Biggest Card Catalog

How would you like to take a walk-through tour of the Metropolitan Museum of Art? Search the file archives looking for 14th century poetry? Get sound clips from Louis Armstrong's last recorded concert? Perhaps you're interested in sports, medicine, law, or parenting. Maybe you'd like to fix an authentic Tibetan recipe for your visiting guru.

The Internet is an inexhaustible source of information. Using a variety of search tools, you can find and download files, read through conversations, subscribe to online publications, and gather groups of information about topics you're interested in.

SIDE TRIP

SEARCH TOOLS FOR FINDING WHAT YOU WANT

The Internet provides you with a number of ways you can search for the information you seek:

* *Gopher* is a search engine created at the University of Minnesota that tunnels for the information you seek through Internet channels. The result of your Gopher search is displayed in a menu so you can easily choose the items you want to view.

* A Veronica search is a version of a Gopher search. *Veronica* stands for Very Easy Rodent-Oriented Net-wide Index to Computerized Archives. The Rodent-Oriented bit has to do with how Veronica uses Gopher servers. Veronica maintains an index of Gopher sites so you don't actually have to go though menu after menu seeking information; you can have the information brought to you. You enter text in a message box describing the topic you want to find and a menu of *hits* (files that match your search information) are displayed for your selection.

(continued)

SIDE TRIP

SEARCH TOOLS FOR FINDING WHAT YOU WANT (continued)

* A *WAIS* search (Wide Area Information Servers) helps you locate files with the content for which you search. For your paper on Persian literature, for example, you could enter the word "Persian" and get a list of files that have the word somewhere in the body of the document. This means, of course, that you will also get information on Persian donuts, Persian rugs, and Persian cats, but you're moving in the right direction.
* The World Wide Web provides one of the easiest ways to search, and one of the most diverse. You can use search tools such as Activa and Yahoo! to locate Web pages with the words you enter.

Find Yahoo! at:
http://www.yahoo.com
Find Activa at:
http://www.activa.com

Kids on the Net

The Internet is a natural for kids—with some controls. Kids love to explore sites, do searches, talk in teen chat rooms, and so on. But kids can also stumble onto sexually explicit material and have conversations with stalker personalities, so if you're planning to let your kids loose to surf the Net, you might want to go over the following guidelines with them first:

* Agree on an allowable time limit
* Set guidelines for where the kids can visit and where they can't—let them know you want them to stay away from adult forums or games you don't like
* Make sure they know not to give out their home address or phone number
* Explain the reason for caution and make sure they know to contact you if they are concerned with any online behavior they encounter
* Check on them during their Internet time to make sure they are visiting sites that you find acceptable

TIP A number of Internet utilities are available that can lock out any Internet sites you don't want your kids to visit. Programs like SurfWatch keep an eye out for keywords you select and block access to sites associated with them.

E-mail for Everyone

You can easily send and receive e-mail using your Internet hookup. Your ISP should provide you with an e-mail utility, such as Eudora, which is shown in Figure 16-3. You'll also be given an Internet address so others can send e-mail to you.

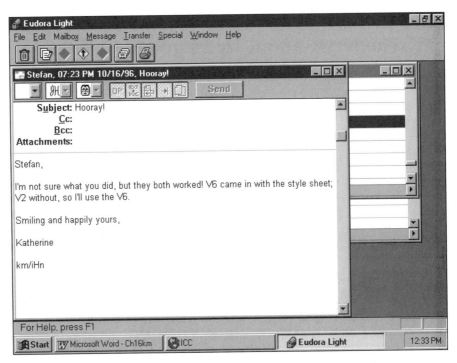

Figure 16-3 Your Internet Service Provider will give you an e-mail utility you can use to send and receive mail.

You can send e-mail using any messaging program, whether or not you have an account with an Internet Service Provider. If you use CompuServe, America Online, The Microsoft Network, or any other commercial service, you already have e-mail capability.

> **NOTE** Each commercial service may have its own addressing rules about how to send your message on the Internet. For example, if you want to send an e-mail message from CompuServe to an Internet address, you include "internet:" in the address. Check with your commercial service to find out about any addressing particulars that may affect you.

If you use Windows 95, you have the messaging utility Microsoft Exchange available for your use. You can send and receive messages and faxes from all popular commercial services and directly through an ISP. If you use Windows 95 but don't have Microsoft Exchange installed, you can add it by displaying the Control Panel, choosing Add/Remove Programs, and clicking the Windows Setup tab. Click Microsoft Exchange in the features list box to select it, and click Add to begin the installation process.

The News About Newsgroups

Another popular feature Internet access brings you is the availability of newsgroups. A *newsgroup* is a discussion group that participates by sending messages based on a particular topic to others in the group. You'll find newsgroups on everything from the study of ancient languages to motor sports to wine-making.

Subscribing to a newsgroup is easier than mailing in a postage-paid card. You simply send a message with the word *subscribe* in it to the newsgroups' subscription address (which is usually fairly easy to find—look in the FAQ, or Frequently Asked Question List, to find this information). When you no longer want to subscribe to the list, you simply send another message to cancel your subscription. While you're subscribed, you'll find your electronic mailbox constantly filling up with messages from complete strangers, many of whom you'll get to know better as time goes on.

How do you know where to find the newsgroups you are interested in? First, your Internet service provider already makes certain newsgroups available for subscription; contact them to find out which ones. Your ISP also provides you with a program called a newsreader that enables you to read the newsgroup messages. Similarly, commercial services have their own stock of current newsgroups that you can view online as part of your subscription to the service.

SIDE TRIP

SAMPLE NEWSGROUPS

alt.music.beatles
alt.book.reviews
alt.politics.economics
biz.jobs.offered
news.announce.newsgroups
misc.education.multimedia
alt.support.cancer

alt.politics.elections
rec.models.railroad
misc.kids
rec.travel.europe
alt.fan.monty-python
rec.scuba

While the newsgroups listed here are pretty safe, there are many, many different kinds of newsgroups out there, with more appearing daily. Not all these newsgroups will appeal to you. Read through some of the message threads before you subscribe to them. Some newsgroups are completely goofy, such as alt.my.head.hurts and alt.alien.vampire.flonk.flonk.flonk.

One of the best ways to find the groups you like is the tried-and-true trial and error method, or you can read about sites in books and magazines.

Discover the World Wide Web

The World Wide Web is the Internet for the rest of us. Although standard Internet searches are great, and finding the files you seek by selecting them from a series of dry menus gets the job done, it's not nearly as entertaining, interesting, serendipitous, or enlightening as using the World Wide Web. Where's the excitement, the glamour?

The World Wide Web livens things up by displaying information in what are called *Web pages*. Each page has *links* or colored and underlined bits of text that take you to other pages of related information. Each page includes text (in any number of colors and formats), graphics, and sometimes video and music. Web pages may include photos of a person (especially if it's someone's personal home page), book covers, product information, and more. Some Web pages include buttons you can click to sign the guest book (letting the page owner know you've been there), order products, download a program, and so on.

What Do I Need to Get on the World Wide Web?

Similar to basic Internet access but different, the World Wide Web needs a kind of program that enables you to see graphics such as a rooster crowing when you click a button or a video clip of a flower unfolding as the page comes into focus. The program also needs to understand and carry out hyperlinks—so when you click a link the program knows to read the Web address at that link and take you there. This type of program is called a *Web browser*.

The major commercial services give you access to the World Wide Web with browsers that are built right into their software. You may have heard of Netscape, which was making CNN headlines not too long ago as the package that was almost synonymous with the World Wide Web. Today, Microsoft has put itself more solidly in the market by creating the Internet Explorer.

A Web browser enables you to navigate the pages on the World Wide Web and find the information you need. Your Internet Service Provider may provide a browser as part of the software utility package you receive for subscribing. Figure 16-4 shows WinWeb, a Web browser that is simple to use.

Figure 16-4 A Web browser enables you to move among the Web pages with a click of the mouse.

There's No Place Like Home (Page)

The page you start with, when you first use your Web browser to access the World Wide Web, is your service provider's *home page* (see Figure 16-5). Whether you are establishing a presence on the Web as a business or an individual, your home page gives visitors a starting point, telling something about you or your business and providing links to additional pages with more information.

How do you get your own home page? Some Internet Service Providers give you the ability to create your own home page free when you subscribe. It's up to you to create it the way you want and upload it to the provider so they can make it accessible to browsers on the Web.

Home pages are getting more and more creative. Put your favorite artwork, photos, music, and more on your Web page. Include a photo of yourself, if you dare. Personalize away.

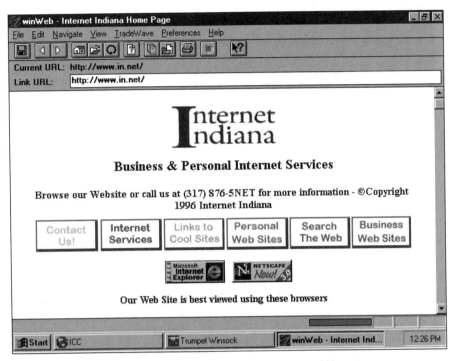

Figure 16-5 The first page you start with when you use your browser to access the World Wide Web is your service provider's home page.

How Do You Create a Home Page?

A home page is really nothing more than a page with codes embedded in it to take care of the formatting, fonts, colors, placement of pictures, and more. The codes in the document are in HTML, or Hypertext Markup Language, and they take care of making sure everything goes where you want it to go and stays there.

You create a home page by entering the codes in any word processor. Or, if you don't want to mess with codes, you can use a Web page editor to do it for you. Many popular programs—Word 7.0 is one example—can turn regular documents into Web pages with basically no help from you. Lotus Freelance Graphics for Windows can turn a presentation you've prepared into a Web page, complete with links in place, which is great if you have just finished a presentation explaining your business and want to make the most of it on the Web.

Examples of Web page editors include the following programs:

* Internet Creator by Foreman Interactive
* FrontPage by Microsoft
* Netscape Navigator Gold Edition
* PageMill from Adobe
* HoTMetal PRO from SoftQuad

Navigating the Web

You get around the pages in the World Wide Web by clicking links. A link is a *hot spot* on the page you click to get to a new location. When you position the pointer on the link, the address appears in the URL message line in your Web browser (see Figure 16-6). When you click the link, you move to the new URL address.

WEB PATH URL is an acronym for Universal Resource Locator, and it's an Internet way of saying *address*. Microsoft's Web page address, or URL, is:

    http://www.microsoft.com

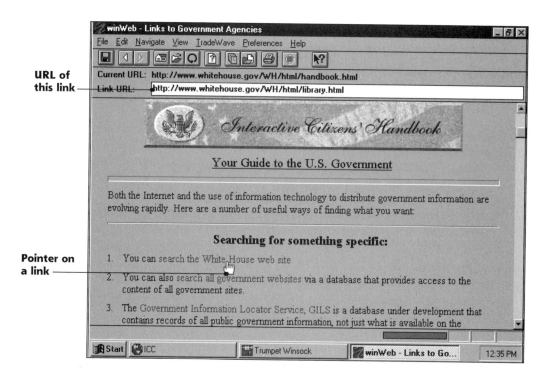

Figure 16-6 When you position the pointer on the link on a Web page, the new address appears in the URL message line.

Your Web browser also has navigational commands and buttons. The commands are probably in a menu called Go or Navigate. Buttons on the toolbar take you back to the pages you've already visited, or back to the home page of your service. One of your biggest challenges is remembering where you were and getting back to that point whenever you want to. Most likely, your Web browser has a command that enables you to save the URL so you can jump to it again another time. You can also store favorite Web addresses for future reference and continued exploration offline.

However, the Web is not static; pages are routinely updated, and some disappear. People who manage their own pages do so out of sheer love (if they're not employed to do so), not just for profit. Pages are therefore worthy of repeat visits to see what (if anything) has changed since you were there last. It's like browsing a huge magazine rack — issues change over time, some new ones crop up, and some favorites disappear.

BONUS

Web Page Organizers

Once you begin exploring the World Wide Web, you'll find there's more to explore than you ever dreamed possible. Some programs enable you to capture and organize Web pages and even Web sites — which include multiple pages. These programs are called Web page organizers, and here's a couple that are available now:

* HotPage by DocuMagix
* Web Buddy by Data Vis

Summary

This chapter investigated of the newest frontiers of the PC age: the Internet. Although the Internet began developing almost 30 years ago, only in the last several years has it become a graphical worldwide system that you and I can navigate to find files, download programs, play games, visit Web pages, and more. We can be sure that however far-reaching, creative, and intriguing the Internet is today, it will be more so tomorrow. Get up there and start surfing — and hang on!

Some Web Sites to Hit

 The WEB magazine, via PC World:
http://www.pcworld.com/

ZDNet Whole Web Catalog:
http://www5.zdnet.com/zdwebcat/

PART FOUR

PREVENTING PC PITFALLS

THIS PART CONTAINS THE FOLLOWING CHAPTERS

CHAPTER **17** COMPUTER CARE 101

CHAPTER **18** PC PROBLEM SOLVING

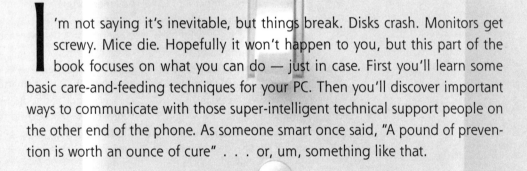

I'm not saying it's inevitable, but things break. Disks crash. Monitors get screwy. Mice die. Hopefully it won't happen to you, but this part of the book focuses on what you can do — just in case. First you'll learn some basic care-and-feeding techniques for your PC. Then you'll discover important ways to communicate with those super-intelligent technical support people on the other end of the phone. As someone smart once said, "A pound of prevention is worth an ounce of cure" . . . or, um, something like that.

THE "EYES" HAVE IT: COMPUTERS IN SCIENCE

Everyone should have an eye doctor like Dr. Michael Mangas.

Dr. Mangas started using computers in 1994, when he bought an inexpensive program, FileMaker Pro, to take care of organizing some of the data needs of his office. Little did he know that he was not only buying a program, he was buying into a whole new way of life for his optometry practice. Today Dr. Mangas uses six computers to take care of a myriad of tasks — from recording basic patient information to handling financial matters to helping him with research and diagnoses.

Once Dr. Mangas began using FileMaker Pro, he was sold. "It's like Lincoln Logs," he said, "It's really easy to do." He began putting together new uses for his computers, networking the systems he had and standardizing record-keeping. Now he could enter information directly into the computers in the exam rooms —no longer would his employees have to read his writing! He also discovered that by keeping all data in one carefully designed file, he could easily spot data trends that could indicate things like future glaucoma, giving him the opportunity to observe and treat conditions early. He's most excited about what the computers mean for his patients—better service, better care, better follow-up.

Dr. Mangas uses removable hard drive cartridges to store all his data, so he can literally "take the office home" and have access to all the data he needs, at any hour. In the future, he is considering adding sound capability so he can record notes directly into the files and the possibility of videocam support so he can file away videos of various eye test results for his patients.

When asked what he would say to someone in his profession who is considering whether to buy a computer, he says, "You really can't do without it. It's the first piece of equipment you should purchase." His computers, he says, help him work smarter and more efficiently than he's ever worked before. And he can provide better care and follow-through for his patients, which really is the name of the game.

CHAPTER SEVENTEEN
COMPUTER CARE 101

KEY GOALS IN THIS CHAPTER

WHAT YOUR SYSTEM NEEDS   PAGE 224

DIVERT DISPLAY DISASTERS   PAGE 225

TIPS FOR KEYBOARD CARE   PAGE 225

MOUSE MOTHERING   PAGE 226

PROTECT YOUR PRINTER   PAGE 227

PROTECT YOUR SOFTWARE AND YOURSELF   PAGE 228

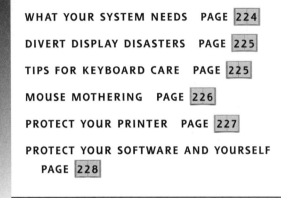

You've purchased your computer, set it up, turned it on, loaded some software, and started creating things. Soon you will have files—and more files, and more files—that are important to you. You'll want to keep them. This chapter offers you some preventative maintenance techniques and care, as well as feeding suggestions that will help you keep your computer happy and your data healthy.

A Basic System Self-Care Guide

The best way to keep your PC functioning for a long period of time is to set up good practices right from the start. By following some common-sense procedures and getting in the habit of cleaning and checking your system, you can help keep your computer virus-free and make sure it doesn't surprise you by running out of disk storage without warning.

The following are some basic PC care guidelines to remember:

* Remove, compress, or archive files and programs you no longer need. Even if you purchased a gigabyte of storage in your new PC, that hard disk will eventually fill up. Get in the habit of removing or archiving files and programs you aren't using anymore to free up hard disk space.
* Run a virus check on all new files and programs. It's especially important that you check files you download from the Internet for viruses; you don't know where they've been! Several different virus-protection utilities are available (such as Norton Anti-Virus) and they are simple to use.
* Use ScanDisk to check your disks and drives. ScanDisk is a utility available with Windows and versions of DOS after 6.0. You can use ScanDisk to check the surface of the disk and look for errors and bad spots. Run ScanDisk periodically to make sure everything is in order.
* Use Disk Defragmenter to clean up your hard disk. Disk Defragmenter pulls files together on your hard disk and cleans up any lost clusters littered around the storage space, taking up small amounts of memory.
* Set a particular day and time to do routine system maintenance tasks.

What Your System Needs

Keep the lid on. Unless you're a certified computer technician (and you wouldn't be reading this book if you were), don't attempt to pop the cover off the system unit and fix anything yourself. Not only does poking around in the system unit risk damaging your PC, but it may void your warranty.

Don't push the system up against a wall. The fan needs room to breathe, and pushing the system unit up against the wall blocks the air passage. This could result in a meltdown that would curl your hair.

Don't stick foreign objects in the disk drives. Seems pretty obvious, doesn't it? It's the old peas-in-your-ears warning (yes, we've been talking to your mother). But what do you do when you push a disk in the drive and the label gets caught? Dig it out with a paper clip, right? Wrong. If you can't reach it with your fingers, wait for the computer repair person to do it for you, and only put one disk in the drive at a time.

Count to ten before you start over. If you and your computer are having a power struggle and you need to turn everything off, count to ten before flipping that power switch back on. During the shutdown process, give the fan and every other internal thing time to shut down completely before you give it a new power jolt.

Power down in thunderstorms. When there's a severe storm in the area, unplug your PC. In fact, unplug everything you can. Better to be safe than fried.

Be kind to cables. Cables are pretty hardy creatures, but they shouldn't be stretched to the max over a long period of time. Avoid letting them get tied in knots, too, which can result in broken wires and a bad cable down the road.

Diverting Display Disasters

Save that screen. A screen saver appears in place of the software display when your computer is unused for a certain length of time. The image on the screen moves continually, which saves your monitor from burn-in; a condition that occurs when a screen that is continually displayed on the monitor gets burned in to the screen's phosphor permanently.

Let it breathe. Again, those little slots along the back, sides, or top of the monitor are important air holes that allow for necessary circulation. All that video circuitry can get pretty warm in there. Make sure the monitor is away from a wall or shelf so the air can move around the monitor easily.

The monitor isn't a knickknack shelf. Many people put various articles atop their monitor. They learn, sooner or later, that there are better places for mementos. Things fall over, they gather dust, and they block necessary air flow. Keep liquids away from monitors. It makes them burn out very quickly.

Check with your monitor manufacturer for updated drivers. From time to time, monitor manufacturers upgrade the driver used to tell your display how to communicate with the software on your system.

Keyboard Care

Keyboard cleaning. Every once in a while, pick your keyboard up, turn it over, and shake it lightly (*really* lightly). Then turn it back over and blow the gunk out from between the keys. You might not see any big chunks of anything, but your keyboard will feel better.

And occasionally, wash behind the keys. If you get really gunky stuff beneath or between the keys, you can clean it out by using a cotton swabbed with alcohol. Just remember to unplug the keyboard first.

Don't eat and type at the same time. Yes, it's tempting — those brownies Sara in marketing brought in and left on the table, just outside the door. Surely you can hold one and eat it carefully while you finish that e-mail message you've got to send out—oops! Where'd that crumb go? Crumbs and sticky fingers sooner or later take their toll on your keyboard. For best results, don't mix business and snack time.

Mouse Mothering

Check those mouse connections. It happens suddenly; one minute you're pointing and clicking happily, and the next, your mouse is dead. Check the mouse connection where it plugs into the back of your system unit. A little tightening should do the trick.

A clean mouse is a happy mouse. After a period of time, your mouse will pick up lint, crumbs, and other substances from your desktop. You can clean the mouse easily by unplugging the mouse, removing the ball, and swabbing the rollers inside with alcohol. You may also want to remove the mouse ball and use tweezers to remove the lint from the rollers inside. Doing this every three to four months—or whenever your mouse begins behaving oddly—should be sufficient.

SIDE TRIP

WHAT PC CLEANING SUPPLIES SHOULD YOU HAVE ON HAND?

- Cotton swabs
- Alcohol (but use it carefully)
- Tweezers
- A small Phillips screwdriver
- A small straight-slot screwdriver
- Canned air (a small aerosol can of air you can use to clear out dust in places you can't reach: beneath or between keys, in the PC fan, etc.)

Come on over to my pad. Every mouse should have a pad. If you haven't already purchased one, you can shop for a style that reflects your personality, such as Bugs Bunny, *Star Trek,* and even Monet. A pad saves wear and tear on the mouse and cuts down on other mouse foes such as static electricity.

Watch that mouse cord. Why does my dog love to chew computer cables? Who knows. When she was small, she felt a strange attraction to the mouse cord. When she was older, it was the PC power cord. For your mouse's protection (and your dog's as well), put cords up out of the reach of those who might chew, tangle, or trip over them.

Protect Your Printer

Time to turn the printer off. Turn the printer off whenever you need to do anything to your printer, such as change the ribbon or the toner, fix a paper jam, and so on.

Use the brush! Inside your laser printer is a small brush you can use to clean toner off the wires. Most people never touch it. Use the brush every few months to get cleaner printouts and prolong the life of your printer.

Know when it's time for a change. Most of us run our toners, ink cartridges, or ribbons down to nothing. Keep a spare or two on hand so you can change before your printer starts leaving out characters on the page.

Recycle your toner cartridges. It's the environmentally friendly thing to do. Many manufacturers now offer reconditioned toner cartridges or reduced rates for cartridges you return yourself. Canon even includes a shipping label with its toners so you can return your used toner free of charge.

Watch out for potential paper jams. Especially in dot-matrix printers, continuous-feed paper can get jammed as it passes through the printer. If you plan to start your printer and walk away, be sure to check on it periodically to make sure the document is printing successfully.

Paper weight makes a difference. When you purchase paper for your printer, you have a choice of several different weights. If you use an ink-jet printer, it may be sensitive to paper weights that are too light, sending two or more pages through at a time and causing pages to be printed partially on one page, partially on another.

What Your Software Needs

Safe storage. Stores sell disk boxes with the express purpose of keeping them safe from magnetic fields and miscellaneous other dangers.

Magnetic fields erase data. Remember the magnetic paper clip holder you keep right beside your PC? You might want to move it. Magnetic fields can erase or garble data on a disk.

Send in your warranty card. When you first purchase a new program, fill out the information card and return it to the manufacturer so that you will be a registered user. Then, if you ever need technical support, you're already entered in their system.

Don't forget your backups. Keep copies of all important files and programs somewhere safe so that in case the horrible happens and your hard disk crashes, you have everything you need to reinstall important applications.

What You Need

A break. Especially if you're new to computers, you need to stand up and walk around, getting your eyes off the screen, every half hour or so. Computer ailments are becoming increasingly prevalent, and a little prevention could keep you from becoming a statistic.

Regular exercise. There are stretches and simple exercises (such as neck rolls, wrist turns, finger stretches) you can do while at your desk. This keeps you moving, helps you relax, and sharpens your thinking.

A comfortable chair. Don't expect yourself to sit eight hours a day on a chair that is too tall, too short, or lacks the padding you need to be comfortable. There *are* areas you can skimp on office furniture, but your chair shouldn't be one of them.

Wrist pads. Worried about carpal tunnel syndrome? A wrist pad, a long rectangular pad that stretches beside the keyboard of your PC, can take some of the pressure off your wrists as you type, which in the long run means healthier hand and wrist muscles.

BONUS

Back Up the Easy Way

Backing up your files is one of the most important care and feeding tips you can follow. When you back up your files, you can also archive the ones you don't need, thereby freeing up more space on your hard disk and making your files easier to navigate.

Seagate Backup is a program that can handle backups for you. Whether you save to disk or to a tape backup unit, Seagate Backup leads you through the process step by step.

Summary

This chapter focused on some practical how-to tips for keeping your PC healthy and functioning. With just a small investment in time and effort, you can make sure you're getting the most out of your PC and are set to take care of disaster if it occurs.

The next chapter helps you solve more common PC problems.

Some Web Sites to Hit

WEB PATH

An Ounce of Prevention Computer Services:
http://www.anounce.bc.ca

TechTools:
http://techweb4.web.cerf.net/tools/utilities/utilties5.html

CHAPTER EIGHTEEN
PC PROBLEM SOLVING

IN THIS CHAPTER YOU LEARN THESE KEY SKILLS

PREVENT COMMON PC POTHOLES   PAGE 231

HANDLE HARDWARE HEADACHES   PAGE 236

SURVIVE SOFTWARE STRUGGLES   PAGE 236

KNOW WHAT TO TELL TECHNICAL SUPPORT BEFORE YOU CALL   PAGE 237

GET THE BEST PC ADVICE   PAGE 238

In a perfect world, we wouldn't need a chapter on PC troubleshooting. Everything would work correctly all the time. There would be no such thing as an error message. Disks would never fail, and RAM would never max out. Until we reach that PC utopia, however, we've got some hard realities to deal with. Things break. Disks die. And sometimes, for no good reason, error messages arise to haunt us. This chapter focuses on those unfortunate—but fortunately infrequent—computer happenings.

Ten Common PC Potholes

Some problems are common to everyone at some point or another. Things like dwindling RAM, lockups, printers that don't print, and modems that don't dial plague us all from time to time. The following are a few of the most common PC maladies.

Problem: Low on RAM
Solution: Upgrade the amount of memory in your PC or close some applications

Running short on memory can cause your computer to do lots of things it wouldn't ordinarily do. Programs stop working. Images freeze on your screen. Buttons just sit there after you click them.

What can you do to correct the problem? In the short-term, close some of the programs you are running. In the long-term, consider adding more memory. Your local computer store has information on how you can upgrade the memory in your computer and how much it's going to cost you. You can add the memory yourself, if you're ready for a technical adventure, but for a minimal extra cost, having a technician do it and guarantee it works is one less thing you have to worry about.

Problem: Out of disk space
Solution: Get a larger hard disk or add a larger storage device to your computer setup, such as a Zip or tape drive

When your hard disk is getting pressed for space, you'll find that things you ordinarily accomplish effortlessly, such as saving a file, copying a file, or downloading a file, become impossible. At first your system slows down, and then you get an error message saying the operation cannot be completed.

Your only real answer to maxing out your hard disk is to get more hard disk space. You can do this one of three ways. You can clean your hard disk, removing all old files and programs you no longer need; you can compress the data on your disk to get more room from the same amount of space; or you can get a larger hard disk.

The best and safest answer is a combination of cleaning off what you don't need and adding more storage. Although some PC users are happy using disk compression, in general it tends to present more problems than it solves. Your machine may run slowly, and you risk losing data if your compression utility has problems.

Problem: S l o w PC
Solution: Your computer may be running low on memory; check your memory resources and upgrade if necessary

The first step in resolving memory trouble is making sure you've closed all programs except the one you are currently working with. This may require disabling any programs that load automatically. (Check your Startup window if you're using Windows, or your AUTOEXEC.BAT file if you're using DOS, to see what programs, if any, are loaded automatically.)

SIDE TRIP

HAVE YOU CHECKED THE OBVIOUS?

* Is the computer plugged in?
* Is the keyboard connected to the system unit?
* Is the monitor turned on?
* Is everything connected?
* Did you flip the wall switch?
* Does the outlet work?

Problem: Dead Disk

Solution: Attempt to recover the files on the disk or reformat the disk

If you get an error when trying to save a file or read a file, there may be something wrong with the disk. You can run a diagnostic program on the disk (Norton's Disk Doctor has a great utility for this, and ScanDisk is included with Windows 95) to see what's wrong, or you can simply reformat the disk and start over. Only reformat if you know you don't need the data on the disk. If there's something you need on there, attempt to recover the data using a recover utility instead.

We're talking about floppy disks here; a hard disk is a disk of a different matter. Formatting a hard disk wipes away all the programs and data files stored there, including all your directories and subdirectories (or folders and subfolders), all the utilities, and everything else. Never format a hard disk unless you've tried absolutely everything else and are still having problems. And even if you feel it's warranted, talk to a technical support person first and investigate other options, including saving whatever data you can before the reformat.

TIP Popular utilities for checking and repairing disks are found in programs such as Norton Utilities, PC Tools, and First Aid 95.

Problem: Lockup!

Solution: Reboot (have your startup disk handy); run ScanDisk and DiskDefragmenter

When your system is seriously low on system resources, RAM, or disk storage space, your system is in danger of lockup. If you haven't experienced this yet, you'll know it when it happens. Your system simply freezes. You won't be able to open menus, click buttons, click the close box, or do anything else. You can press Ctrl+Alt+Del to reboot your computer, but inevitably you will lose any unsaved data in your file.

If you are using Windows 95, pressing Ctrl+Alt+Del brings up a warning screen that gives you the option of waiting 20 seconds to see whether the system stabilizes. If the system does not stabilize, which means it remains locked, you can click the End Task button in the dialog box and then try closing tasks one by one in the dialog box displayed. If and when your system unlocks, close all remaining programs and shut down your computer. Count to 10 before restarting. And keep an eye on the number of programs you run at any one time to keep the RAM usage as low as possible.

Problem: Goofy files
Solution: Make sure you are using a file format that's right for your software

One of the more confusing things about PCs, although it's getting better, is that not all files work with all programs. It's very possible that one day you'll open a file and find a bunch of goofy-looking characters. Just because a program enables you to work with text, for example, doesn't mean that every program that works with text will be able to read that file. If you have downloaded a file from the Internet, opened a file created in another program, or tried to view an e-mail message using your regular word processor, you might see strange characters and very little real text in there. Pay close attention to the last three characters, the *extension,* in the filename, and try to save files in your word processor's standard format whenever possible.

TIP Some files are zipped or encoded. A zipped file, a file that's been compressed with the file utility PKZIP or WinZip, needs to be unzipped before you can use it. An encoded file, such as those often sent over the Internet, needs to be decoded before it can be viewed. You can get utilities such as PKZIP and Xfer Pro by using an Internet search to locate them and download them to your computer.

Problem: No modem, no sound, no nothing
Solution: If you're running Windows, check out the Control Panel and find out what Windows sees

Especially when you first add an item to your computer, such as a sound board, a new modem, or a new trackball, the risk that things won't work the way you expect them to runs pretty high. This was particularly true with PCs before Windows 95. Windows 95 includes what's called Plug-and-Play technology, which means that if the device you're adding is Plug-and-Play compliant, it will install its drivers directly into Windows 95 so the operating system knows what you've added as soon as you've added it.

If you're having trouble with a device you've recently added to Windows 95, open the Control Panel, choose the System icon, and select the Device Manager tab. You'll be able to see what devices Windows 95 sees as installed on your system and perform tests to see what's responding and what isn't.

Problem: Huge files
Solution: Compress or zip files before moving, copying, or sending them over the Internet

With the blossoming popularity of multimedia, files aren't getting any smaller. It's not unusual for files with video clips, sound bites, and high-quality photos to be more than 1MB apiece. The only answer is to compress the data in some fashion. One method is to use PKZIP to compress the files before you copy them to disk or transmit them. Another method—and one that many multimedia professionals choose—is a portable hard disk or a Zip drive, which enables you to store files on 100MB disks and move them from system to system as needed.

Problem: Error messages
Solution: First write down the error message and what you were doing when you got it; then exit the program, if possible, or reboot

Error messages appear most often because of low system resources. You might also hit an error message when you've found a bug in the program, when you've tried to perform an "illegal operation," or when too many operations are piling up on the processor. There's not much you can do except whatever the error message tells you to do (which is usually just click OK); but first, write down the error message and make a note of whatever you were trying to do. That way, if this message repeats itself later, you'll have more evidence to lay on the technical support staff.

Problem: The printer isn't printing
Solution: Check all the connections; make sure the printer has paper, is turned on, and is online

The first few times you print may test your patience, or your file may print correctly from the start. If you send a file to the printer and nothing's happening, first check to make sure your computer is connected by cable to the printer, that the printer is plugged in, and that the printer has paper. Also make sure the printer doesn't have a paper jam. If the printer is a laser printer, you should see a flashing light indicating that data is being sent to the printer. If the printer is a dot-matrix printer, you need to make sure the printer is online and ready to receive data.

If you are using Windows, open the Print Manager and see whether the printing has been paused. If so, click the Resume button to continue printing. You can also cancel printing, turn off your printer, wait several seconds, and turn the printer on again. Now try printing a second time.

Hardware Headaches

When hardware goes south for the winter, it's a pretty big deal. A dead hard disk is a major tragedy. (Backup! Backup! Backup!) A fried monitor (they don't like water), a gummed-up mouse, and a keyboard dropping characters are nothing to be ecstatic about, either. This section provides you with a few lists of common causes, solutions, and preventions you can practice to ward off the evil hardware spirits.

Common causes of hardware headaches:

Unplugged connectors

Use and abuse

Drops, bangs, and bumps

Symptoms to watch for:

Erratic acts

Squeaks and beeps

If you have to hit it to make it work

Ways you can prolong your hardware life:

Treat it gently

Eat your cookies away from the keyboard

Have it serviced at least every 12 to 15 months

Don't move it around a lot

Make sure the environment is as hazard-free as possible

Software Struggles

Software gives a whole different set of struggles to deal with. When something goes wrong with a program, it may not be as obvious as a hardware problem. You may get an error here, or hit a program glitch there. At times, you may have major problems — like the thing just won't start or won't let you exit.

Common causes of software struggles:

Not enough RAM

Dwindling storage space

Incompatible program versions

Software with problems (bugs)

Viruses (not common, but something to watch for)

Operator error (not *you*, someone else who uses the computer)

Symptoms to watch for:

Slow response times

Menus not opening when you click them

Screen colors that change for no reason

File-saving procedures that take forever

Error messages

Ways you can live happily with your software:

Know what to tell your tech-support person

Learn how the program *should* behave

Make sure your PC has enough RAM to run the program

Clean all unnecessary files off your hard disk

What You Need to Tell Tech Support

Calling technical support is something few people really love to do. You often spend 30 minutes on hold (and not always on their dime) and may have to pay in the neighborhood of $35 to ask a single question.

Most hardware and software manufacturers, thankfully, are not relying on their technical support department for the lion's share of their income. You get a certain amount of free support (usually 60 or 90 days from your first tech support call) after you purchase a new device or program.

Still, when you call, you want to have the following information ready to tell the technical support person:

- The software you are using
- The software serial number (if you're calling with a software problem)
- The type of PC you are using
- The amount of RAM your system has
- How much disk storage is available
- What type of modem (speed and type)
- What you were trying to do when the problem occurred
- What you tried, if anything, to fix the problem without success

TIP Many people find the help they need online in user forums related to the computer devices or software they've purchased. You can search through a library of messages related to your question or pose your question in an e-mail message to the forum *sysop* (that's *system operator*, the leader of the forum). You will find help forums for all the major hardware and software vendors on your favorite online services, including CompuServe, America Online, and The Microsoft Network.

The Best Troubleshooting Advice Ever

Common sense, as they say, isn't all that common. But as you continue working with your PC, keep five simple ideas in mind to help keep cool in the face of PC pandemonium:

Know that problems will happen occasionally. They will. Just when you need that printout *now*, the printer jams. When you are minutes away from the deadline, your modem will stop working and you won't be able to send the file. It won't happen often, but it *will* happen.

Solve the problems you can before they happen. Some things you can anticipate and avoid before they happen. You know you're asking for trouble if you try to run Windows 95 on a computer with only 4MB of RAM. You can avoid that by getting more RAM installed on your system or by not using Windows 95.

Have a system in place to deal with the problems you can't. Make sure you've got a boot disk to start your PC if it crashes, and know where you can use other options, if necessary. Can you hook up to a coworker's printer? Is there another system you can use to send that file? In any event, you still need to get the primary PC fixed, but having another plan to get you past a crisis moment can be a great stress reliever.

Always have a backup. Make sure you follow a routine; every week or two, back up all files that have changed. That way, in the unhappy event that your hard disk goes south, you have your data saved safely away.

Don't wander too far away from your nearest tech-support contact. Know when to throw in the towel and contact the experts. If you're on the road, make sure you've got tech-support numbers tucked away somewhere in your briefcase so you can get to them even if your system is down. If you rely heavily on your technical-support person, find out about different support plans and choose one that fits the amount of time you need and the amount you want to pay.

BONUS

First Aid 95

Your computer is so smart it should be able to fix its own problems, right? That's what CyberMedia hopes you'll think if you've got their program, First Aid 95. This program works with Windows 95 and anticipates and circumvents crashes and lockups. It also kick-starts your PC when you can't get the thing booted, restores your previous window configurations after a crash, and links you to the Web sites of software you have installed on your PC. First Aid 95 is available through most mail-order companies.

Summary

This chapter gave you a glimpse of the different types of problems you may have during your PC work sessions. You learned about a few common problems, and what to do about hardware and software troubles. Rest assured that you will run into more than these, but the answers are out there. Think through your technical support options so you'll know whom to call when PC calamity strikes.

This chapter winds up *Discover PCs*. Following this, you'll find an appendix of helpful commercial online forums and Web sites, and how to reach them. Now we're ready to push you out of the nest to continue discovering on your own.

Remember, the PC is a tool—a great tool, but only a tool. The *real* magic is in your imagination.

Some Web Sites to Hit

Hard Drive Data Recovery & Repair Center:
http://fox.nstn.ca/~nstn2879/repair.html

Willow Pond Multimedia Garage:
http://www.willowpond.com

Microsoft (to contact technical support):
http://www.microsoft.com

IBM Computer (to contact technical support):
http://www.pc.ibm.com.com

DISCOVERY CENTER

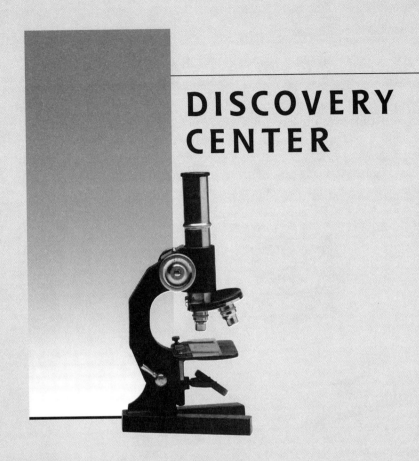

The Discovery Center serves as a handy reference to the most important topics discussed in this book. There is a lot of information spread throughout *Discover PCs*: buying and setting up your computer; understanding the system unit, keyboard, and mouse; using modems and monitors; deciding which programs to get; traveling with your computer; getting on the Internet; and troubleshooting your computer.

For this reason, the most important information about these topics has been distilled from each chapter into the following pages. Also included are pet peeves you might encounter as you begin to work more closely with personal computers, followed by solutions to the problems. Although the Discovery Center is self-contained, we've provided page numbers to steer you to the relevant parts of the book where you can get more details about each subject.

CHAPTER 1

Welcome to the Personal Computer (page 10)

Such a small contraption, and such potential power. Don't let it intimidate you. The personal computer on your desk, or on the kitchen table, or still sitting on the store shelf — it's your personal link to an easier life in which letters get written without spelling errors, checkbooks balance, numbers add up, and mailing labels print almost without any effort at all.

PCs Make Your Personal World More Powerful (page 11)

Whether you plan to use your computer for home, business, school, or all three, the personal computer gives you access to thousands of programs that will help you learn, explore, and perform tasks.

PCs Make Experiencing the World More Personal (page 12)

If your PC is equipped with a modem, you can literally reach around the world through your phone lines, trading e-mail with users all over the globe and visiting university libraries, museums, and more from cultures near and far.

PC Peeve

"The hardest thing about getting started with my computer was making the purchase. I put it off for a long time, saying I wanted to save the money until I absolutely needed it. Now I can't believe we waited so long. I wish I'd started using PCs a long time ago!"

Don't wait unnecessarily to buy your computer. If you don't think you have much use for a PC, you haven't read this book carefully enough.

CHAPTER 2

What You Need to Know Before You Buy (page 22)

Some of us inherit our PCs from friends, relatives, or coworkers who have moved on to a more powerful system. The rest of us are in a position to make an educated decision about the PCs we purchase. The most important things you need to know about the computer you purchase are:

* What programs do you need to run?
* What computers do you need to trade files with?
* What do you like?

New System, Used System, Leased System (page 30)

A system that's new to you doesn't necessarily mean never-been-used new. You can buy the PC right off the Wal-Mart shelf or you can order one from a mail-order house. Other options include purchasing used systems from a used computer store (be sure to ask about a warranty) or leasing a system for a certain period and then buying it outright or trading it in on another system. (Or you could always run next door and use your neighbor's — no, bad idea.)

PC Peeve

"I'm drowning in details! I don't know which features I've *got* to have and which features just would be *nice* to have. How do I find out what's important and then choose a computer I'll be happy with?"

Any amount of time you spend educating yourself about the computer you eventually choose will be time well invested. Read PC reviews in magazines. Go to the stores and try using different systems. Arm yourself with information and you'll be more likely to make the best decision for your needs.

CHAPTER 3

When You Need a Desktop Computer (page 37)

* You plan to work only at your desk
* You want a full-sized keyboard
* You are impressed by PC size
* You want a larger monitor than a notebook has to offer
* You plan to add a number of peripherals, including a printer, a modem, a CD-ROM, and more
* You prefer comfort to portability

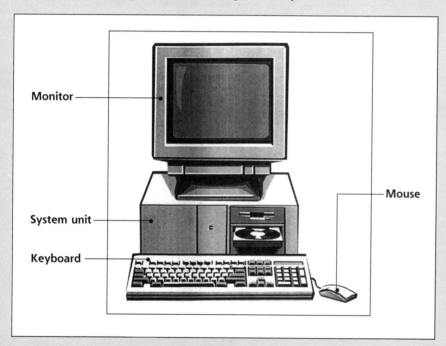

When You Should Get a Notebook Computer (page 41)

* You need computing power on the run
* You plan to use your notebook part time

* You don't want to give up valuable desk space to a full-sized system
* You would benefit from being able to move your computer easily

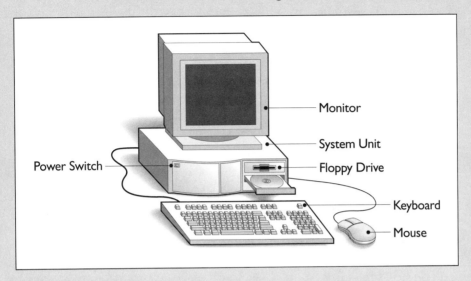

PC Peeve

"I inherited a notebook computer from a coworker that I use on my desktop. The only problem is that I can't get used to the small screen."

Get another monitor to plug into your notebook for those times when you want to use the notebook as a desktop system.

CHAPTER 4

What Makes Up the System Unit? (page 50)

The *system unit* is the power center of your PC. It's here that all the data crunching goes on. When you click the mouse and type at the keyboard, those actions are interpreted and processed by your computer's brain, the microprocessor, which is housed inside the system unit.

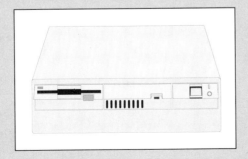

The Microprocessor (page 53)

The microprocessor is a single computer chip that does all the processing. Your microprocessor might be a 386, a 486, or a Pentium processor.

Peripherals (page 53)

When you add items to your system — such as a modem, mouse, printer, and so on — the service technician adds a board for that item inside the system unit. This board enables the hardware to work with the rest of the system.

Power Switch (page 59)

The power switch is no surprise: It turns the system on and off. Remember to save your files and exit any open programs before you turn your computer off.

PC Peeve

"Once I let my three-year-old put a disk in the drive, and now he wants to do it all the time. I've pulled everything from business cards to Post-It notes out of the drive slot."

Don't let your young children play with your disk drive. Would you let them play with your stereo?

CHAPTER 5

The Lowdown on Disk Drives (page 64)

Drives are all about storage. Storing programs. Storing files. Moving files from one place to another. Loading files into your machine. Taking files off your machine.

Three different storage devices are called *drives:* floppy disk drives, hard disk drives, and CD-ROM drives. (Two other types of drives are tape drives and CD-R drives. They are helpful for more professional storage uses.)

Floppy Disk Drive (page 67)

The floppy disk drive lets you store programs and files on disks that you insert in the drive. The great thing about having a floppy disk drive is how easily you can move files from one computer to another.

Hard Disk Drive (page 69)

The hard disk drive enables you to store a greater amount of data, many times that of a floppy disk. The hard disk is enclosed within the system unit.

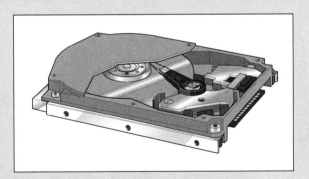

CD-ROM Drive (page 71)

A CD-ROM gives you the benefit of accessing mega volumes of data, but you can't store files on it the way you can on a disk.

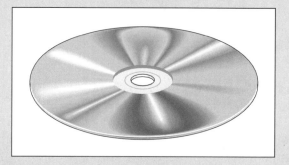

PC Peeve

"I'm tired of getting the 'Insufficient disk space' message when I try to copy a group of files to a disk."

Compress files before copying them if they are large or if you're trying to put a bunch of files on a single floppy disk.

CHAPTER 6

The Computer Monitor (page 77)

Without a monitor, your computer wouldn't be worth much. You wouldn't see what was going on. You could still click the mouse and type at the keyboard, but what would the point be? The monitor is your window to your work.

The Video Adapter (page 78)

The video adapter is the card that plugs into the motherboard of your system and controls the video data sent to the monitor. Common video adapters are VGA and SuperVGA.

Monitor Component	Function
Dot pitch	Affects the quality of the display; the smaller the dot pitch, the sharper the screen image
Pixel	A single dot on the video display
Resolution	Number of pixels used to produce the display, which affects the quality, or sharpness, of the screen
Video RAM	Memory included on the display adapter to help speed up video display

PC Peeve

"I sit with my back to an outside window, and every time the light changes, I've got to readjust the brightness control on my monitor."

Get good blinds and indirect lighting.

CHAPTER 7

The Standard Keyboard (page 85)

The keyboard is one of the first parts of your PC you'll become actively involved with. It is also one of the least threatening. If you've ever used a typewriter, a calculator, or a touch-tone phone, you can figure out a keyboard.

The standard keyboard is a relatively complete set of *alphanumeric keys* (that's letters and numbers), along with punctuation keys, cursor keys, and perhaps a separate keypad for entering numbers.

The Notebook Keyboard (page 87)

The notebook keyboard is substantially smaller than the standard keyboard included with a desktop system. The cursor keys and function keys are combined. Another space saver: no separate numeric keypad. Sorry, you'll have to use the row of numbers just below the function keys.

PC Peeve

"My husband eats Doritos while he works at the computer and gets crumbs between the keys. Every so often the keys jam and I have to take the keyboard in for repair."

Two possible solutions: Retrain your husband to eat away from the keyboard (which may or may not be possible — M&Ms are my weakness), or periodically hold the keyboard upside down (preferably over his head) and lightly shake the crumbs out. If that doesn't work, you can (carefully) use a vacuum cleaner (put on the attachments first!) or unplug the keyboard and use a Q-tip dipped in isopropyl alcohol to clean between the keys.

CHAPTER 8

The Mouse (page 98)

Here's a mouse that will be welcome in your house. The mouse is a small handheld pointing device that enables you to move the pointer around on the screen and easily select folders, files, and programs.

The Trackball (page 104)

The trackball is also a pointing device but you don't move it around on the desktop like you do the mouse. With the trackball, you move the ball itself to move the pointer on the screen.

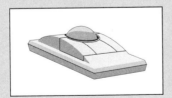

The Touchpad (page 106)

The touchpad is a touch-sensitive panel hooked up to your PC that enables you to point at the item you want by pointing to the corresponding area of the touchpad.

PC Peeve

"I hate it when I move the mouse and the cursor stands still on the screen. Sometimes I have to bang the mouse on the table to get it to respond."

Clean the mouse's trackball, check the cable connection, or get a better mouse if the problem persists.

CHAPTER 9

The Printer (page 110)

You use your PC's printer to print letters, memos, budgets, newsletters, checks, mailing labels, and all sorts of other things. The type of printer you select depends on the quality of printout you need and the amount you are willing to spend. There are many different printer types to choose from, and many good printers are available at a low cost.

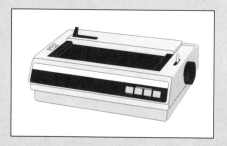 

Print Quality (page 111)

You won't need high-quality print for all your documents. Some printers give you readable but not great text:

```
This text is readable but not necessarily high-print quality
```

Other printers give you letters that rival professionally printed text:

High-quality text, which is easy on the eye but not necessarily the wallet, offers sharply defined characters

PC Peeve

"I always forget which side of the stationery goes in first when I'm printing letters on my laser printer. Invariably, the letter is printed on the wrong side!"

Write an *X* on the back of a piece of regular paper and then print a sample letter. When the printer outputs the letter, make a note of which side the *X* was on. You can even go so far as to tape "front down, top first" on a Post-it note on the back of your printer, so when you forget next time you're one step ahead of the game.

CHAPTER 10

The Modem (page 125)

It's hard to believe that something so small and inexpensive inside (or outside) your system unit can link you to computers across the world. Your modem translates your data into audio signals and the modem on the receiving end does the reverse. Voilà — telecommunications!

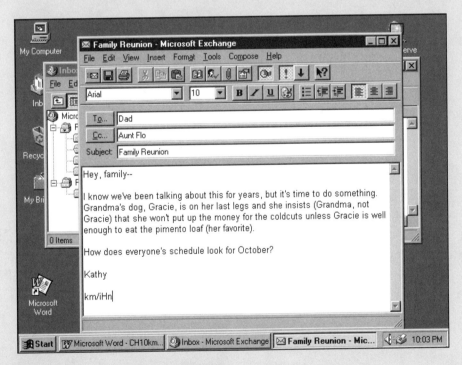

What's a Fax/modem? (page 131)

You know what a fax is, and now you know what a modem is. Mix both talents together in the same PC board and you've got a fax/modem.

DISCOVERY CENTER **253**

> **PC Peeve**

"Downloading programs with a modem that's too slow!"

Get a faster modem. Today's standard is 28,800 baud. Tomorrow's will undoubtedly be faster.

CHAPTER 11

The Scanner (page 134)

If you've been wanting to find some way to turn those photos into files you can use on your PC, you're in luck. A scanner will do the job. A scanner does just what its name implies — scans a document, photo, drawing, whatever — and turns it into an electronic file you can use in your PC programs.

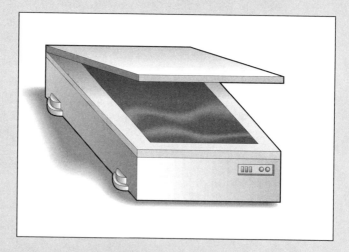

The Graphics Tablet (page 137)

If you're artistically inclined, you'll love a graphics tablet. Although a mouse makes an awkward drawing tool, a graphics tablet is an electronic device based on the old pen-and-paper idea, which makes it easy to preserve all your doodles and designs.

The MIDI Keyboard (page 138)

Set the composer in you free to write, record, and annotate music right on your PC. If your computer has a sound board and you've got a MIDI cable and a MIDI-equipped keyboard, you can play music on your PC.

PC Peeve

"I've got too many peripherals and not enough ports to plug them into."

Unfortunately, PCs have only so many ports for expansion. Make sure you've got the most important items connected. You may wind up getting a backup system for the others!

CHAPTER 12

This, too, could be yours . . . (page 144)

Functional yet inviting. Space-saving yet roomy. Sound like a home infomercial? It could be your office if you plan it right. Get out that paper and pen. Make a few sketches. You don't have to be a Frank Lloyd Wright — just put some thought into how you want your workspace designed before you move in and start typing.

A Few Things to Think About (page 145)

When planning your space, think about the following:

- Where the light comes from
- What type of lighting is available
- Which side of the system your mouse is on
- How much room you need for the system unit, keyboard, and room for opening a front-loading CD-ROM drive
- Where the printer goes
- What kind of power supply you have (quantity of outlets and quality — is it spike-protected?)
- How far the cables reach
- Where you can sit comfortably
- Where you are either protected from or accessible to the kids (or pets)

PC Peeve

"I run my small business from a corner of my dining room, and boy, am I cramped! I have to move the keyboard just to free up enough desktop space so I can move the mouse or write something out by hand."

Get a keyboard drawer to attach underneath your desk or table that lets you slide the keyboard out of the way when you're not using it. It's inexpensive, easy to assemble, and can add much-needed space (more breathing room) to your small office space.

CHAPTER 13

Somewhere inside the mysterious workings of your computer system, the operating system performs its vital tasks. Without an operating system, you wouldn't see the Windows desktop when you powered up your computer. Without the operating system, you wouldn't be able to find out what's on a disk, start a program, or work with files. The operating system basically tells the microprocessor how to carry out the tasks you want done.

The operating system bridges the gap between the programs you use and your PC. It includes the user interface, which gives a common look and feel to all the disk and file procedures you perform.

Duties of the Operating System (page 152)

- Gets in touch with the keyboard, mouse, disk drives, and screen
- Parcels out your computer's RAM so your programs can run
- Loads programs into memory when you start them
- Saves files
- Opens files
- Deletes files
- Renames files
- Determines where to save files to disk
- Prints files
- Takes care of multitasking

OS Terminology (page 156)

Operating system: The software that works behind the scenes to communicate the commands to your PC hardware and coordinate activities in the programs you run. Examples: MS-DOS, Windows 95, System 7 (Macintosh), UNIX, OS/2, and Windows NT (for networked, rather than stand-alone, PCs).

Operating environment: Versions of Windows or Windows-like programs available before Windows 95 that relied on DOS to perform the functions of the full operating system. Also called a *graphical user interface*.

User interface: The portion of the operating system that controls the way the user interacts with the computer. The Windows 95 interface includes the Taskbar, the program and group folders, and the cascading menus. Also called a *shell*.

Multitasking: The ability of the operating system to run multiple tasks simultaneously. The operating system controls the processing so that each active program gets the focus it needs to continue operating smoothly.

CHAPTER 14

Do Something! (page 167)

You purchased this PC with a goal in mind. You wanted to do something: print letters, organize recipes, surf the Internet, write your congressperson, balance your checkbook, control and maintain your client list, and so on.

The part of the computer equation that enables you to *do* whatever it is you want to do is the software. You may use one program all the time or you may use many, depending on your needs. And, depending on the PC you've purchased and how much RAM and disk storage it's got, you may be able to use several at the same time.

Suites for the Sweet (page 168)

The software suite is the Swiss Army knife of the software industry. Designed with the idea that you can get everything you need (or close to it) in one set of programs, the software suite includes several powerful applications that can easily share features and data and are packaged neatly together in one bundle. Microsoft Office is one extremely successful software suite, including word-processing, spreadsheet, database, presentation graphics, and communications programs. Other popular suites include Lotus SmartSuite and WordPerfect Suite 7, by Corel. Low-end suites — often called *integrated packages* — include Microsoft Works and ClarisWorks.

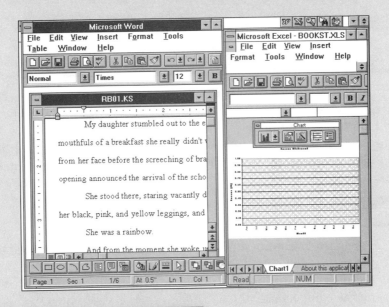

Ready, Set, Install! (page 187)

Installing a program is a scary undertaking if you've never done it before. But it's simply the process of getting the program files you need on your hard disk so you can run the program you have purchased. You may have purchased your computer with the programs already installed, but sooner or later you'll have to install something yourself. Just make sure you've backed up important files on your compute and have enough storage space to install the new program; then take a deep breath and follow the installation instructions included with your software.

PC Peeve

"Whenever I try to call the technical support number for the software I've purchased, I get stuck in their automated phone system for an hour. How can I get answers to my questions without sitting on hold forever?"

There are a few tricks to reaching some technical support departments. Don't call before 10 A.M. or between 3 and 6 P.M. — those are the busiest times of the day. If the support line is open after normal working hours, call late. Another option is to search online for your software program and find support groups and technical support forums on services like CompuServe, the Microsoft Network, and America Online. You could also buy a product-specific book from IDG Books!

CHAPTER 15

Your PC: You Can Take It with You! (page 195)

Picture this: You've got an opportunity to turn in a bid on a project that could really get your small business moving. You plan a meeting with two other entrepreneurs to discuss the best way to approach the bid. You know the ideas are going to be flying hot and heavy. You can take your legal pad and your ballpoint pen and hope that you'll be able to read your scrawled notes later, or you can take your PC and type in the ideas as soon as they are born.

Portable Computing (page 195)

Several important changes in the world of computers have made portable computing popular. The size of the computer is one of the most important issues. If you can imagine carrying a full-sized desktop PC through an airport, you'll appreciate the convenience notebook computers have to offer. Small enough to fit in the average briefcase, a notebook computer doesn't weigh you down. Equipped with a modem, it gives you access to both computing power and up-to-the-minute messages at a moment's notice.

PC Peeve

"Whenever I travel with my PC, I'm concerned about the X-ray machine zapping the data on my disks."

At the security checkpoints in airports, ask the attendant to check your computer case without sliding it through the X-ray machine. Even though X rays aren't likely to harm your data, it's better to be safe than sorry. Airport security will check all the pockets in your PC case, too, so save yourself some hassle by using those pockets only for essentials that you can remove and put back easily.

CHAPTER 16

Internet Basics (page 206)

The Internet is not only a network, it is a world-wide network of networks. Using the Internet is no more threatening than using any computer program, but once you're on the Internet, you can perform searches, participate in conversations, play games with users literally across the world, and much, much more.

World Wide Web (page 215)

The World Wide Web puts a friendly face on the Internet. Using a series of links that you activate by clicking, you can move from one Web page to another, browsing through pages or using search tools to locate a specific topic. Web pages are visually inviting and easy to use — you simply point and click your way through cyberspace.

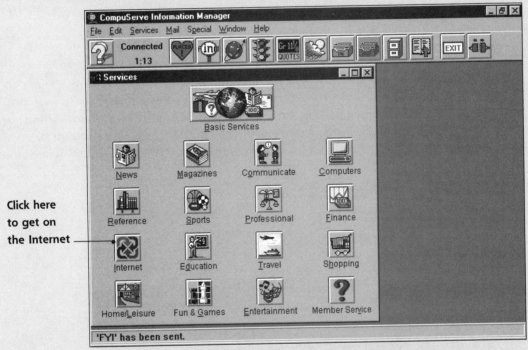

Click here to get on the Internet

What Can You Do on the Internet? (page 211)

* Send e-mail to a friend
* Search for information for your dissertation
* Join a newsgroup on your favorite topic
* Buy a new car (really!)

DISCOVERY CENTER

- Get help with a troublesome software program
- Chat with people who have similar interests
- Play games by yourself or with others
- Download programs and files of video, music, fonts, clip art, and more

PC Peeve

"I'm confused by the number of options available. What's better, an online service or a direct account with an Internet provider?"

The answer depends on what you want to do. An account with an Internet provider gives you a greater number of hours for a smaller charge, and provides local access so you don't have long distance charges. However, you won't get the range of forums and services available in one friendly package as you will with an online service.

CHAPTER 17

Caring for Your PC (page 223)

If you're the type of person who kicks vending machines, you've got some relearning to do. PCs don't like thumps. They're sensitive to sudden power outages, cat hair, magnetic fields, and poor air circulation. When you write that check and take the PC home, you're starting a relationship with a major piece of equipment that will work well for you for a long time to come if you follow some basic guidelines for keeping it healthy and happy.

General Tips (page 228)

- Send in your warranty card
- Know your tech support phone number
- Backup your important files regularly
- Use a virus checker program to make sure your files are safe

PC Environmental Hazards (page 225)

- Dust
- Magnetic fields
- Drinks
- Crumbs
- Static electricity

PC Peeve

"I don't have a backup utility or a tape drive and I don't usually remember to make copies of important files. I know someday my data will get fried and I won't have a backup."

Backup utilities are really inexpensive (some are available as freeware or shareware on the Internet). You don't have to have a tape backup unit in order to do regular backups. Just copy out the important work files to floppy disk until you put a more formal backup routine in place. Get yourself in the habit of backing up the files by doing it the same time each week, such as just before you stop work on Friday afternoon.

CHAPTER 18

How to Sleuth Out a Problem (page 232)

1. Describe the problem.
2. Write out any error messages that appeared.
3. What were you doing when the problem occurred?
4. How much RAM does you PC have?
5. How much disk storage is available?
6. Is the problem related to a program you were using or to the operating system?

What to Do When Your System Acts Strangely (page 236)

1. Save your file immediately.
2. Close any open programs.
3. If you're using Windows 3.x, exit to DOS; if you're using Windows 95, select Start → Shut Down.
4. Turn off your computer.
5. Wait ten seconds before restarting your computer.

Tech Support Web Sites to Know and Love

Apple   http://www.apple.com
Borland   http://www.borland.com
Claris   http://www.claris.com

Compaq	http://www.compaq.com
Corel	http://www.corel.com
Dell	http://www.us.dell.com
IBM	http://www.ibm.com/
Intel	http://www.intel.com/
Lotus	http://www.lotus.com
Microsoft	http://www.microsoft.com
NEC	http://www.nec.com/
Netscape	http://www.home.netscape.com
Packard Bell	http://www.packardbell.com/index.html
Toshiba	http://www.toshiba.com

PC Peeve

"My computer never has the same problem twice!"

If you keep having continual trouble and all the problems are different, your PC may need a general cleaning. Remove all unnecessary files from your hard disk, run ScanDisk to check for errors, and use Disk Defragmenter to organize the data. If that doesn't clear things up, use a virus scan utility to make sure there aren't any bugs lurking around in there playing hide and seek.

INDEX

A

accessing the Internet, 207-210
  commercial online services, 208-209
  Internet Service Providers, 209-210
  modem speed, 208
accessing the World Wide Web, 215-216
AC current, international travel with PCs, 201
Activa, 212
active matrix screens, 17, 27, 82
add-on touchpads, 106
addresses
  e-mail, 214
  Web sites. *See* Web site addresses
Addresso keyboards, 87
advertisements, reading carefully, 15-18
alphanumeric keys, 89
Alps Enhanced Windows 95 keyboard, 88
ALT key, 92
America Online, 177
anti-virus utilities, 187
aperture grille pitch, 80
Apple computers
  Apple Newton Message Pad, 41
  peripherals, 42
application software, 154
ARPANET, 207
arrow keys, 90

AUTOEXEC.BAT file, 153, 162, 164
auto-execute files, 158, 164
automated voice-mail, 12

B

backing up
  files, 6, 229
  software, 228
  tape backup units, 66
backslash (\) key, 93
Basic Input/Output System. *See* BIOS (Basic Input/Output System)
batch files, 158, 164
batteries, 60
  testing life, 201
baud rate, 124
Better Photography: Learning to See Creatively, 185
BIOS (Basic Input/Output System), 52-53, 155
  definition, 51
  startup, 152
bits, 66
boot process, 152
breaks, importance, 228
business cards, printing, 120-121
business uses of PCs, 11-12
bus mouse connector, 98-99
buttons
  mice, 99
  trackballs, 105

265

buying PCs, 2
    compatibility issues, 23-24
    expansion capability, 24
    memory amount, 28
    preferences to consider, 25-28
    questions to ask, 31
    reading advertisements, 15-18
    software considerations, 23
    where to buy, 2, 29-30
bytes, 66

C

cables, 148
    care, 225, 227
cable ties, 148
CAD (computer aided design) programs, 179
call-waiting, modem use, 131
cameras, digital, 136-137
CAPSLOCK key, 92
cards, 51, 57-58
carpal tunnel syndrome, 94
cartridges, printers, 115, 120
CD caddies, 72
CD-R drives, 44, 64, 71-72
CD-ROM drives, 43-44, 64, 66, 71-73
    costs, 44
    definition, 51
    desktop computers, 37
    options, 72
    speed, 44, 72
    uses, 17
    working of, 72-73
cellular phones, 200
chairs, 145, 228
chat rooms, 124
children, Internet use, 212-213
chips. *See* microprocessors; RAM (random-access memory)
circulation, 225

Cirque GlidePoint Desktop touchpad, 106
Cirque keyboards, 87
CIS:Mail, 130
ClarisWorks, 169, 172
cleaning supplies, 226
clicking, 100, 101
clip art programs, 178
clip-on trackballs, 105
color graphics adapter (CGA) monitors, 81
color monitors, 79
commercial online services. *See* online services
communications software, 176-177
compatibility
    hardware, 23, 24
    software, 24
COM ports, 58, 99
CompuServe, 126, 177, 208
computer aided design (CAD) programs, 179
computer games, 13, 174-176
computer magazines, 19, 30
computers. *See also* desktop computers; notebook computers; PCs
    description, 10-11
Computer Shopper, 30
computer system care, 223-228
    guidelines, 223-224
    keyboard, 225-226
    mice, 226-227
    monitors, 225
    printers, 227
    software, 228
    system unit, 224-225
conferencing, virtual, 124
CONFIG.SYS file, 153, 162, 164
connecting modems, 131
Connectix VideoPhone, 137
Conversions Plus for Windows, 183

converters, electric current, 201
copy clips, 83
copying
    disks, 74
    files, 6
Corel/WEB.DESIGNER, 178
costs
    CD-ROM drives, 44
    chairs, 145
    desks, 150
    desktop computers, 37-38
    ISPs, 209
    keyboards, 26
    laser printers, 117
    modems, 43
    multifunction centers, 118
    notebook computers, 39-40
    printers, 42, 43, 110, 113
    printer supplies, 120
    QuickCam, 137
    scanners, 134, 135
    spreadsheets, 173
    tempered glass filters, 83
    uninterruptible power supplies, 62
    word-processing software, 171
    Zip drives, 75
CTRL key, 92
cursor keys, 90
cyberspace, 124

D

DARPANET, 207
databases, 173-174
data compression, 70-71, 235
Day Timer Organizer 2.0, 182
DC current, international travel with PCs, 201
defragmenting disks, 224
DEL key, 92
demodulation, 124

density, floppy disks, 69
desks, 149-150
desktop computers, 35-38
    advantages, 37
    keyboards, 36, 86
    options, 36-37
    prices, 37-38
desktop publishing programs, 180-181
desktops, organizing software, 192
desktop scanners, 134, 135
device drivers, 152
digital cameras, 136-137
directories, DOS, 158, 159
disk boxes, 45
Disk Defragmenter, 200, 224
disk drives, 52, 63-76
    care, 60
    definition, 51
    desktop computers, 37
    disk densities, 69
    notebook computers, 39
    protecting, 224
    saving files, 64-65
    types, 64, 65-67. *See also* CD-R drives; CD-ROM drives; floppy disks; hard disks
disk maintenance operations, 162
disks. *See also* floppy disks; hard disks
    copying, 74
    erasing, 74-75
    evolution, 14
    formatting, 73, 233
    labeling, 74
    lack of space, 232
display adapters, 77-78, 81
docking stations, 143
DOS, 158-160
    copying disks, 74
    erasing disks, 74
    formatting disks, 73

(continued)

DOS *(continued)*
   function keys, 91
   identifying programs loading
      automatically at startup, 153
   RAM requirement, 164
   shell, 158
   starting programs, 188
   types, 156, 158
   user interface, 153, 154
   Windows 3.1, 155-156, 159-160
   Windows 95, 156, 159-160
dot-matrix printers, 42, 110, 119
   paper, 119
   working of, 112-114
dot pitch, 80
dots-per-inch (dpi), 135
double-clicking, 100, 101
downloading, 124
dragging, 100, 102
drawing programs, 178
drives. *See* CD-R drives; CD-ROM
   drives; disk drives; floppy disks;
   floppy drives; hard disks
DriveSpace, 70
dual-scan screens, 17, 27, 82
DX chips, 53-54

E

ECCO Pro 3.0, 182
educational software, 183-184
educational uses of PCs, 12
edutainment software, 184-185
EGA (enhanced graphics adapter)
   monitors, 81
electrical outlets, international travel
   with PCs, 202
electrical storms, 225
electric current, international travel
   with PCs, 201

electron guns, 78
   refresh rate, 27, 81
e-mail, 125-126, 213-214
   definition, 124
   software, 130, 176
Em@iler, 177
END key, 93
Enhanced graphics adapter (EGA)
   monitors, 81
Enter key, 89-90
environments, operating systems
   compared, 155-156
Erase-Eaze key, 88
erasing disks, 74-75
error messages, 235
   during printing, 6
   while opening files, 6
Escape key, 93
ESC key, 92
Eudora, 176
Eudora Light, 130
Everything Weather, 185
Excel, 172, 173
Exchange, 130, 177, 199, 214
exercise, importance, 228
expansion
   importance, 24
   notebook systems, 40
expansion slots, 18
Extended VGA graphics cards, 81
extensions, 234
external modems, 129
eyestrain, reducing, 83

F

Family PC magazine, 19
fans, 59, 224
FastTrack Schedule, 182
FAT (file allocation table), 67, 73

Fax, 176
fax/modems, 131
fields, 174
file allocation table (FAT), 67, 73
file-compression programs, 70-71, 235
file maintenance operations, 162
files
    AUTOEXEC.BAT, 153, 162, 164
    backing up, 6, 229
    batch, 158
    batch (auto-execute), 158, 164
    CONFIG.SYS, 153, 162, 164
    directories in DOS, 158, 159
    extensions, 234
    huge, 235
    incorrect format, 234
    opening, 6
    saving on disk, 64-65
    spreadsheet, 172
filters, monitors, 83
First Aid 95, 239
flat-bed scanners, 134
floppy disks, 14, 65, 67-69
    damaged, 233
    density, 69
    handling, 68
    importance, 17
    sizes, 64, 67, 68
    3.5-inch, 67-68
    traveling with PCs, 201
FLOWERscape, 185
FocalPoint, 177
font manipulation programs, 179
fonts, 169-170
formatting
    disks, 73, 233
    word-processing software functions, 169-170
forums, 126
Fractal Design painter, 138
FrameMaker, 181

freeware, 187
FrontPage, 178
function keys, 91
functions, spreadsheets, 172
furniture, 145, 149-150

G

game pads, 139-140
games, 13, 174-176
gigabytes (GBs), 14, 66
GlidePoint WaveKeyboard, 87
Golf Tips: Breaking 100, 185
Gopher, 211
graphical user interfaces, 153
graphics cards, 77-78, 81
graphics programs, 178-180
graphics tablets, 137-138

H

hand-held scanners, 134
hard disks, 52, 64, 65, 69-71
    capacity, 14
    data compression, 70-71
    defragmenting, 224
    formatting, 233
    freeing space, 70-71, 224
    removable, 70
    working of, 69-70
hardware. *See also* specific hardware devices
    compatibility, 23, 24
    problems, 236
Hewlett-Packard 550C printer, 114
high-resolution mice, 102, 103
HOME key, 92
home pages, 216-218
    creating, 217-218
home uses of PCs, 12-13
hot spots, 218

household management, 12
HP ScanJet, 135
HTML (Hypertext Markup Language), 217

I

IBM Enhanced Keyboard, 87
IBM ThinkPad Slimline, 38
IC chips, 53-54
impact printers. *See* dot-matrix printers
information services, 124
infrared transceivers, 16
inkjet printers, 42, 110, 111, 114-115
    paper, 119
INS key, 92
installing software, 187-188
    operating systems, 161-162
interfaces, 151
    DOS, 158
interlaced monitors, 82
internal modems, 129
international travel with PCs, 201-203
Internet, 127-128, 205-220. *See also* Web pages; Web site addresses; World Wide Web
    accessing. *See* accessing the Internet
    children, 212-213
    evolution, 207
    search tools, 211-212
    software source, 186-187
    speed, 207, 208
    uses, 211-215
Internet Explorer, 130, 177
Internet Phone, 177
Internet Service Providers (ISPs), 209-210
Internet tools, 176

J

joysticks, 139

K

keyboards, 3, 10, 85-95
    add-ons, 95
    care, 93-94, 225-226
    carpal tunnel syndrome, 94
    cursor keys, 90
    desktop computers, 36, 86
    Enter key, 89-90
    Escape key, 93
    function keys, 91
    manufacturers, 87-88
    MIDI, 139
    notebook computers, 39, 87
    Num Lock key, 91
    Pause key, 91
    personal preferences, 25-26
    Print Scrn key, 92
    QWERTY keys, 88-89
    remapping, 93
    Scroll Lock key, 91
    specialty keys, 92-93
    typewriters compared, 86
    typing skills, 89
Kid Phonics CD, 184
Ks (kilobytes), 66

L

labeling disks, 74
LANs (local area networks), 206
Laplink, 198
laptop computers, notebook computers compared, 196
laptop printers, 203
laser printers, 43, 110, 116-118
    care, 227
    paper, 119

workings of, 116
The Learning Advantage, Library 1 and 2, 184
links, 128, 218
live video, 137
local area networks (LANs), 206
locking up, 6
   solutions, 233-234
Lotus Freelance Graphics, 217
LPT ports, 58
luggable computers, 38

M

MacLink Plus/Easy Open, 183
magazines, 19, 30
magnets, 60, 228
Mail, 130, 177
mail ordering
   PCs, 30
   software, 186
mail programs, 130
mainframes, 10
MathBlaster: IN Search of Spot, 184
MBs (megabytes), 66
MDS mice, 102
MechWarrior 2, 176
megahertz (MHz), 13, 29
memory. *See also* RAM (random-access memory)
   amount, 14
   importance, 17
   ROM, 14, 51
MHz (megahertz), 13, 29
mice, 36, 98-104
   care, 226-227
   cleaning, 102-104
   clicking, 100, 101
   double-clicking, 100, 101
   dragging, 102
   number of buttons, 99

options, 102
personal preferences, 26-27
pointing, 100
serial and bus, 98-99
solving problems, 6
working of, 99
microcomputers, 11. *See also* desktop computers; notebook computers; PCs
microprocessors, 52, 53-54
   definition, 51
   evolution, 13
   speed, 17, 29, 53-54
Microsoft Network (MSN), 126-127, 177
Microsoft programs. *See* specific programs
MIDI (Musical Instrument Digital Interface), 138-139
MILNET, 207
minicomputers, 11
modems, 15, 43, 123-132
   call-waiting, 131
   connecting, 131
   costs, 43
   definition, 124
   description, 123-124
   extras, 131-132
   Internet access, 208
   software, 130, 176-177
   software needed, 125
   speed, 130, 208
   types, 128-130
   uses, 125-128
modulation, 124
Money, 182
money managers, 182-183
monitors, 3, 10, 77-84
   active matrix, 17, 27, 82
   add-ons, 83

(continued)

monitors *(continued)*
   care, 225
   desktop computers, 36
   display adapter, 77-78
   dual-scan, 17, 27, 82
   interlaced versus noninterlaced, 82
   monochrome versus color, 79
   notebook computers, 39
   as peripherals, 42
   personal preferences, 27-28
   positioning, 147
   posture for using, 82-83
   reducing eyestrain, 83
   refresh rate, 27, 81
   resolution, 27, 80-81
   screen savers, 225
   size, 79-80
monitor stands, 82
monochrome monitors, 79
Mosaic, 130
motherboard, 53-57
   definition, 51
   microprocessor, 53-54
   RAM chips, 54-57
mouse. *See* mice
mouse pads, 45, 107, 227
mouse pockets, 107
mouse suits, 107
moving mice, 100
MSN (Microsoft Network), 126-127, 177
multi-disk changers, 72
multifunction centers, 118-119
multimedia generation programs, 179
multimedia software, 184
multi-user PCs, 192
Musical Instrument Digital Interface (MIDI), 138-139
MYOB Accounting, 183
Myst, 176

N

navigating the Web, 218-219
Netscape, 176
Netscape Navigator, 130, 177
networks, 206. *See also* Internet; Web pages; Web site addresses; World Wide Web
newsgroups, 214-215
   definition, 124
Noninterlaced monitors, 82
Norton Anti-Virus, 187
Norton Navigator 95, 192
Norton Utilities, 183
notebook computers, 2
   advantages, 41
   batteries, 60
   docking stations, 143
   keyboards, 39, 87
   laptop computers compared, 196
   trackballs, 105-106
   travel. *See* traveling with PCs
Notepad, 171
Now Up-to-Date, 182
numeric keypad, 90
Num Lock key, 91

O

OCR (optical character recognition) software, 136
offices. *See* workspace
office uses of PCs, 11-12
Okidata LED laser printer, 43
online, meaning, 11
online communication services, 126-127
online services, 130, 177
   addressing rules, 214
   Internet access, 208-209
opening files, 6

operating systems, 151-166. *See also*
 DOS; Windows 95; Windows 3.1
 environments compared, 155-156
 functions, 154-156
 installing and upgrading, 161-162
 layers, 154-155
 multiple, using simultaneously, 165
 OS/2, 160, 162
 shell, 151
 startup process, 152-154
 UNIX, 160, 162
 Windows NT, 162
optical character recognition (OCR)
 software, 136
optical mice, 102
organizing software, 192
OS/2, 160, 162

P

page description language, 117
PageMaker, 181
Paint, 180
painting programs, 178
palmtop computers, 41
paper
 dot-matrix printers, 119
 inkjet printers, 115, 119
 laser printers, 117, 119
 weight, 119, 227
paper feed mechanisms, inkjet
 printers, 115
paper jams, 227
parallel ports, 16, 58
Passage to Vietnam, 185
Pause key, 91
PCL (language), 117
PC Magazine, 30
PCMCIA cards, 129
PCMCIA slots, 58, 129

PCs. *See also* desktop computers;
 notebook computers
 evolution, 13-14
 historical background, 10-11
 manufacturers, 45
 turning on, 51, 60-61, 224
 users, 13
 uses, 11-13
Pentium Pro, 53-54
peripherals, 42-44
personal information managers
 (PIMs), 181-182
personal uses of PCs, 12-13
PGDN key, 92
PGUP key, 92
photo and image editing programs,
 179
PIMs (personal information
 managers), 181-182
pixels, 80
PKZIP, 70, 235
Planet Earth: Explore the Worlds Within,
 185
Poetry in Motion, 185
pointing, 100
pointing devices, 97-107. *See also* mice
 need, 97
portable computers, 38-41. *See also*
 notebook computers
 palmtop, 41
ports, 16, 57-58
POST (Power On Self Test), 53, 152
PostScript printers, 43, 110, 116, 117
posture for monitor use, 82
PowerDesk, 183
powering down, 61
Power On Self Test (POST), 53, 152
PowerPoint, 180
power supply, 52, 59-60
power surge protector strips, 45
power switch, 51

preinstalled software, 152-153
prepackaged software, 4
presentation graphics programs, 178
prices. *See* costs
print cartridges, inkjet printers, 115
printers, 42-43, 109-121
   care, 227
   cartridges, 115, 120
   choosing, 110-112, 113
   costs, 42, 43, 110, 113, 117
   ease of use, 113
   laptop, 203
   maintenance costs, 113
   multifunction centers, 118-119
   paper, 119-120
   positioning, 148
   print quality, 110-111, 113
   problems, 6, 235
   ribbons, 120
   speed, 113, 114
   switching between, 120
   thermal, 118
   toner, 117, 120, 227
   types, 110
   working of, 112-118
print head, 113
Print Scrn key, 92
Print Shop Deluxe II, 181
problem solving, 6, 231-240
   First Aid 95, 239
   hardware problems, 236
   software problems, 236-237
   technical support. *See* technical support
   troubleshooting, 238-239
programs. *See* software; specific programs
Publisher, 181
purchasing PCs. *See* buying PCs

Q

QuarkXPress, 181
QuickBooks, 183
QuickCam, 137
Quicken, 182
QWERTY keys, 88-89

R

RAM (random-access memory), 14, 52
   amount to buy, 28
   definition, 51
   determining amount, 55-56
   DOS requirements, 164
   functions, 55
   limitations, 55
   low, 232
   running out of, 56-57
   video, 17, 78
   Windows requirements, 162
RAM chips, 54-57
read-only memory (ROM), 14, 51
read/write hole, 67, 68
rebooting, 6, 233-234
reconditioned PCs, 30
records, 174
refresh rate, 27, 81
remapping keyboards, 93
removable hard disks, 70
resolution
   laser printers, 116
   monitors, 27, 80-81
   scanners, 135
responsiveness rate, mouse, 26, 103
retail stores
   buying PCs, 29-30
   buying software, 186
ribbons, printers, 120
ROM (read-only memory), 14, 51

S

saving files on disk, 64-65
ScanDisk, 200, 224
scanners, 134-136
schedulers, 182
screens. *See* monitors
screen savers, 225
Scroll Lock key, 91
search tools, Internet, 211-212
serial ports, 16, 58
   mice, 98-99
setting up PCs, 4, 146-148
   cables, 148
   listing components, 146
   monitor position, 147
   printer position, 148
   system unit position, 146-147
shareware, 187
shells, 151
   DOS, 158
SHIFT key, 92
shutters, 67, 68
Sidekick, 182
SIMM (Single Inline Memory Module) chips, 53-54
size of PCs, 14
slimline keyboards, 88
Smartcom, 177
SoftQuad HoTMetaL PRO, 178
software, 167-193. *See also* operating systems; word-processing software; specific software packages
   application, 154
   care, 228
   choosing PCs, 23
   communications, 176-177
   compatibility, 24
   databases, 173-174
   desktop publishing programs, 180-181
   educational, 183-184
   edutainment, 184-185
   e-mail, 130, 176
   evaluating, 187
   file-compression, 70-71, 235
   finding, 185-187
   games, 13, 174-176
   graphics programs, 178-180
   installing, 187-188
   loading automatically at startup, 152-153
   memory, 28, 56-57
   modems, 125, 130
   money managers, 182-183
   multimedia, 184
   organizing, 192
   PIMs, 181-182
   preinstalled, 152-153
   prepackaged, 4
   problems, 236-237
   running programs simultaneously, 28, 56
   scanners, 136
   schedulers, 182
   spreadsheets, 168, 172-173
   starting programs, 5, 188-189
   technical support, 190, 191
   traveling with PCs, 196, 197, 199
   upgrading, 190-191
   utilities, 183
   Web page design programs, 177-178
sound boards, 16
speakers, 16
special effects programs, 179
specialty keys, 92-93
Spectacular 3D Web Workshop, 178
speed
   CD-ROM drives, 44, 72
   computer, slow, 232-233
   Internet, 207, 208
   microprocessors, 29, 53-54

(continued)

speed *(continued)*
    modems, 130, 208
    printers, 113, 114
spreadsheet files, 172
spreadsheets, 168, 172-173
standard keyboards, 87
starting programs, 188-189
starting up PCs, 4-5
    international travel, 203
    operating system, 152-154
stores. *See* retail stores
style sheets, 170
stylus, 137
SuperVGA graphics cards, 81
Supra Sonic 288 modem, 132
SurfWatch, 213
surge protectors, 147
switch boxes, 120
swivel bases, monitors, 83
SX chips, 53-54
System Commander, 165
system lockup. *See* locking up
system maintenance, 224
system operators, 238
system units, 3, 10, 49-62
    BIOS, 52-53
    care, 60-61, 224-225
    components, 50-52
    definition, 51
    desktop computers, 36-37
    motherboard. *See* motherboard
    ports. *See* ports
    positioning, 146-147
    power supply, 59-60
    purpose, 50

T

Tab key, 92
tape backup units, 66
task chairs, 145
technical support
    hardware, 30, 59
    information needed, 237-238
    software, 190, 191
telephones
    cellular, 200
    Connectix VideoPhone, 137
    international travel with PCs, 202, 203
    Internet Phone, 177
tempered glass filters, 83
text editors, word-processing software compared, 171
thermal printers, 110, 118
3D Pinball, 176
thunderstorms, 225
Timeslips Deluxe, 183
toner, printers, 117, 120, 227
touchpads, 16, 27, 106
tower configurations, 36-37
trackballs, 3, 26-27, 39, 104-106
trackpads, 16, 27, 106
traveling with PCs, 195-204
    computer preparation, 200-201
    constant travel, 197-198
    extras needed, 199
    hardware needs, 198
    international travel, 201-203
    occasional travel, 197
    printers, 203
    software needs, 196, 197, 199
    testing battery life, 201
    virtual offices, 196
troubleshooting, 238-239
Truform Ergonomic Keyboard, 87
typewriters, keyboards compared, 86
typing skills, 89

U

UltraVGA graphics cards, 81
Uninstaller for Windows 95, 183
uninterruptible power supply (UPS), 61-62
Universal Resource Locators (URLs), 218
UNIX, 160, 162
upgrading
   computer systems, 28
   operating systems, 161-162
   software, 190-191
uploading, 124
UPS (uninterruptible power supply), 61-62
URLs (Universal Resource Locators), 218
used PCs, 30
user interfaces, 153-154
users, 13
utilities software, 183

V

Veronica, 211
VGA graphics cards, 81
video, live, 137
video cards, 57-58
video RAM, 17, 78
viewable area, monitors, 79-80
virtual conferencing, 124
virtual offices, 196
viruses, 187
   detecting, 224
voice-mail, automated, 12

W

WAIS (Wide Area Information Servers), 212
wall plugs, international travel with PCs, 202
WANs (wide area networks), 206
warranty cards, software, 228
wave keyboards, 87
Web browsers, 130, 176, 216, 219
Web page design programs, 177-178
Web page organizers, 219
Web pages, 128, 215
   home, 216-218
Web site addresses
   add-ons, 140
   buying PCs, 33
   choosing PCs, 19
   computer system care, 229
   Internet, 220
   keyboards, 95
   modems, 132
   monitors, 84
   operating systems, 166
   PC furniture, 150
   PC manufacturers, 46
   pointing devices, 107
   printers, 121
   problem solving, 240
   software, 193
   system unit, 62
   traveling with PCs, 204
WebTalk, 177
Wide Area Information Servers (WAIS), 212
wide area networks (WANs), 206
WinCIM, 126, 177, 208
Windows 3.1, 157
   copying disks, 74
   DOS, 155-156
   erasing disks, 75
   formatting disks, 73
   function keys, 91
   games, 174

(continued)

Windows 3.1 *(continued)*
  identifying programs loading automatically at startup, 153, 162-163
  RAM requirement, 162
  starting programs, 188, 189
Windows 95, 157-158
  communications software, 176
  connecting modems, 131
  copying disks, 74
  DOS, 156
  e-mail, 214
  erasing disks, 75
  formatting disks, 73
  function keys, 91
  identifying programs loading automatically at startup, 153, 163
  installing and removing programs, 188
  Microsoft Network, 126-127
  RAM requirement, 162
  starting programs, 188, 189
Windows NT, RAM requirement, 162
WinWeb, 177, 216
WinZIP, 70
WordPad, 171
word-processing software, 169-171
  cost, 171
  formatting and enhancing using, 169-170
  style sheets, 170
  text editors compared, 171
  word-wrapping, 89
workbooks, 172
Works, 169, 172, 176
worksheets, 172
workspace, 143-150
  choosing, 144
  furniture, 145, 149-150
  PC setup, 146-148
  planning, 144-145
  usability, 149
  virtual offices, 196
workstations, 150
world current voltage, 201
World Wide Web, 128, 212, 215-219. *See also* Web pages; Web site addresses
  accessing, 215-216
  home pages, 216-218
  navigating, 218-219
wrist injuries, keyboard use, 94
wrist pads, 45, 228
wrist rests, 95

Y

Yahoo!, 212

Z

Zip drives, 75
Zip-It, 183
Zork Nemesis, 176